D0983897

WITHDRAWN

Sub-Saharan Africa

Sociology of "Developing Societies"
General Editor: Teodor Shanin

967
Su14a

Sub-Saharan Africa

edited by Chris Allen and Gavin Williams

Monthly Review Press
New York and London

Selection, editorial matter, and Introduction copyright © 1982
by Chris Allen and Gavin Williams
All rights reserved

Library of Congress Cataloging in Publication Data

Main entry under title:

Sub-Saharan Africa

  (The Sociology of ''developing societies''; 2)
  Bibliography: p.
  Includes index.
  1. Africa, Sub-Saharan—Social conditions—
Addresses, essays, lectures. I. Allen, Christopher.
II. Williams, Gavin. III. Series.
HN773.5.S9   967   81–16902
ISBN 0–85345–597–X   AACR2
ISBN 0–85345–598–8 (pbk.)

Monthly Review Press
62 West 14th Street
New York, N.Y. 10011

Printed and bound in Great Britain
at The Pitman Press, Bath

For Thomas Hodgkin
(1900–82)

$88 - 3130$

ALLEGHENY COLLEGE LIBRARY

Contents

Series Preface

The question of the so-called "developing societies" lies at the very heart of the political, the economic and the moral crises of the contemporary global society. It is central to the relations of power, diplomacy and war of the world we live in. It is decisive when the material well-being of humanity is concerned; that is, the ways some people make a living and the ways some people hunger. It presents a fundamental dimension of social inequality and of struggles for social justice. During the last generation it has also become a main challenge to scholarship, a field where the perplexity is deeper, the argument sharper and the potential for new illuminations more profound. That challenge reflects the outstanding social relevance of this problem. It reflects, too, an essential ethnocentrism that weighs heavily on the contemporary social sciences. The very terminology which designates "developing" or "underdeveloping" or "emerging" societies is impregnated with teleology which identifies parts of Europe and the USA as "developed". Images of the world at large as a unilinear rise from barbarity to modernity (or vice versa as a descent to hell) have often substituted for the analysis of actuality, as simplistic metaphors often do. To come to grips with a social reality, which is systematically different from that of one's own, and to explain its specific logic and momentum, is a most difficult conceptual and pedagogic task. It is the more so, for the fundamental questions of the "developing societies" are not of difference only but of relationships past and present with the countries of advanced capitalism and industrialization. It is in that light that we encounter as analysts and teachers not only a challenge to "sociology of development", but also a major challenge to radical scholarship itself.

The Sociology of "Developing Societies" series aims to offer a systematically linked set of texts for use as a major teaching aid at university level. It is being produced by a group of teachers and scholars related by common interest, general outlook and commitment sufficient to provide an overall coherence but by no means a single monolithic view. The object is, on the one hand, to bring relevant questions into focus and, on the other hand, to teach through debate. We think that at the current stage "a textbook" would necessarily gloss over the very diversity, contradictions and inadequacies of our thought. On the other hand, collections of articles are often rather accidental in content. The format of a conceptually structured set of readers was chosen, sufficiently open to accommodate variability of views within a coherent system of presentation. They bring together works by sociologists, social anthropologists, historians, political scientists, economists, literary critics and novelists in an intended disregard of the formal disciplinary divisions of the academic enterprise.

Three major alternatives of presentation stand out: first, a comparative discussion of the social structures within the "developing societies", focusing on the generic within them; second, the exploration of the distinct character of the main regions of the "developing societies"; third, consideration of context and content of the theories of social transformation and change. Accordingly, our *Introduction* to the series deals with the general issues of comparative study, other books cover different regions, while a final volume is devoted to an examination of basic paradigms of the theories of social transformation. They therefore represent the three main dimensions of the problem area, leaving it to each teacher and student to choose from them and to compose their own course.

The topic is ideologically charged, relating directly to the outlook and the ideals of everyone. The editors and many of the contributors share a broad sense of common commitment, though there is among them a considerable diversity of political viewpoint and theoretical approach. The common ground may be best indicated as three fundamental negations. First, there is an implacable opposition to every social system of oppression of humans by other humans. That entails also the rejection of scholastic apologia of every such system, be it imperialism, class oppression, elitism, sexism or the like. Second, there is the rejection of "preaching down" easy solutions from the comfort of air-conditioned offices and campuses, whether in the "West" or in "developing societies" themselves, and of the tacit assumption of our privileged wisdom that has little to learn from the common people in the "developing societies". Third, there is the rejection of the notion of scholastic detachment from social commitments as a pedagogy and as a way of life. True scholarship is not a propaganda exercise even of the most sacred values. Nor is it without social consequences, however conceived. There are students and teachers alike who think that indifference improves vision. We believe the opposite to be true.

TEODOR SHANIN

Acknowledgements

The editors and publishers wish to thank the following who have kindly given permission for the use of copyright material:

Africa-Studiecentrum, Netherlands, for the article ''African Migration and Peripheral Capitalism'' by Drs Victor Piché and Joel W. Gregory from *African Perspectives*, 1978.

Basil Blackwell Publisher Ltd for an extract from *Freedom and Labour* by P. Harries-Jones (1975).

Cambridge University Press for extracts from *Rural Hausa* (1972) by Dr Polly Hill; *Saints and Politicians* (1975) by D. O'Brien; ''The Second Independence: A Case Study of the Kwilu Rebellion in the Congo'' by Renée C. Fox, W. de Craemer and J. M. Ribeaucourt, from the journal *Comparative Studies in Society and History*, vol. 8, part 1, and ''Nigeria'' by Terisa Turner from *West African States: Failure and Promise* edited by J. Dunn (1978).

Canadian Association of African Studies for extracts from the article ''Corporate Interests and Military Rule'' by M. Martin, in the *Canadian Journal of African Studies*, 7, 2, 1973.

Centre for Developing-Area Studies, McGill University, Montreal, for the article ''The Wrong Side of the Factory Gate: Casual Workers and Capitalist Industry in Dakar'' by Chris Gerry, originally published in *Manpower and Unemployment Research* (now called *Labour, Capital and Society*) vol. 9, no. 2. November 1976; an extract from ''The Labouring Poor and Urban Class Formation'' by Richard Sandbrook and Jack Arn published in Occasional Monograph Series, No. 12, and the article ''The Labouring Poor, Trade Unions and Political Change'' by Jeff Crisp, originally published in *Manpower and Unemployment Research* (now called *Labour, Capital and Society*) vol. 11, no. 2, November 1978.

Rex Collins Ltd for an extract from *Nigeria: Economy and Society* by Gavin Williams.

The Controller of Her Majesty's Stationery Office for an extract from ''The African Middle Class'' by T. L. Hodgkin, in *Corona*, 8, 3, 1956.

Croom Helm Ltd for an extract from "Domestic Labour and the Household" by Maureen Mackintosh from *Fit Work for Women* edited by Sandra Burman (1979).

Mrs V. Dudley and the Ibadan University Press for the article "Instability and Political Order" by the late Professor William Dudley.

Dr C. Gerry for his paper "Urban Poverty, Underdevelopment and Recuperative Production in Dakar, Senegal" (1977).

Robert Gordon for extracts from his book *Mines, Masters and Migrants* (1977).

Heinemann Educational Books for extracts from *Colonialism and Underdevelopment in East Africa* by E. Brett, and with University of California Press for extracts from *Underdevelopment in Kenya* by C. Leys.

Heinemann Educational Books and Africana Publishing Company for an extract from *Black Mineworkers in Central Africa* by Charles Perrings.

History Workshop, for an extract from the article "Lord Milner and the South African State" by Shula Marks and Stanley Trapido from *History Workshop Journal*, vol. 8, 1979.

The estate of T. L. Hodgkin for an extract from the article "Mahdism Messianism and Marxism in the African Setting" in *Sudan in Africa* edited by Y. F. Hasan.

Professor Allan Isaacman for an extract from his paper *A Luta Continua: Creating a New Society in Mozambique*, no. 1, Southern Africa Pamphlets, a joint enterprise of Fernand Braudel Center for the Study of Economics, Historical Systems and Civilizations, State University of New York at Binghamton; Africana Studies and Research Center, Cornell University; Centro de Estudos Africanos, Universidade de Eduardo Mondlane, Maputo.

Claude Meillassoux and the International African Institute for an extract from the Introduction to *The Development of Indigenous Trade and Markets in West Africa* (1971).

The Merlin Press Ltd for extracts from "Capital Accumulation, Class Formation and Dependency" by Colin Leys from *Socialist Register* (1978).

Mouton Publishers for extracts from "Pragmatists or Feminists?" by Carmel Dinan in *Cahiers d'études Africaines* (1978).

Oxford University Press for extracts from "The Afrikaner Broederbond 1927–1948" by Dan O'Meara in the *Journal of Southern African Studies*, vol. 3, no. 2 (1977) and "Migrant Labour and Changing Family Structure in the Rural Periphery of Southern Africa" by Colin Murray from *Journal of Southern African Studies*, vol. 6, no. 2 (1980).

Penguin Books Ltd and Little, Brown & Company for an extract from *Africa in Modern History: The Search for a New Society* by Basil Davidson (US edition *Let Freedom Come: Africa in Modern History*).

Pluto Press Ltd for an extract from *Chibaro* by Charles van Onselen (1975).

Presence Africaine for an extract from *The Damned* (1963) by Frantz Fanon, originally published as *Les Damnes de la Terre*.

The Review of African Political Economy for an extract from "Hidden Forms of Labour Protest" by Robin Cohen.

Routledge & Kegan Paul Ltd for an extract from *Religious Change in Zambia* by W. van Binsbergen.

The Royal African Society for "Political Radicalism in Africa" by Richard Jeffries from *African Affairs*, 77, 308, 1978.

Sage Publications Inc. for extracts from two articles "From Peasant to Workers in Africa" by Robin Cohen and "Taking the Part of Peasants: Rural Development in Nigeria and Tanzania" from *The Political Economy of Contemporary Africa* (vol. 1, Sage Series on African Modernization and Development) edited by Gutkind and Wallerstein. Copyright 1976.

Sociologische Gids for the article "Controllers in Rural Tanzania" by Thoden Van Velzen (*Sociologische Gids*, 19, 2, 1972).

Stanford University Press for extracts from *Women in Africa: Studies in Social and Economic Change* edited by Nancy J. Hafkin and Edna G. Bay. Copyright © 1976 by the Board of Trustees of the Leland Stanford Junior University.

The University of Chicago Press for extracts from *Urban Policy and Political Conflict in Africa* by Michael Cohen.

Introduction

In editing this collection we have tried to make our selection systematic and coherent, able to stand on its own as an introduction to the sociology of Africa, and serve as a part of a series united, as Teodor Shanin's Preface points out, by shared interests, outlook and commitment.

Sub-Saharan Africa, as a unit of study, is marked both by local variation, the product of ecology and precolonial history, and by broad uniformities, the product of colonial history. We have focused on the common aspects of African social structures and processes, while not denying or ignoring local variation. In particular we have included material on South Africa. In its level of development (notably in industry and agriculture), in the completeness of the proletarianization of its African population, and in the sophistication and effectiveness of its state, South Africa is anything but typical of Africa in general. Yet such features raise analytical and methodological issues common to the study of all developing societies, while the history of their attainment in South Africa is both of particular comparative interest for the study of contemporary Africa, and has had a major impact on the entire southern (and Central) African region (see *Marks and Trapido, Murray, van Onselen, Gordon, O'Meara*, below).

Precolonial African societies were characterized by marked differences, even to some extent within the same ecological zone, in their changing forms of agricultural production and political arrangements, and in the nature and significance of their involvement in trade networks (see Davidson, 1969; Davidson, 1978; and for case studies Iliffe, 1979; Meillassoux, 1967). The dual impact of European capitalism and colonial rule imposed a degree of uniformity on these diverse patterns, without wholly eradicating them. This uniformity can be seen in economic and political structures, in the social transformations resulting from them, and in ideology.

Colonial economic development in "black" Africa was relatively modest in scope and intensity, focusing on mineral exploitation, and on peasant production, sometimes combined with settler production, as in East-Central Africa (Brett, 1973; Cowen, 1979; Palmer, 1977) and in nineteenth-century South Africa (Bundy, 1979). Outside South Africa, production is still largely reliant on mining and peasant agriculture rather than on manufacturing industry and large-scale commercial agriculture, where growth has been recent and limited. Thus those social categories and processes characteristic of development and industrial growth are less conspicuous in Africa. Even rural society has not been wholly transformed into a peasantry economically and politically incorporated within a capitalist economy and state (Klein, 1980; Hyden, 1980). The African working class is small, relatively ill-defined, and in social and cultural terms not distinct from the broader mass of the urban poor (see Part V). Similarly the bourgeoisie is of recent origin, small and weakly capitalized. It tends to accumulate through political ties and corruption rather than through efficient use of capital, and has been and is currently subordinate to foreign and state capital (see Part VI).

Politically, colonial rule relied heavily on existing systems and holders of political authority, incorporated, transformed and even created to form part of an integrated and subordinate administrative system, staffed by African officials known uniformly as ''chiefs''. Peoples with different systems of kinship, languages and forms of political integration and organization were differentiated and designated as distinct units, as ''tribes'', forming one basis of the politicization of ethnicity characteristic of post-war Africa.

The predominance within society of rural communities created for colonial governments problems of incorporation and control, and led to more or less successful attempts to increase the central capacity of government (well illustrated in Iliffe, 1979). This was necessary to recruit and regulate labour, to tax peasants, and to dictate the terms of trade for their produce. Once a function of chieftaincy, in post-war Africa it has been increasingly based on the spread of state apparatuses in the countryside through ''rural development''. Shaped and legitimated by a common ideology of development involving the external provision of inputs, goals and management, such rural development strategies (and their effects on rural class structures and relations) recur across geographical and temporary boundaries (Heyer, 1981). A similar stress on the elaboration and expansion of state machinery and state role arose from post-war concern with economic development (often identified with industrial development). This requires the creation of an effective bureaucracy and revenue base, as well as machinery for recruiting and disciplining a wage labour force. South African history exemplifies the key role of the state in the creation of capitalist farming and industrial expansion, while several other African states illustrate the contradictions involved in attempting this without adequate central capacity (see, for example, Fransman, 1981). State institutions in Africa are often weak and poorly developed, unable to articulate and regulate relations between classes, or effectively to intervene in and manage economic, social and political life.

The persistence of a particular conception of development illustrates the ideological effects of colonial rule, particularly on the elite, educated – as Fanon (1965) so acidly argues – for collaboration in both colonial rule and decolonization. Equally important has been the displacement and transformation of traditional religious belief and organization (see Davidson, 1969) by the world religions of Christianity and Islam. These have had profound effects on political consciousness, and have provided vehicles for political action (see Part IV). Together with the relative weakness of urban class formation, the result has been that political consciousness and attitudes have been only feebly influenced by class consciousness. Awareness of inequality, while widespread, is associated not so much with class antagonism as with the desire for, and the mythology of, individual advancement through the intervention of patrons, good fortune, and the like. Rural political life is less a matter of clashes between landlord and peasant, or conflict between the peasantry and the coercive apparatus of the state, as much as the interaction of religion, communal identity, the operations of patrons (public or private) and resistance to further incorporation into the state (see Parts III and IV).

The study of African societies has been shaped by paradigms of wider application which are designed to help our understanding of developing societies generally, and which are discussed by *Brett* (p. 3). Two paradigms have been particularly prominent. In the USA variants of "modernization" theory have been dominant, but while its assumptions have been damagingly exposed by several critiques (Frank, 1969; Taylor, 1979), this has not deterred people from continuing to use the ideas and imagery of the supposed transition from "tradition" to "modernity". A radical counter-imagery was offered by the sociology of "underdevelopment", arguing that Europe and North America were not the source of progress, but had deprived the Third World of its "surplus" and blocked development (Frank, 1967). Marxist critics of this latter approach, discussed by Bernstein in the *Introduction* to this series, have tended to revert to the evolutionist assumptions of orthodox Marxism (Warren, 1980: see Palma, 1978; Leys, 1975; Williams, 1978).

Drawing on this tradition, Phillips (1977) has argued convincingly that the proper focus of study should be the development of capitalism in all its forms. This cannot be limited to the instances of Britain, West Germany, the USA and Japan; conversely, the study of African societies must draw on studies of Europe and North America for relevant comparisons, and not only those of Asia and Latin America. South

Africa, but not as yet the rest of Sub-Saharan Africa, has been exposed
to such comparative scrutiny (Trapido, 1971; Greenberg, 1980;
Burawoy in Nichols, 1980); unfortunately the study of South Africa has
itself been isolated from studies of East or West Africa. In a small way
we hope to contribute to remedying this weakness in this volume by
presenting material on southern Africa within an African context.

Studies of Africa, and more generally of developing societies, have
been marked by the strengths and weaknesses of a distinctly partisan
scholarship. Underdevelopment theory, or the "revisionist" (i.e.
Marxist) historians of southern Africa, have opened new ways of
understanding African societies which are exemplified in this collection
(and see Marks in Samuel, 1981). Yet such partisan scholarship has also
been defensive, determined to sustain its own assumptions in the face of
the enemy. Its aim has been to convert, and to reassure the converted,
rather than to convince, which has inhibited writers from exploring
problems and evidence which their assumptions cannot readily
accommodate.

This is well illustrated by the liberal–Marxist "debate" over South
Africa. The debate has been defined both by the ways in which the
protagonists understand societies, and by their political commitments.
Liberal arguments have been notable for their wishful thinking and
restatement of the paradigms of neoclassical economic theory
(Bromberger in Leftwich, 1974; Lipton, 1979). Marxists, who have
convincingly demonstrated the relations between capitalism and the
racist political and social institutions of South Africa (Legassick, 1974a,
1974b; Johnstone, 1970; Davies, 1980; *Marks and Trapido*, p. 10)
remain, however, uneasy in their handling of the sociological category of
race (see Rex, 1970) and are only now developing an appreciation of the
contradictions within the present structure.

Obviously, as with the selection of items for this volume, our own
values and theories will define what we choose to study and how we
choose to do it. The validity of our analysis does not, however, depend
on whether it conforms to a theoretical problematic (however
sophisticated), but on its capacity to lay bare and comprehend the
phenomena it seeks to explain. In our choice of extracts we have
therefore preferred material derived less from the practice of theoretical
debate and more from the experience of field research and the attempt to
synthesize and present analytically a wide range of empirical material.
We have tried at the same time to avoid dogmatic prescription and
sought for simplicity, clarity and brevity in the extracts chosen.

To keep the book short but coherent we concentrate on one major
aspect of African sociology, that of social structure. Thus we have not,
for example, drawn on social anthropology, concerned as it generally is

with community rather than class and with culture rather than politics. Nor have we paid much overt attention to the sociology of interpersonal relations, whether arising from the roles of spouse, parent, friend, client, "tribesman" or employee – though all of these are treated in our extracts. Instead we consider the most important divisions within African society, those of gender, class and race. Thus, following a section on the way in which these divisions have been shaped by colonialism and capitalism (which should be read in conjunction with the *Introduction* to this series), we have sections on women, peasants, the urban poor and the bourgeoisie. In keeping with our concern for empirical scholarship, the selection overall has a descriptive flavour which we hope will convey something of the vividness and particularity of African society as well as its attraction to Africanists. We have also aimed to achieve a regional balance, avoiding the concentration of much sociological research, on English-speaking West Africa, and giving due weight to southern Africa.

Each of the social categories with which we deal is discussed from three standpoints: its origin and nature, the forms of consciousness with which it is associated, and its characteristic forms of politics. We do not suggest that each category is sharply defined, with an unambiguous relationship with other categories (see, for example, the introduction to Part V), and with a definite form of political consciousness or strategy. Class concepts should not only refer simply to exclusive, economically defined categories, but also to relationships between members of the same or different classes. Hence our concern is with workers, not "the working class", or with peasants, not "the peasantry". Class membership is one of several ways in which people identify themselves collectively, and forms one of the sources of collective action. Political actions arising out of the experiences and exigencies of specific class situations may yet be articulated in other terms, such as those of religious movements, as several of our excerpts in Parts IV and V will show. Class relations and forms of social identity are continually changing, and we have tried to convey a sense of the historical depth of the process of class formation and of class relationships, especially in our material on southern Africa.

Both consciousness and politics reflect in their ambivalence and flexibility the variety of possible relationships between classes and the importance of divisions within them, most notably within the bourgeoisie. Relationships between classes may indeed be less significant in many instances than, for example, such relationships as those between rural society as a whole and the state (Part III) or between the urban poor and the urban privileged (Part V; *Cohen* in Part VI). Class consciousness is not necessarily either the commonest or the dominant form of consciousness: religion, ethnicity, status and race are all important influences. The latter three are illustrated below in a variety of contexts from mines and urban politics to peasant revolt. We devote special attention to religion in our material on peasant consciousness and politics (Part IV), both a means of responding to exploitation and a means of securing peasant subordination to rural patrons and the colonial and postcolonial state. During the peasant revolts and armed liberation struggles of the post-war period such religious forms of consciousness have been superseded (as are ethnic forms) by a more explicitly national and class consciousness (see, for example, *Davidson* in Part IV; Marcum, 1969, 1978; Isaacman, 1978).

In explaining political activity neither liberal nor Marxist analysts have come to terms successfully with the variety of phenomena which have been lumped together under the blanket terms of "ethnicity" or, more crudely, "tribalism". Pluralist theories (Kuper, 1969) have tended to treat such phenomena as *sui generis* and thus requiring no explanation, though, as Melson (Melson and Wolpe, 1971) argues, tribalism cannot be treated as an independent or fundamental variable in analysing political conflict, being itself either an outcome or a mode of such conflict. We are, however, no nearer to a satisfactory account of why conflict should take such a form in some contexts rather than others, though Kasfir (1976) and Young (1976) have made determined efforts. Similarly, Marxists tend to have recourse to the claim that tribalism is just ideology (Mafeje, 1971; see also Leys, 1975), or to make the phenomenon vanish by redescribing it in terms of class, religious or other forms of conflict (see Mamdani, 1976; and discussion in Saul, 1979).

The concept of the state has led a similarly shadowy existence in studies of politics. Often it becomes reduced to the notions of "government" or "administration", seen both as institution and as actor. Marxists, particularly in African contexts, generally try to treat the state as the political manifestation of a class (Jessop, 1982); the problem is then to identify which class. Since the class which informs the state has often proved peculiarly elusive, they have been driven to nominate metropolitan classes, or class alliances (see the material on the "overdeveloped" postcolonial state in Goulbourne, 1980; and discussion in Leys, 1976; Saul, 1979), while Leys in his work on Kenya has drawn on Marx's theory of "Bonapartism" to explain the Kenyan state and its activities in terms of the balance of class forces (Leys, 1975, 1978, and in Fransman, 1982). It is more fruitful to study the various ways in which state activity intervenes in class relations, shown, for example, in rural development (Part III), industrial relations (Part V), and the accumulation of private capital (Part VI), before attempting to conceptualize the state; Leys, again, is probably the best example of this to date.

Although we have arranged our material according to our chosen social categories, the discussion of each category is not confined to its particular section, and certain major topics – ethnicity, state activity, nationalist politics, etc. – arise in most sections. To use this book effectively, therefore, it should be read as an integrated text; for convenience the index identifies these and other recurring themes, as do the introductions to each part. The book should also be read as an introductory text, for it aims in part to encourage readers to follow up the topics and authors mentioned. In order to keep within the limits of space allowed us while covering a wide range of material and authors, we have cut many of the pieces included, by condensing some passages and omitting others while retaining the flow, sense and style of the argument and (wherever possible) empirical illustration of the analysis presented. A first step, therefore, in following up our selection is to return to the original texts; the full references can be found in the bibliography at the end of the book.

A second step is to consult the introductions to each part, which also function as guides to further reading, listed again in the bibliography; for simplicity a work with several authors is cited under the first author only. In citing further reading we have tended to choose material that is likely to be available in university libraries; that is, in English (though there is a mass of important work in French), and which itself acts as a guide to more literature. Novels are often the most vivid and intuitively satisfying portrayals of social phenomena available, and several are therefore mentioned. Our listings are severely limited by both shortage of space and by the structure of the book, and some earlier bibliographical guides may still prove helpful (Allen in Gutkind, 1976 and in Gutkind, 1977; McClelland in R. C. O'Brien, 1979). Keeping up with new literature is best done by consulting the list of recent publications in the *Review of African Political Economy,* while the most useful journals to read regularly are the *Canadian Journal of African Studies, Cahiers d'études africaines,* the *Review of African Political Economy,* and for southern Africa the *Journal of Southern Africa Studies* and the *South African Labour Bulletin.*

Part I

Colonialism and Class Formation

Introduction

African societies have been transformed by the impact of colonial conquest, the commercialization of production and the response of Africans to these challenges. The first section outlines some of the changes which have taken place and the variations among them in different parts of Africa. *Brett* takes up the debate about the impact of capitalism on the development/underdevelopment of African and other countries. He argues that colonialism in East Africa created the conditions for and set limits to the subsequent development of societies' productive capacity. (See also Kjekshus, 1977; Kitching, 1980; and for West Africa Suret-Canale, 1971; Williams, 1976.) Brett shows how different forms of agriculture – settler, plantation and peasant – involved different forms of labour control, capitalist enterprise and surplus appropriation, and elicited different forms of political response. He also argues that colonial administration was central to the formation of classes, allocation of resources and development of a bureaucratic ideology in the colonial state and its contemporary successors (Lee, 1967; Iliffe, 1979; Allen, forthcoming; and *Leys* below).

In West Africa, foreign merchants and colonial rulers reoriented production and commerce towards the Atlantic export trade in slaves and later agricultural commodities. European firms dominated the import-export trade, in which Africans were able to operate in a subordinate position (Hopkins, 1973). *Meillassoux* points to the existence of an indigenous network of traders in products locally consumed and produced, but threatened by displacement by foreign imports and confined by state intervention (Harriss, 1979). They are more capable of adapting to changing patterns of trade and state policies than Meillassoux suggests.

Marks and Trapido identify the conditions for the development of capitalism as they were established by the British imperial administration and mining capital in South Africa after the Anglo-Boer War. This required a far-reaching programme of social engineering. First came the capacity to procure, direct and cheapen the cost of labour. Capitalist development also required the creation of a modern bureaucracy to regulate society and competition among capitalists, and to promote production of cheap energy and food. It depended on a class alliance of mining and agricultural capital – the "marriage of gold and maize" (Trapido, 1971; Fransman in Fransman, 1981). Lacey (1981) shows how difficult it was to create this alliance, to which white workers were recruited after the defeat of the 1922 Rand mine strike had smashed their resistance (Johnstone, 1976, Davies, 1979) and to which manufacturing interests were accommodated (Davies, 1980).

Cheap labour depended on restricting the development of peasant production (Arrighi, 1973, Bundy, 1979, Vail, 1980, Palmer, 1977, criticized by Cooper, 1981 and Ranger, 1978); it also drew migrants from reservoirs of labour, thus cheapening wage costs, as almost all the papers in this part show (cf. First, 1982; Burawoy in Nichols, 1980). More generally, as *Gregory and Piché* show, colonialism promoted the movement of people as well as goods in the direction it required (von Binsbergen, 1978; Aghassian, 1976), even to the European metropole itself (Adams in R. Cohen, 1979). Most studies focus on migration for wage labour to mines and plantations, and their consequences for rural communities and kinship structures, which *Murray* analyses carefully below and in Murray, 1981, and on people seeking urban employment. Less attention is paid to the massive movements of farmers between rural areas which opens huge areas to crops for local and foreign markets (e.g. Hill, 1963).

Colonial rule and capitalist penetration formed the class structure of colonial Africa. They set in motion the twin processes of peasantization (Post, 1972) and proletarianization (*Cohen,* below), transformed indigenous political institutions into appendages of the colonial state, generated commercial and bureaucratic bourgeoisies, created the distinctive cultures and social structures of settler societies and, not least, altered the forms of domestic life and relations between the sexes as *Murray*, and the excerpts in Part II show.

Colonialism and Capitalism

Teddy Brett, *Colonialism, Underdevelopment and Class Formation in East Africa* (1973)

We have distinguished three major theoretical positions with respect to the impact of contact with the West upon social change in the Third World. The older tradition of imperial history and the more recent literature in the behavioural social sciences assumes that the relationship has produced essentially beneficial results since contact has tended to diffuse the values and techniques required for "modernization" to backward and isolated societies which would otherwise have found it much more difficult to obtain access to them. At the other extreme that contact is essentially exploitative, that an increase in such contact can only increase servitude and that a process of genuine development will only be possible when Third World societies can cut the connections which tie them to the dominant Western powers altogether. Between these two extremes lies the classical Marxist position which argues that the impact of the relationship is profoundly ambivalent; that it tends on the one hand to create exploitation and subjugation while on the other it produces new forces in colonial societies which will be capable of overthrowing external dominance and of using the positive achievements of the developed world as a basis for the elimination of their own backwardness and subordination.

External dominance in the Third World meant that the commanding heights of the new economy and administration were occupied by expatriate groups from the beginning; expatriate groups, moreover, with access to resources derived from their metropolitan base which were far in excess of anything which indigenous groups could hope to acquire in the short run.

Whatever the differences between them, the dominant expatriate groups in the colonial political economy derived their ability to exploit East African resources from the power of the colonial state on the one hand and the inability of members of the indigenous society to compete with them on the other. These two factors were closely related to each other. Where indigenous classes had already acquired skills and capital the power of the state could be used to destroy this to allow expatriate interests full play – the destruction of India's textile industry in the nineteenth century is perhaps the most notorious example of this kind.

Where, on the other hand, pre-colonial society was relatively undeveloped – [as] in the East African interior – skilled personnel would have to be imported in the first instance to man the administrative, educational and economic institutions required to integrate the region into the international system of exchange. . . . Would the system of dominance established during this period tend to perpetuate itself or to produce indigenous groups capable of replacing it and establishing a genuine independence? And here the role of the colonial state was clearly crucial – because it determined access to resources it also exercised a very direct influence over the prospects for development of the indigenous population.

The new system of production must be described as at least partially capitalistic because it was mainly controlled by private individuals and directed to the market. But access to the productive resources which determined success or failure on the market was directly controlled by the state. The state, in turn, was not an independent force but directly dependent on the balance of social forces in the system which it notionally controlled, and most especially upon the dominant economic forces in the metropolitan country and their local representatives. The colonial state can therefore be viewed as the managing agent of the dominant private interests in the capitalist system, with a vested interest in maintaining their dominance inside colonial society. If this is true – and I would argue that the concrete cases reviewed in this book (i.e. Brett, 1973) do substantiate this position – it is possible to argue that the dominant forces in the colonial system were bound to use their power to limit the access of indigenous groups to resources required for autonomous development and hence to perpetuate the underdeveloped nature of their condition. . . .

Colonialism required the creation of an export sector in the local economy, and this in turn required the evolution of a rural class with the resources required to sell some part of its production on the international market. In fact the growth in agricultural exports in East Africa between the wars was very considerable in terms of quantity (although not necessarily in terms of value because of the effects of the Depression of the thirties). The rapidity of this growth can be largely attributed to the relatively favourable terms on which the British authorities provided the infrastructure services which sustained it – in this respect East Africa certainly benefited considerably from its association with what was still the wealthiest of the European colonial powers. The productive capacity represented by these exports (which were to rise rapidly in value during and after the Second World War) is, however limited, the foundation on which future economic change will have to be based.

But any analysis which confined itself to the examination of growth rates would be likely to obscure more than it revealed; these have to be examined in relation to the changes in the structure of production, distribution and political control which such growth induces and which is then influenced by them in turn. The crucial structural issue in agricultural development in East Africa related to the mode of production and in particular whether this was based upon settlement, plantations or the peasantry – this choice in turn determined the evolution of rural social structure and political control since each strategy involved sharply differing processes of class formation. The *settler strategy* required a process of capital accumulation in that sector based upon a net transfer of capital and of labour to it from the peasant sector. This process, which can perhaps best be viewed in terms of Marx's analysis of primitive accumulation, produced a rural structure based upon large-scale expatriate capital employing African wage-labour in the settler sector, and was combined with the continued existence of subsistence-based precapitalist production in the African reserves, which served to maintain and reproduce the reserve army of agricultural workers when they were not required in the capitalist sector itself. The *plantation structure* which co-existed with this in Kenya and was the leading expatriate sector in Tanganyika, required very little capital from the peasant sector, but depended upon the availability of cheap labour which in turn depended on the inability of farmers in certain areas to produce directly for the world market because of poor infrastructure services. It too produced a structure based on large-scale capital, African wage labour and a subsistence sector disconnected from the market. The *peasant strategy*, on the other hand, was based upon small-scale production mainly dependent on family labour with subsistence production co-existing with production for the market. . . .

Planatation development was justified by its proponents for crops which required large-scale processing facilities. The fact that these could not be found locally was thought to legitimate expatriate control, provided that all this initial capital was in fact brought in from the outside and not extracted from the African population. But the assumption that plantation development was cost-free from the point of view of the local population must be looked at in the wider context of its sources of labour and of its effects upon the development of the areas from which this labour was drawn. In East Africa plantations depended upon the failure to open up these areas, since an extension of cash crops there would have reduced the supply of labour or increased its price to a level which only the most efficient producers could have paid. The situation thus strongly reinforces Myint's general conclusion (1971, see rest of this section) that "the existence of an indigenous subsistence agricultural sector seems to have worked, at least in the transitional stage, for the *lowering* of the wage in mines and plantations''; and further, ''that the colonial powers have been able to maintain low wages in the mines and plantations by neglecting and impoverishing the subsistence agricultural sector''. The whole effect, much reinforced by the strength of the political representation given to plantation interests both locally and in London, would therefore be cumulatively to strengthen regional inequalities and hence the development of a system of dualism involving ''servile exploitation''. The system, based as it was upon expatriate capital, also probably made a small contribution to the stimulation of more advanced forms of economic production in other sectors of the economy.

All these negative effects of plantation development were much intensified in the case of settler development. The predominance of plantations in Tanganyika only extended to a limited range of crops and regions and did not preclude the emergence of a dynamic process of peasant development in a number of areas. In Kenya settler dominance virtually excluded peasant development, it required a net transfer of resources from the African to the European sector, and it required that the former sector be reduced to an underdeveloped labour reservoir for the latter. The most reactionary aspect of the settler strategy stemmed from the fact that they contributed virtually nothing to the development of the exchange economy which existing peasant producers could not provide as well or better. This fact, combined with their demand for the style of life of the English gentry, meant that the whole force of the state had to be brought to bear in order to extract the resources from the local population which were required to maintain their position.

The development of the settler sector depended directly and heavily upon the support of the colonial state. While Africans in the remote regions of Tanganyika who were forced to walk 300 miles or more to work on the plantations could not be expected to realize that this was the outcome of particular aspects of colonial policy, those in Kenya subjected to the Kipande system, land alienation, and a prohibition on cash-crop production, could not avoid making this connection. They learnt very quickly that their poverty and dependence was the direct result of the relationship between the settlers and the colonial state. This fact also forced them to realize that liberation could not be derived simply from an involvement in ''tribal'' politics at the local level, but would require a movement which could direct pressure against the colonial centre where all the crucial decisions were taken. Further, European politics were based upon the need to maintain their racial monopoly over the key developmental resources; they could allow neither Africans nor Asians access to their privileged domain in the White Highlands. This monopoloy meant that Africans could not hope for upward economic and other forms of mobility on an individual basis – they would be excluded because they were African and could therefore only hope to progress within the broader context of the African community as a whole. For the African élite as well as the masses, therefore, nationalism was an imperative.

African nationalism was to emerge as a political force throughout colonial Africa after the Second World War, but the conditions from which it arose differed sharply. It invariably required the existence of a small Western-educated élite within the African population capable of organizing a national movement which could deal with the colonial authorities on their own terms. It also required the support of large sections of the rural population, which would only be forthcoming where they could be shown that their interests had come into direct conflict with the policies of the colonial state. In the peasant-dominated areas of Uganda and Tanganyika this conflict did not arise out of policies related to control over agricultural production because the peasant strategy tended, if anything, to increase the resources going into the African sector rather than to diminish them. In these cases opposition was to arise out of issues derived from processing and marketing which took much longer to mature. But the creation of settler dominance drew large sections of the rural population directly into anti-colonial struggle from the earliest stages of the evolution of the cash economy, a fact which explains the relatively early emergence of nationalism in Kenya, its violence and its ability to mobilize wide strata of the population, notably in the areas most directly affected by the settler presence. But the effects of this situation went even further than this. The dependent subsistence sector had to be administered, and this was only possible through the maintenance of the authority of "traditional" institutions like the chieftainship. African agents had to be found to man these institutions – chiefs, headmen, clerks and so on – and these were rewarded with superior access to the benefits of the colonial world. They were then expected to maintain the authority of the colonial system in the reserves and were assumed by officialdom to represent the interests of the African population as a whole. Their position was necessarily to bring them into opposition with the emerging nationalist forces, which were challenging the colonial structure that gave them their privileges. This tendency also emerged in areas of peasant development – for example, in the Lake Region of Tanganyika – but it was far more intense in Kenya because of the much greater exploitativeness of the system as a whole. Thus the conflicts engendered by the system were not confined to those which existed between Africans and Europeans, but were also developed inside the African community itself – as was to emerge very clearly during the Mau Mau movement, when loyalists were a prime target for attack. . . .

The colonial administration, standing at the point of intersection of the political pressures emanating from British society on the one hand and local society on the other, was expected to manage the whole system although not to run it. With certain limited exceptions, the means of production and distribution were controlled by private interests whose position had therefore to be taken into account when policies were decided. Government could make choices between the options presented by the conflicts between the needs of private groups, but could never free itself from its fundamental dependence on the capitalist system itself. Its influence, which must not be underestimated for this reason, was therefore confined to the choice between alternative strategies for capitalist development, which it could exercise by providing one group of entrepreneurs with opportunities to operate as against another – settlers rather than peasants, processors rather than middlemen, importers rather than domestic producers, and so on. The outcome of these choices was clearly critical for the long-term evolution of the social system, and the basis on which they were made as well as their long-term implications must therefore be looked at with care. Further, the administration in East Africa was accorded great social status and provided a high percentage of opportunities of employment at all levels in the non-agricultural sector. Its impact on the evolution of social attitudes and on social change inside the local population was therefore also to be crucial.

Colonial administration constantly operated within an unresolvable contradiction – on the one hand the demands of the cash economy required that Africans be drawn out of their old routines and systems of social organization; on the other, they could only be effectively kept in order provided traditional habits of deference were maintained. Change was both essential and dangerous. . . . This led both the peasant and the settler theorists to advocate the maintenance of traditionalism institutionalized in the Indirect Rule system. This tendency was, of course, fully compatible with the maintenance of the dualistic development described earlier in this section – if Africans could be persuaded to limit their incursions into the new world to growing a few strands of cotton or coffee or to working for wages for a few months of the year, it would mean that they could both retain their loyalty to the local authority structure and provide the resources required to keep the settlers, processors and traders in business. On the other hand, if they moved out of these lowly roles and acquired the mobility and resources derived from economic entrepreneurship they would threaten not only the profits of expatriate enterprise, but also the authority of the traditionalistic systems of rule to which they were subjected on the local level. While Indirect Rule assumed that "traditional" authorities were to develop independently of central political authority they had necessarily to operate within the broad context of the colonial value-system, more especially in the areas most strongly affected by the growth of the cash economy. This meant that the authority of the chief had, in the last resort, to be subordinated to that of the District Commissioner, and he therefore ceased to depend on his standing with his own people, to whom he was now only nominally responsible. . . .

The presence of the administrative apparatus itself created a new élite which was superimposed upon the whole of indigenous society, and yet derived its values and its life-style from its metropolitan base. . . . The central administration was monopolized at the decision-making end by Europeans, but lower-level positions in the executive and clerical grades were filled either by Asians or, as the educational system developed, Africans in increasing numbers. Because of the limitations imposed on African mobility in the economic sector this class of literate clerks was to occupy a very prominent position in the evolving structure of African society. They became a part of the "modern" sector and were able to learn at least some of its techniques of organization and control. Further, the racial division of labour within the administration prevented their upward mobility beyond the lowest level and thereby ensured that their loyalty to the colonial systems would be less than complete. Members of the group played a leading role in the formation of pressure groups and parties. Perhaps more important, the need to educate a class of clerks and technical assistants led to the expansion of the educational system, and this was ultimately to produce people who chose not to go into administrative service, but into nationalist politics instead.

Finally, there is little doubt that the bureaucratic theory introduced into East Africa by the administrative class strongly reinforced the tendency to favour large-scale monopolistic forms of organization, which emanated from the dominant expatriate economic groups. . . . An essentially bureaucratic approach to problems of economic organization saw competition as "wasteful" and assumed that these problems could be solved through the application of "rational" techniques to organizations which occupied monopoly positions. It attributed great virtue to size, assumed that only large organizations could provide efficient and modern services, and considered that the abuses deriving from monopoly power could be controlled through the supervision of the state. The social base for this view was, of course, the large expatriate enterprise, where it served to justify the claims of settlers, processers and, subsequently, industrialists, to monopoly privileges. The bureaucracy, with its ideological roots in the tradition of scientific administration, and its social identification with the expatriate business and agricultural class, strongly supported this latter position;

the more so because of its dislike of the Asian trading class, which it suspected of dishonesty, and of its desire to stop Africans from moving out of their traditional pursuits into the modern sphere. The end result was a tendency to intervene to substitute centralized bureaucratic controls for free competition on the market in virtually every sphere of economic life.

This tendency has exerted a powerful influence over the subsequent evolution of the East African economy, which is still heavily influenced by its commitment to bureaucratic forms of centralized organization and hostility to the development of small-scale entrepreneurship through free access to the market. It began with the need to shelter expatriate capital from the small-scale competition of Asian or African entrepreneurs; it thereby created a structure in which almost the only channels of upward mobility were through these large-scale organizations which depended so directly upon administrative support. This meant that Africans, once they reached the point where they could move out of the agricultural sector, could only think of doing so by moving into these organizations, since the opportunities for entrepreneurship at levels which they could manage without assistance from the state had been so severely limited. The educational system, in its turn, was evolved to train Africans for these bureaucratic roles rather than for entrepreneurial ones by stressing academic rather than practical training which would have improved skills in agriculture, business and small-scale manufacturing. And the continued strength of this tendency, strongly reinforced by the continued dominance of the Western powers and the multi-national corporation, serves to perpetuate reliance on imported and capital-intensive technology and forms of organization. In this sense the bureaucracy was a primary agent in the creation of the contemporary state of underdevelopment in East Africa.

Shula Marks and Stanley Trapido, *Lord Milner and the South African State*
(1979)

The context of this extract on the reconstruction of the South African state after the Anglo-Boer war was an attempt to reinterpret a major area in imperial and South African historiography. Contrary to much of the literature, we were concerned to show that the Anglo-Boer war was not simply the outcome of the machinations of a single individual, Alfred Milner, but needs to be understood as the outcome of the late-nineteenth-century crisis in British economic and social life. Milner did not stand alone, but represented a major response to this crisis; the social imperialism which arose out of, on the one hand, the anxieties and fears of the middle class in the 1880s, confronted by the long depression and the rising tide of working-class discontent and militancy which erupted in 1886–7; on the other, through the growing awareness, during the 1880s and 1890s, that British economic supremacy was being increasingly challenged by Germany and the USA at almost every point. Part of the resolution of this crisis consisted in a greater dependence on formal and informal empire for economic support. In this situation the discovery of gold on the Witwatersrand gave the drive for British supremacy on the subcontinent a peculiar importance. Increased gold production was necessary to underpin the expanded trade of the late nineteenth century, while at the same time the Rand itself was a major area of both international investment and trading competition. The nature of the state within which the mining industry found itself, was thus of vital importance both to the mine magnates and their shareholders, whether British or European, and to the sections of the British state/ruling class.

At the end of the nineteenth century, a peculiar disjuncture existed between the enclave capitalist mode of production, based upon the most advanced and sophisticated technology and high concentrations of European finance capital (which arose quite dramatically and suddenly in the middle of the veld of the Transvaal as a result of the mineral discoveries), and political/state power which remained in the hands of Afrikaner notables, themselves largely dependent on their landholdings. The form of the state in the late-nineteenth-century Transvaal still reflected the preindustrial agrarian society of the Afrikaners, and the sudden intrusion of masses of capital together with the demands of development were not, in the first instance, unlike the effects of multinational corporations on third-world countries today. Although Kruger tried, through his concessions policies, to create an independent industrial base, these attempts simply led to an increase in the possibilities for corruption among the small bureaucracy emerging out of the class of notables, most members of which still retained the ideology, life-style and kinship obligations of the earlier agrarian mode of production. Although there were very real signs in the 1890s that the South African Republic was capable of "reform" – that is, "modernizing" – and that individual Afrikaners were undoubtedly making the transition to capitalism, it was an earlier entreprenuerial and individualistic form of capitalism which was remote from that demanded by the new concentration of economic power on the Rand, and the demand of the mining magnates for a new form of centralized and, effectively, coercive state apparatus. Through the 1890s, the demands which the major mining houses were making on the Kruger Republic really added up to this and, in the final analysis, could only be resolved by war. The war itself meant that the state, which was established in the last days of the war and which lasted until Milner's departure from South Africa in 1905, was in many ways a ''conquest'' state and that the ideology of social imperialism was therefore given a freer reign than might have otherwise been possible. Given the very clear perception and breadth of the demands which were being made there was no way in which Kruger could produce the reforms demanded without giving away, as he realized, ''his state''. . . . In some respects the economic conditions which came with the peace were notably different to those which existed before the war. The price of gold, when measured against the cost of stores, fell between 1899 and 1908, and while speculative capital, which had been an essential part of the mining industry before the South African war, made one brief appearance, in 1903, it then shied away from the goldfields. Nevertheless the one overriding anxiety of the mining houses remained: the widespread existence of low-grade ore which could only be mined if the whole cost structure of the industry was significantly changed. Still in a number of areas the mine magnates were making demands of the state which Kruger could not fulfil – and which, despite their short-term disagreements with the reconstruction regime, Milner was bent on securing. As important was that Milner's successors, first Lord Selborne and then more significantly the Afrikaner-led cabinet of the self-governing Transvaal, were equally determined to maintain these essential conditions in which the mining industry could thrive.

There is not space here to elaborate on these at any length. Let us simply set out the demands of the pre-war period and then look at some of the most crucial changes inaugurated during the reconstruction period. Foremost among the demands was the call for the transformation of the machinery of state; for a modern bureaucracy, particularly a Native Affairs Department, an effective police force and an uncorrupt judiciary. Next was the call for the elimination of the concessions policy and the operation of free trade with reduction and elimination of tariffs. Third, there were the calls for the mechanisms to control and direct labour. Fourth, there was the need to ensure the reproduction of the work force, both black and white, and associated with this the need to reduce the cost of essential foodstuffs, housing, and to ensure health and sanitation. Fifth, the magnates themselves sought a ring-keeper who would reduce and eliminate competition among themselves, and between themselves and commercial farming and commercial capital. Sixth, to reinforce the coercive machinery of state and to reduce the need for it, they sought institutions which would create ideological supports for the new economic order. These included a compliant press as well as a suitably adapted educational system. The reform of the educational system, we should add, was essential if the stabilization as well as the reproduction of the white working class was to be achieved.

Of these, the most readily remedied, and certainly amongst the most publicized grievances, related to Kruger's concessions policies, in particular the dynamite monopoly and the railway concession granted to the Netherlands South Africa Railway Company, both of which bumped up crucial costs. . . . Clearly, although individual capitalists were not averse to making the most of the concessions while they existed, in the overall interest of accumulation, what the magnates wanted was the establishment of conditions for the free movement of goods within the region. Hence their opposition to the concessions policy; hence their interest in unification.

Far more complex and related to most other aspects of policy were the labour needs of the mines; indeed these can be seen as the most important demands being made by the industry upon the state. Paradoxically this issue was not only the one in which the Kruger regime seemed both unable and unwilling to assist the mining companies, but it also revealed the companies' need to have a strong state to prevent their setting their own short-term interests against the long-term interests of the industry. . . . The 1890s when attempts by the Chamber of Mines to coordinate recruiting, impose a maximum average wage and prevent the poaching of labour from one mine to the next constantly broke down. The same problem was to recur after the war, when the magnates – Wernher-Beit in particular – appealed for state intervention to impose some uniform action on the industry's labour recruiting policies. As had been the case before the war, the Robinson group had broken rank with the mine-owners' recruiting organisation, the Witwatersrand Native Labour Association (WNLA), threatening as a result to raise the price of labour. . . . So pressing had been the Chamber of Mines' demands for labour before the war that the liberal anti-imperialist J. A. Hobson (1900: 230) was persuaded that Britain's war aim could be reduced to the "one all-important object" of securing "a full, cheap, regular, submissive supply of Kaffir and white labour". Given the suddenness and speed with which the mining industry grew up, it needed a state to create its proletariat. . . . From the point of view of the Chamber of Mines, the weaknesses of the Kruger administration related to its inability to enforce controls over the drunkenness and desertion of the existing work force, to impose a uniform policy in terms of recruitment on the industry, and above all to lower the costs of the reproduction of both the white and to some extent the black working class. On every one of these issues, the Milner regime took action in the post-war period, with a greater or lesser degree of success. Sometimes it was a matter of administering existing laws more efficiently (as with pass laws or prohibition); more often it involved large-scale social engineering.

One of the most dramatic examples of social engineering, as Peter Richardson (1982) has shown, involved the securing of a huge army of Chinese workers. This in spite of the fact, realized at the time, that the Chinese labour policy threatened to jeopardize what have conventionally been seen as Milner's political objectives. Chinese workers were required to replace Africans who resisted post-war attempts both to reduce their wages and to have imposed upon them new technology and production routines. These had become necessary if the mines were to make use of low-grade ore to which they had committed themselves in their pre-war speculative operations. Employing Chinese workers involved, between 1903 and 1907, the huge task of recruiting 60,000 men and transporting them 12,000 miles to the Witwatersrand. In the short term they added to the cost structure, yet by substituting Chinese for cheaper black labour it became possible to work lower-grade ore and still make a profit. Chinese labour was more expensive because the combined cost of recruiting, transport, wages, food, social infrastructure and accommodation exceeded the cost of African labour.

There were, however, a number of conditions which contributed to the greater profitability of Chinese labour power. To begin with they were contracted for much longer periods than African workers, three years against six months. Because they were on the mines for this much longer period they were able to acquire the skill and experience to use the more efficient hand drill rather than the compressed air drill used by the short-term African workers. The hand drill permitted much narrower stopes – the work place from which ore is extracted – reducing working costs and enabling the companies to mine much lower grades of ore than had been economically possible before the South African War. This was because essential to narrow stoping and hand drilling was an additional degree of coercion which was absent from the relationship even between African workers and mine management. Short-term African workers resisted the unpleasant and arduous conditions of hand drilling by the simple expedient of desertion. The inadequate policing of the South African Republic could do little to stop this. Chinese workers, who were banned from working outside of the mine to which they were assigned, let alone outside mining, were confronted by the more thoroughgoing police force of the new regime. The greater coercion provided by the new state as well as the inability of the Chinese workers to find refuge beyond the purpose-built mine compounds, meant that they had little alternative but to remain at their place of work.

This coercion also meant that their labour could be distributed in a more rational way and they were systematically sent to the working (rather than the developing) mines of the more profitable groups, who in practice controlled the Chinese labour schemes. But it was not only the new effectiveness of the state in the Transvaal which made it possible to employ Chinese labour profitably. It was also its capacity to call on the imperial state to negotiate Chinese recruitment. Not only could the South African Republic not have undertaken the international negotiations itself; it is also doubtful whether it could have placated white public opinion. It should, however, be noted that opposition to Chinese labour brought the former Boer generals to create a populist Afrikaner organization, Het Volk (The People). With this development British strategy for incorporating the citizens of the ex-republics changed and eventually internal self-government was conceded to them. The impact of Chinese labour on the working conditions of the Transvaal mines outlasted their presence. African workers, reduced in importance for almost five years, found their bargaining power undermined when economic necessity returned them to the lower wages and more difficult working conditions which had, by 1908, become the norm. Moreover, the success of Chinese labour, shortlived as it was, was not only to undermine the bargaining position of black workers, but also to ensure (notwithstanding the high rate of white unemployment on the Rand at the time, and Milner's desire to swamp Afrikaners demographically) that white workers would not be used in unskilled non-supervisory work. For ideological justification Milner turned to the arguments of the eugenics movement to bolster his case:

> Our welfare depends upon increasing the quantity of our white population, but not at the expense of its quality. We do not want a white proletariat in this country. The position of the whites among the vastly more numerous black population requires that even their lowest ranks should be able to maintain a standard of living far above that of the poorest section of the population of a purely white country. . . .

The mine-owners were equally clear that a mass substitution of white for black unskilled labour was unacceptable, and this for two related reasons. The majority of the Afrikaner unemployed in the towns were seen as unacceptable because they were too proletarianized. Unlike the Africans they might have replaced, they were landless, and the wage they required had to provide not only for their own keep, but also for their families' subsistence and reproduction. Nevertheless, some of the earliest Afrikaner miners were, like their African counterparts, migrant labourers. In the months immediately after the war, however, when they were faced with a great shortage of labour, and, at the same time, with

ALLEGHENY COLLEGE LIBRARY

large numbers of unemployed white workers in the towns, the Johannesburg representatives of the mining companies contemplated the use of a limited number of unskilled white workers. The London principals warned against their employment and Percy FitzPatrick writing to Julius Wernher in London, assured him that he recognized

> as a cardinal and acknowledged fact . . . the appalling position that we should be in if we were to work towards Mr Seddon's New Zealand ideal or the 'working man's paradise' and have this industry throttled by labour unions. I never for one moment forget this danger. . . . Nothing will persuade me that white labour can displace black here. . . .

But even if white labour were not to displace black, it could not itself be dispensed with. And this posed a danger which had been revealed by the weakness of the Kruger state. This was seen most dramatically when in 1897 the Robinson group of mines declared a lock-out against their own men – . . . and found themselves at the mercy of strikers who destroyed extensive company property because the South African Republic's police could not hope to protect the far-flung mines. In the pre-war period anti-capitalist feelings among white workers were extremely strong. . . . When the war was over the British army, the local town police, and soon the Union Defence Force (that is, the South African army) would safeguard mining property. But this defence was poorly undertaken if left only to the coercive powers of the state. The incorporation of white workers was essential if the new state was to ensure the capitalist property relations would go unchallenged. Equally both the Afrikaner party, Het Volk, and the rival political associations representing the mine-owners (Progressive Association) and the commercial and professional middle classes (Responsible Government Association) saw the need to get white working-class support. The result, when responsible government was finally conceded to the Transvaal, was a franchise which admitted virtually all adult white males. If white workers were not subjected to the same degree of exploitation as were black workers, this was because their manifest capacity for militant action was both feared and where necessary deferred to.

At the same time the anti-capitalist class consciousness of white workers had to be blunted by other means. Before the war the mine-owners had seen the *Standard and Diggers News* as a major source of working-class mistrust and antagonism. . . . Not surprisingly the *Standard and Diggers News* was closed down with the British occupation of Johannesburg in 1900. Under the new order the press was to help create those attitudes to mining property which would make the white working class accept them as legitimate. . . . With the coming of the new state the *Star* was given a clear run to establish its ideological hegemony. The

Star, it should be said, belonged to the Argus group of newspapers which in their turn were a subsidiary of the Wernher-Beit group. When Basil Worsfold was employed by the Argus group the parent company dispensed with the formality of separate notepaper in giving their new editor his instructions:

> We do not think it is the wish of the Company to lay down any specific lines upon which it is their desire that you should edit the paper referred to, but, generally speaking, the proprietors are desirous of supporting the Imperial and Local Governments in their work of administration in the Transvaal, and in their general policy regarding the South African Colonies.
>
> As you are aware, in the present condition of South Africa the Mining Industry is of paramount importance, the prosperity of the country being practically dependant upon its expansion and success. You would, therefore, be expected in general to support the policy of that Industry as formulated by the Chamber of Mines.

In spite of this brief, or because of it, Worsfold came into conflict with his employers because he defended a series of measures taken by the administration at which his employers in the Chamber took offence. Within a very short while he was to resign as editor.

At a whole variety of other levels, which have recently been most notably explored by Charles van Onselen (forthcoming), the state and the mining industry intervened in these years to shape the geography of class on the Witwatersrand. These interventions ranged all the way from transforming municipal government and fiscal policies to housing and sewers. Most were related to the need to reduce the costs of the white working class by stabilizing it on the Rand. Thus, among the first schemes blessed both by Chamberlain and Milner and by the mining magnates (who with Lord Rothschild also financially backed the scheme) was to import women domestics to the Rand from the United Kingdom. This project had the virtue of simultaneously "releasing" black males from domestic service to work in the mines, and of supplying a potential source of wives for the white working class which would both stabilize the work force and provide for its domestic labour needs more cheaply.

One of the most important long-term interventions by the state in the period of reconstruction was its attempt to reduce the very high death rate which resulted from working and living on the mines. The Witwatersrand Native Labour Association reported these deaths as "wastage", but the Chamber moved in only in a dilatory way to reduce this even though it was in its own interest to do so. The state to begin with acted with some circumspection. There was no conflict between its paternalism and its desire to reduce the mortality rate on the one hand, and on the other its promise to shelter the industry from adverse publicity and its willingness to forgo improvements in low-grade mines or in mines nearing the end of their productive lives. In spite of this forbearance, however, the industry did little to improve conditions and in 1905 the state found it necessary to enact the Coloured Labourers' Health Ordinance. This prescribed minimum conditions for maintaining health in compounds and gave the Native Affairs Department power to enforce compliance. . . .

A further way of cheapening the cost of labour (white as well as black) was . . . through a transformed agriculture. Again at almost every level in agrarian society the post-war administration attempted to introduce far-reaching changes. Not all its policies were immediately successful: war, drought and cattle disease were obstacles. Nor can rural social relations be transformed by administrative fiat. Yet in the long run the intervention of the regime was to be decisive in a number of areas. After the war (and sometimes before it was over) the state made itself felt in the rural society and economy, but it was always constrained by the need to strike a balance between economic necessity and political possibility.

Departments of state were created with the specific task of directing and guiding the rural economies to a more productive condition. Both colonies were given Land Boards – which grew out of the exigencies of reconstruction – and these soon became departments of land with a general responsibility for transforming the arable and pastoral economies by advancing social, technical and scientific changes on a scale never before envisaged in any of the states of South Africa. The Transvaal acquired a commissioner of Lands from the Western Australian government and a director of agriculture from the Colonial Office. Both men saw their task as depending on the state and having long-term consequences which could not be measured by any immediate return on the large amounts of capital being invested. . . . Science began to play a part in the agriculture of the new colonies such as had never been possible before. We have only to compare the way in which rinderpest, swine fever, and East Coast fever were dealt with before and after the war to recognize that we are dealing with administrations of a qualitatively different order. Yet it would be wrong to see this merely in terms of technological inputs. For the new state the primary task was to transform social and political relationships. To do this involved a variety of strategies, not all of which achieved the same long-term success, but collectively they contributed to bringing a new rural order into being. The best-known of these various schemes were the attempts to bring English-speaking settlers to the rural Transvaal and Orange River Colony. This was the least effective of all the attempts at social engineering and probably owed as much to the eagerness of the land companies (many closely associated with the mining houses) to realize at least a part of their assets, as it did to the political and social considerations of the Milner administration. But for all that the settlement schemes did not achieve Milner's objectives, they did bring over a thousand rural households to the new colonies, and no proper measurement has yet been made of the effect which this had on the economy. Quite apart from the £500 on average which each settler brought in savings, their presence also encouraged a general and perhaps incalculable assistance to the countryside which might not otherwise have been proffered.

In seeking its economic objectives the colonial state hastened the establishment of local agricultural societies, setting them into being as well as financing them. Although a few such societies existed before the war they had limited their activities to arranging local shows. Now they joined in seeking scientific and technical solutions to farmers' problems as well as proposing administrative and political objectives. Quarantine committees, launched to place some of the responsibility for controlling animal diseases upon rural society, had a similar effect to the agricultural associations of strengthening the notables of the countryside.

The condition of the rural white poor had reached a point of crisis before the war. . . . After the war the incoming regime inherited a situation exacerbated by physical destruction as well as the weakening of communal obligations and commitments. What were therefore essentially schemes for famine relief were also seen to present the possibility of shifting political allegiances. The best-known of these was the Burgher Land Settlements which made the white poor the "Bijwoners [sharecroppers] of the State". It may be that these schemes failed . . . because unlike the urban social change which the regime was forwarding, rural schemes had not been studied sufficiently before being put into operation. There was, indeed, no rural Toynbee Hall to use as a model. It was more likely however that the rural poor were not transformed into sturdy yeomen because they lacked the resources essential for rural or any other enterprises. They could claim neither capital nor labour from the state or elsewhere, and as hardworking as the majority of participants were (stereotypes to the contrary), the Burgher Land Settlements failed because of these two critical shortcomings.

In any event the Burgher Land Settlements did not encompass all the poor and the drift to the towns continued, helping to swell the ranks of the unemployed, adding to the class of "poor whites", "breeding apathy, squalor, crime and discontent". This created serious anxieties about the urban stability of the Transvaal towns. To meet such concern Lord Selborne, who replaced Milner as High Commissioner in 1905, proposed to cope with the disaffection of the poor, as well as that of the rural propertied, by attempting to revive at least a part of their previous class structure. In proposing a Land Bank he hoped to benefit the rural notables and to get them to accept the status quo. But he hoped also to recreate the system of clientage which had incorporated the white poor in an earlier period. The success of such a policy must be judged by both its long-term as well as by its short-term results. In the long term these poor could not be kept out of the towns and the effects of their proletarianization would be among the most dramatic known to South African history. Within the short term the outcome was nevertheless substantial. Het Volk . . . accepted the concessions of Selborne . . . and rather than challenging the colonial regime became the "willing ally" of both the mining industry and British imperialism. Yet these political and social successes, though they must be seen as preceding, are not to be separated from the success of the botanist and the veterinary surgeon. By 1908 the new seed, new methods of preparing the soil, inoculation, quarantining and stock improvement, had turned the agricultural and pastoral short-falls of the decade before the war into the surplus stocks of maize and beef of that year. The ex-republics rather than having to find imports for the Rand markets were now forced to find export markets for their own crops.

One direction of social policy was to have very long-term and far-reaching consequences. Milner's administration set themselves against tenancy arrangements, whether for cash rents, sharecropping or even labour; they seemed determined to transform all black tenants into wage labourers. Although they were arguably influenced by theoretical considerations about the superiority of wage labour, it is abundantly clear that they were primarily concerned to free potential black labour for the gold mines. . . . It was left to the South African Native Affairs Commission which in its report drafted one of the most far-reaching schemes of social engineering, to propose the elimination of all tenancy arrangements although it allowed labour tenancy as the most suitable bridge to the final stage of wage labour.

If the Milner and Selborne administrations had to come to terms with the realities of existing class relations in the countryside and worked within the framework in relation to white farming, to some extent the evolution of a policy of "reserves" for African occupation, and indeed the territorial limits which were set to the future South African union in these years, were the result of a similar interaction between social engineering and the art of the possible. The utility of a policy which would maintain the "reserves" in order to subsidize the cost of reproducing a migrant labour force was beginning to be appreciated both in official circles and in the intellectual groups which had evolved

around some of Milner's advisors. . . . Among these was an accountant
of one of the mining groups, Howard Pim, who as early as 1905 put
forward a schematic statement on the potential role the reserves could
play in subsidizing the true cost of the migrant's wage:

> let us assume . . . that the white man does turn the native out of one or
> more of his reserves . . . the native must live somewhere. We will suppose
> that he is moved into locations attached to the large industrial centres – a
> theory of native management which receives much support. . . . In the
> location he is more closely huddled together than he would be in his own
> country, and finds . . . himself in surroundings in which his native
> customs have no place and he is compelled to purchase from the white man
> the food which in his own country he raised for himself. What the white
> man gains, therefore, is little more than the labour required to pay for the
> food which under natural conditions the native raised for himself. . . . The
> white man has not yet shown that in South Africa his cultivation of the
> simple crops which the native requires can compete with native
> cultivation. . . . For a time the location consists of able-bodied people, but
> they grow older, they become ill, they become disabled – who is to support
> them? They commit offences – who is to control them? The reserve is a
> sanatorium where they can recruit, if they are disabled they remain there.
> Their own tribal system keeps them under discipline, and if they become
> criminals there is not the slightest difficulty in bringing them to
> justice. . . . As time goes on these location burdens will increase and the
> proportion of persons in the location really able to work will still further
> diminish . . . it is a fair assumption that at the outside one-fifth of the
> location population . . . is able to work. This means that the wages paid by
> the employers will have to be sufficient to support four other persons
> besides the workman. . . .

If Pim's position had not yet been generally accepted, the administration
had nevertheless to accept the necessity of avoiding open confrontation
in the countryside. For this reason it was extremely cautious in its
responses to settlers' calls for outright expropriation of African lands in
the Transvaal and Swaziland. Contemplating a more gradual process of
proletarianization than the immediate demands being made by settlers,
members of the Kindergarten and others proposed a policy based on
"territorial separation". This was most clearly enunciated in their far-
reaching Native Affairs Commission. It was explicitly directed at
formulating "a uniform native policy" in view of the impending
unification of the southern African territories, and aimed to produce a
policy "which would transcend Cape liberalism and the repressive
policies of the Republics. In a number of spheres, but particularly on
land, its recommendations foreshadowed Union policy over the next
quarter-century and more". . . . The new state emerged as the
guarantor of property rights, recognizing the need to orchestrate

economic policy, decisive in abolishing the remaining obstacles to labour recruiting, clearsighted in perceiving that capital needed to be saved from its own shortsighted tendency to bid up the price of labour, cognisant of the necessity to attempt to modify the most disruptive effects of industrial development and of having to provide efficient channels for transactions between states. In fact, in many ways these are roles which, it can be suggested, are required by the modern multinational corporation of the post-colonial state. The reconstruction regime either played a key part in meeting these conditions or prepared the way for meeting them. The Kruger regime with its different economic constituency and rationale, might satisfy one or other of these conditions at any one time. It could not satisfy all of them all the time.

Commerce

Claude Meillassoux, *The Impact of Capitalism on Indigenous Trade in West Africa* (1967)

Capitalism acts in two different ways. On one hand it elicits a sector of production built up in its own image through the presence of capital and its corollaries – private control of the means of production and wage-earning. On the other hand it feeds off the pre-capitalist sectors through the mechanism of primitive accumulation. The introduction of capitalism had the dual effect of maintaining a dependent African commercial sector and of competing eventually with traditional trade.

Imperialism in West Africa was achieved through conquest or reconquest of successive economic sectors (according to the profits immediately available) and through the increasing deflection of accumulated capital towards Europe. . . .

In both Senegal and Sierra Leone in the nineteenth century, after encouraging the growth of a commercial class recruited primarily among literate mulattos and Creoles, the authorities placed obstacles in the way of their development and favoured colonial commerce to their detriment. As a result of this policy the next generation of the African commercial classes sought employment in the administration. Today in Senegal European businessmen concentrate more and more on the export–import business or on wholesale transactions, leaving the retail trade and rural commerce to Lebanese and to a new generation of African traders. The latter are mainly active among African customers in the low-spending bracket. The new Senegalese businessmen have created distribution chains over the greater part of the country. This national commercial capitalism is, however, being blocked by European corporations who have the ear of the Senegalese Government. The result is the refusal to allow local capital to be invested in strategic sectors where foreign capital is dominant: banks, air and sea transport. Since the possibilities of investment are restricted, this later African bourgeoisie is confined to speculative and hazardous ventures or to business under state control, neither of which can develop into a solid and lasting autonomous economic sector. Dependent on European supplies and European transport, deprived of any control over banking, confined to a monetary system based on a distant centre and affected by political decisions influenced by European competitors, Senegalese business has only room to develop within the narrow limits defined by the state.

There is also a commercial network of traders, hawkers, petty-traders, who are involved in the circulation of European capitalist goods and the collection of cash-crops. They are mentioned here so that they should not be confused with those merchants who are the heirs of the pre-colonial trade which does continue up to the present. The persistence of this type of commerce is remarkable. Every year a caravan of several thousand camels transports salt from Taudenit to Timbuktu whence it is distributed through West Africa. Salt mines at Tichit in the west, and Bilma in the east, and others of less importance, also still provide a market for grain, cloth, fish, shea butter, and kola. Cattle also come down from the sahel and the savannah lands to the urban centres and coastal regions; fish from the Niger basins to the coast and kola from the Ivory Coast and Ghana is sold in the savannah. . . .

This commerce has preserved its essential and traditional infrastructure: a network of agents, brokers and middle-men which has been described by Polly Hill (in Meillassoux, 1967). This favours the persistence of cohesion of merchant communities as Abner Cohen (1969) has shown for the Hausa of Ibadan. There is a highly hierarchized selling organization dominated by a few very big traders whose political influence is still considerable. This commerce has indirectly benefited from facilities provided by the capitalist economy. The widespread use of money as a means of payment over large areas of West Africa, the introduction of postal services, banking facilities, railways, roads, the growth of urban populations – all these factors have encouraged commercial growth, led to improvements in methods of payment and commerce, encouraged the formation of commercial capital and accelerated its turn-over.

The position of these merchants appears to be strong and so far attempts by capitalist competitors to take over their distributive networks have failed. Amin and Amselle (in Meillassoux, 1967) describe the case of the Lebanese who attempted to take over the kola trade between the Ivory Coast and Senegal, while Cohen shows how Europeans failed to conquer the Hausa meat trade.

Nevertheless this commerce rests on structural and ideological foundations which are links with the pre-capitalist sector. Islam, for example, one of the strengths of these groups in the past, is today a liability. Moslem culture is not appropriate to the requirements of modern commerce. Administrative formalities, the constant use of telegraphic services and correspondence, the growing need to keep written accounts and the use of a foreign administrative language are all elements requiring a western-educated personnel. Many have resigned themselves to sending their sons to European schools, and thereby run the risk of seeing them lose their faith. At Bamako, the Wahabi sect, which recruits members from among merchants, has set up Franco-Arabic schools which provide adequate education for their children. But this new education often results in school-leavers seeking administrative posts rather than taking on the hazardous life of a merchant. Some of them are even encouraged to do this by their parents, who are aware of the increased difficulties their activities are coming up against, laws and regulations which are becoming more and more strict as well as indirect competition from the capitalist sector.

The social organization of these trading enterprises is described as based on relations of kinship, alliance, and clientage which formerly guaranteed the goods and the payments, ensured loyalty from the employees and maintained the cost of labour at the lowest rate. Now that the young potential merchant has his apprenticeship at school rather than with his employer this paternalistic structure is crumbling away (Amselle in Meillassoux, 1967).

In the end the most important feature of this commerce – its close ties with the non-capitalist sector – will condemn it to eventual death. Kola, shea butter, tobacco, cattle, dried and smoked fish are produced by agricultural communities, pastoralists, and fishermen who exist in self-sustaining economies and only commercialize a fraction of their production. Some change by producing agricultural goods for export, others export manpower and import products. In these cases the supplies of the old intercontinental trade are withering at their source. it is by changing the methods of production of these traditional goods, or substituting new ones from the capitalist sector, that capitalism can overcome the traditional trading sector. This process began long ago for the cloth and hardware market, now industrial tobacco is replacing local tobacco and also kola in urban areas. The capitalist sector is winning other markets, too, such as fish (providing competition from industrial maritime fisheries), and it will soon affect the cattle trade. Traditional commerce rests on its paternalistic structure, its diffusion among the rural masses in villages and small towns, its network of agents in distant districts and the prevailing African taste for their commodities. It is based on the survival of old sectors of production and consumption, which, while contributing to the characteristic style of the West African economy, are doomed to disappear.

Migrants and Proletarians

Joel Gregory and Victor Piché, *The Causes of Modern Migration in Africa*
(Van Binsbergen and Meilink, 1978)

First, the importance of the transformation of agriculture as a cause of migration must be stressed. The plantations set up by colonizers in certain regions of Africa required a substantial labour force and since this was not always locally available immigration was necessary. During the colonial period, and especially before the 1950s, this movement of population was often brought about by force. Commercial peasant agriculture was another important element in the colonial transformation of agriculture and also led to migration. With the advent of individual cash incomes, socio-economic inequality was created and some peasants were able to extend their land while those at the bottom of the ladder were dispossessed of theirs; at the same time peasants who had been successful in acquiring more land, hired agricultural labourers.

Second, colonial intervention in the mining sector produced a similar effect on migration. The need for a substantial labour force led Europeans to form policies and institutions which would guarantee them a labour force with which to man the mines of Central and South Africa. These policies and the widely varying strategies associated with them – ranging from the use of force to industrial paternalism – were designed to drive peasants from their land and attract them to the mining areas.

Third, there was forced migration. This direct exploitation of the labour force took two forms, namely military conscription and forced labour. Not only did colonial recruitment of a young, healthy labour force deprive villagers of a considerable portion of their labour, but it also encouraged others to flee the village. Forced migration, albeit temporary, set patterns for the future.

Fourth, head tax in cash, a fiscal measure introduced by the colonizers and still in use in several countries, also gave rise to migration. Since it was impossible to raise the necessary tax payments from the village, migration of one or more members of a household often seemed to be the only solution to the problem. In this case, as in the case of military service and forced labour, certain villagers (often all) fled the tax by migrating more or less illegally to neighbouring territories.

This leads us to a fifth and final cause of migration, regional disparities of economic growth strengthened by the neocolonial political economy. Because of the export orientation of the colonial and neocolonial economy, location of farming, mining, industrial, and commercial activity bore little relation to the needs of the population, to precolonial demographic and economic patterns, or to current population distribution.

One of the first studies done on rural–urban migration in Africa came to the conclusion that Toucouleur migration to Dakar was neither the result of an attraction to the city (the "bright lights" theory) nor youthful rejection of traditional values, but the result, rather, of the "economic underdevelopment of the Senegal River Valley" (Diop, 1960). Money sent back to the village by the new city dwellers was absolutely essential in maintaining a minimum standard of living in the Valley. . . . This study shows the effects on migration of at least three of the mechanisms identified earlier: agricultural change in the Senegal Valley brought about by the introduction of cash crops such as peanuts and cotton the need for money to pay taxes, and the growth of economic disparities between regions.

The same factors, plus the use of forced labour, are found in the case of migration (of the Mossi in particular) from Upper Volta to Ghana and the Ivory Coast, and more recently to urban centres within the country. Upper Volta was never a classic case of colonial "development". French investment was made primarily in coastal colonies, with Upper Volta being kept as a labour reserve, with the very limited number of jobs in the capitalist sector concentrated mostly in the largest towns. Upper Volta was also the most "favoured" for extraction of forced labour and recruitment for the French army. One of the consequences of this was the flight of a certain portion of the population to Ghana. Finally, since the beginning of the twentieth century Upper Voltans have been subject to a "rigorously" imposed head tax. The result was, and still is, substantial migration to Ghana and more recently to the Ivory Coast, in order to raise the sums demanded. . . .

A final example is temporary migration in South Africa. Indeed, all five causal mechanisms which we have identified come into operation in the case of South African migration. Added to institutionalized structural imbalance, there was complete transformation of agriculture, massive exploitation of mineral resources, and a whole system of coercion, control, taxes, and fines designed to guarantee the exitstence of an unqualified cheap and non-unionized migrant labour force. . . .

African migration also in turn promotes underdevelopment and dependency in several ways. The first concerns the economic effect produced by the departure of people from their villages. By its very nature, labour migration mostly affects young, active (usually male) individuals. Even the short-term absence of members of a household, which usually constitutes the basic unit of production, causes a disproportionate drop in production by the household. In quantitative terms, such lowering of productivity may be extremely important for certain households and collectively for whole villages and regions. The qualitative effect is probably even more drastic. In many cases farming and craft activities are affected by the absence of a dynamic part of the work force. Certain farming activities might therefore be passed over or badly done: for example, clearing of new land; the cultivation of either food or cash crops; cultivation of fields which at certain points in the agricultural cycle require increased labour; the maintenance by women and youths of small individual personal plots the product of which normally provide a substantial margin of security. Similarly craft activity may be cut down by migration. Since craft work is done in the "slack" periods of agricultural activity, and since migration drains away a large section of the labour force, these slack periods can no longer be used for craft work.

Second is the effect of migratory movements on the regional economy. The economic changes occurring in the arrival zones of migration produce a more general transformation in the structure of the regional economy. The mode of production is modified by the penetration of capitalism and the presence of migrants makes possible capitalist agriculture on plantations and large farms. Moreover, other landowners may rent their fields to migrants. It is this transformation of land which has enabled African agriculture to enter international commercial networks. Commercialization of agricultural and industrial products has made Africa more dependent on international markets in which prices are controlled by monopolies and multinational trusts. There is also a change in industrial activity in the arrival zones. The establishment of factories which substitute assembly of semi-transformed products for local manufacture of consumer goods very soon reduces traditional craft work to a minor, sometimes folklore level. Very often migrants provide the cheap labour on which these factories run. . . .

Migration contributes not only to the perpetuation of dependence and underdevelopment, but also to the transformation of classes. In effect, the African peasant, accustomed to cultivating his own land and using his own tools, goes to work for a wage and for the benefit of another. We see in this process the basic element in the proletarianization of African rural masses: they sell their labour to those who have capital, agricultural land, and mineral exploitation rights. Since one is no longer able to generate enough income to provide for one's needs, which include taxes and the purchase of imported goods, a household sends off one or more of its members into migration. By so doing, the means of a household to provide for its own middle-term needs are still further reduced. . . .

The case of Upper Voltan emigration amply illustrates the effect of underdevelopment in home areas. Skinner has enumerated several effects of emigration in Mossi country. The absence of labour forces everyone to work in collective fields, thus neglecting individual fields: during the dry season, when seasonal as well as more permanent migrants are gone from the village, there is not even enough labour for clearing new farms, digging or repairing walls, or weaving cloth (for clothing). He also observes the expansion of a local commercial petty-bourgeoisie, made possible by the accumulation of resources of some returning migrants as a result of their sojourns outside the village (Skinner, 1960). The other side of the coin is seen in the reception areas of the Ivory Coast, a proletarianization of immigrants, especially Upper Voltans, who occupy positions at the bottom of the occupational and wage scales. This plentiful and cheap supply of labour allows for the ''development'' of the Ivory Coast economy; it has, in effect, been responsible for the Ivory Coast ''miracle''.

Colin Murray, *Migrant Labour and Changing Family Structure in the Rural Periphery of Southern Africa* (1980)

Anthropologists and others have long been concerned with the effects of oscillating migration on the areas from which migrants are drawn. Godfrey Wilson (1942) outlined systematic connections between the circulation of labour, the demographic ''disproportion'' between town and country, and the impoverishment of the rural areas; and he related them all to contemporary conditions of uneven capitalist development. Subsequent studies (e.g. Schapera, 1947) broadly endorsed Wilson's substantive findings. The prolonged absence of husbands and fathers was associated with high rates of conjugal breakdown and desertion; it induced a repetitive cycle of illegitimacy and instability in arrangements for rearing children; while the concentration of earning capacity among younger men subverted the authority of the senior generation. . . .

Yet there were apparently conflicting views. Watson (1958) argued that tribal cohesion amongst the Mambwe of Zambia persisted not in spite of labour migration but because of the conditions under which Mambwe participated in the cash economy. There was a surplus of male labour arising out of the imposition of *pax britannica* and the relative interchangeability of agricultural tasks between the sexes, so that co-operative labour relations were able to survive the absence of men. Migrants actively sustained their connections with their rural communities because their access to land there afforded them permanent security, by contrast with the endemic insecurity of life in the towns. . . . (Cf. van Velsen, 1960.)

How can these views be reconciled? First, we should distinguish the domestic economies of northern Zambia and Malawi from the Bantustans and Lesotho: the former have a much stronger agricultural base than the latter. Second, we should distinguish at least the following different levels of analysis: (1) that of "families" identified by reference to the individual household which contains a migrant and his immediate kin; (2) that of "families" identified with reference to the wider kindred or the agnatic lineage; (3) that of the village or rural community as a whole; and (4) that of the larger political community defined by reference to the "tribe" or to the territorial authority of a chief. Separation of these levels is a matter of analytical convenience only. The real consequences of a system based upon the premise "that a human being can be broken into two parts: a "labour unit" working in town, separated from the other part – a man with parents and wife and children, with hopes and aspirations" (F. Wilson, 1972) reverberate through all levels of social aggregation. But it is possible that conclusions which apply at one level of analysis do not apply at another level. For example, Watson and van Velsen observed "tribal cohesion", Wilson and others have observed the destruction of families. A lively consciousness of ethnic identity or a vigorous commitment to traditional values is surely not incompatible with the breakdown of family life, as is evident in the Bantustans. . . .

Studies of migrant labour in the 1970s have been given further impetus by the new historiography in southern African studies, in which underdevelopment in the labour reserves of the rural periphery is analyzed as a corollary of development in the South African industrial core. (Palmer, 1977) In this perspective migrant labour is no longer regarded as an extraneous or incidental phenomenon whose "effects" can be analysed with respect to the integrity or otherwise of a traditional social system. It is, instead, regarded as a result of the penetration of capitalist relations of production under specific historical conditions. . . . The anthropological method of prolonged participant observation offers an invaluable opportunity of revising or elaborating, with appropriate empirical evidence, some of the rather abstract formulations proposed by the radical theorists of underdevelopment.

One such formulation is the "dissolution/conservation contradiction". As applied in southern Africa, this contradiction refers to the dual role of the labour reserve. It had to supply labour and it also had to provide part of the means of subsistence. At different periods in different areas, capital required the penetration of precapitalist social formations in such a way as partially to "free" labour from the land but at the same time to sustain their ability to reproduce the labour force. Hence kinship relations were both "dissolved", in some sense, and "conserved", in some sense (Wolpe, 1972; cf. Clarke, 1977). This was ensured by state policies, or rather the lack of them relating to social security, retirement, the bringing up of the next generation and so on, responsibility for which continued to be vested in social relations in the labour reserve. "Accessibility to the migrant worker of the product (and of the social services) of the Reserves depends upon the *conservation* albeit in a restructured form, of the reciprocal obligations of the family" (Wolpe, 1972: 434).

It is difficult to make sense of such a paradoxical formulation. How can relations be simultaneously restructured (i.e. transformed) and conserved? Is it not simpler to acknowledge that a certain pattern of reciprocal obligations has broken down, and that the onus placed on certain relationships – particularly the conjugal one – has intensified? . . .

Studies of small communities in Botswana (Schapera, 1975) and Lesotho (Murray, 1977) illustrate processes both of conservation and of change. On the one hand, we have evidence of a relatively stable agnatic structure (inheritance from and residence in the households of paternal ancestors) which endures through several generations. On the other hand, we have evidence of high rates of individual mobility, conjugal instability, illegitimacy, desertion and the break-up of families. The significant inference to be drawn from this is that study of the structure of small communities, defined in terms of the relationship between household heads, does not of itself indicate the qualitative disruption of family life that takes place over time. For the changes in kinship relations that I have described are quite consistent with the persistence of the agnatic structure of small communities as assessed in terms of genealogical relationships between household heads. Indeed, far from being contradictory in their implications, both the conservation and the change are rooted in the political economy of the labour reserve. The stability of residential alignments in many areas of the periphery is directly related to the severity of South African influx control and of land shortage. A man does not have the effective option either to move with his family outside the labour reserve, or to move away from his home area within the labour reserve, since he is even less likely to be allocated land elsewhere. On the other hand, the instability of conjugal relationships, the haphazard patterns of socialization and the high rates of illegitimacy are all largely attributable to the circumstances of migrant labour.

. . . A "movement" from the extended family to the nuclear family is commonly alleged to accompany the transition from a "traditional subsistence economy" to a "western-oriented cash economy". An abstract formulation of this kind begs the question of the meaning and existence of either entity, by confounding the discrete functional criteria (co-residence, consumption, reproduction, co-operative labour, distribution of migrant earnings, etc.) by which it is necessary to distinguish observations of family life. It also ignores the developmental cycle of the domestic group, which manifests itself in a statistical diversity of types of household composition at any one time. There is little point in identifying the nuclear family as the basic unit of analysis in circumstances where thousands of husbands and wives are forced to live apart; where frequency distributions of household sizes commonly exhibit two distinct modes (at 2 or 3 and about 6 persons respectively); where many households are headed by widows; where a significant number of women bear children but remain unmarried; and where many children are reared by grandparents in multigeneration households because their parent(s) is/are absent on migrant labour. A contradiction inheres in the attempt to maintain nuclear family integrity. A man's absence as a migrant labourer is a condition of his family's survival. But his absence also undermines the conjugal stability from which his family derives its identity.

. . . Especially in the circumstances of the southern African periphery, a particular conjugal union does not fall readily into a classificatory typology of the married and the unmarried, but must be understood as a temporal process during which its status is constantly susceptible to redefinition.

Thus there is some substance to criticism of kinship analyzes based on the imposition of western categories such as that of the nuclear family. But such criticism is quite gratuitous if it leads the critic, either to insist by contrast but without appropriate evidence on the importance of the "extended family", or to undermine the credibility of evidence – now surely overwhelming – that the enforced separation of spouses generates acute anxiety, insecurity and conflict. . . . The danger is that it effectively endorses the habit of capitalist employers and others who use the phrase the "extended family" in a residual sense to refer to something that allegedly accommodates everyone (the sick, the unemployed, the elderly) in default of decent wages or adequate social security arrangements. There is very little evidence to support such a view. . . . The nuclear family form of household can be identified as one typical phase of the developmental cycle. But statistical surveys exhibit a great diversity of household composition, from widows living on their own to complex three- (or *n*-) generational households which reflect the centrifugal distribution of children between households rather than their centripetal concentration within the households of their parents. Second, evidence from Lesotho suggests that the earnings of migrant labourers are increasingly concentrated within their own households and that households without direct access to an income from wage labour are severely disadvantaged. At the same time there is ample evidence relating to "family" gatherings, court cases, co-operative labour, visiting and mutual support, to identify aggregations of kin outside those incorporated within the household. Third, those networks of kin which are tactically articulated, normatively reinforced and susceptible to observation by the anthropologist are functionally related to constraints and opportunities which vary with phase in the developmental cycle and also with changes at the macro-economic level; for example, in prevailing wage levels, the recruitment policy of the mining industry and the effective export of unemployment by South Africa. In this way the notion of "family structure" must encapsulate diverse temporal processes by which individuals constitute their kinship universe.

Robin Cohen, *The Emergence of Wage Labor* (Gutkind, 1976)

The creation of a stable wage-labor force in Africa is essentially a product of white settlement and the establishment of European colonial administrations. Yet the organized expropriation of labor power had also been widespread in indigenous societies. Various forms of chattel and domestic slavery existed in many precolonial states; customary family labor was common, while itinerant groups of workers engaged in house building or heavy farming on an essentially contractual basis. . . . None the less, the colonial administrators in the early years of colonial rule found it difficult to displace surplus labor and to recruit sufficient laborers with the qualities they wanted and at the price they were willing to pay. Of course some colonial authorities did not attempt to introduce a free labor market and developed instead brutal policies of forced labor. The French did not abolish *prestation*, a labor tax which compelled adult males to work for a number of days a year, until 1946; while the British, although far less culpable in this respect, none the less used unfree labor in the production of essential war supplies, like Nigerian tin, during the Second World War.

Where the buying and selling of labor did take place, administrators were wont to complain about the supposed idleness and cost of African labor, particularly in comparison to Indian labor. As a consequence, farm labor from outside the continent was sometimes introduced. The Indian indentured laborers on the Natal sugar plantations were the largest group of imported laborers, but Chinese constituted 27 per cent of the labor force in the South African gold mines in 1905, while small groups of workers from the Caribbean were also contracted, particularly for work on the railways. Neither forced labor nor recruitment from abroad could, however, meet the demand for labor in the long term. Africans therefore had to be induced to sell their own labor power. Conquest and the dispossession of land rights, notably in Kenya, southern Africa, and the Rhodesias, began the process; the imposition of hut and land poll taxes more generally completed it. . . .

It was the creation of a landless group of rural dwellers, a group who also could no longer meet the cash demands of the colonial administration, who provided the making of an embryonic proletariat. A continuous and stable labor supply none the less remained a problem for the colonial state until the 1930s, for one major reason – colonial governments refused to pay unskilled laborers at a sufficiently attractive rate. Problems of labor recruitment only disappeared in the 1930s due to the effects of the worldwide depression. . . . By the 1930s a stabilized proletariat came into existence – particularly on public works programs, in the mines, in the building of roads and railways, and in the development of harbor and port facilities. Other than unskilled labor, colonial governments had additional manpower needs in accord with their *etatist* character. Soldiers, clerks, court stenographers, sanitary inspectors, policemen, and messengers.

Migrant Labor

A circular movement of migrant labor is involved, as numbers of the labor force shifted off the land (initially in response to the repressive policies of the colonial and white settler regime and later also in response to the 'pull' factors of the city) to join the chain of proletarianization. Many of course did so only seasonally, or for temporary contracts, but over the years the rate of return to the rural areas declined. First, production in the rural areas shifted slowly out of the hands of the community into individual peasant proprietorship. Second, employment opportunities in the cities opened up as industry and administration expanded. Expansion rarely was sufficient to meet job demands, but social aspirations deriving partly from the expansion of education remained high and many unemployed workers prefer to stay in the towns. Finally, the degree of impoverishment which became common in many African rural economies meant that a return to the land was in any case unfeasible for most migrants.

The contemporary patterns of in-migration to the cities are clear. Demographers have noted an upward shift in the median age of town dwellers, while many scholars have commented on the huge and growing pool of unemployed or casually employed labor in the cities and the associated growth of shanty towns and slum conditions. These trends suggest that the pattern of short-term migration is seriously in decay.

Only in southern Africa does an efficient and institutionalized use of migrant labor survive, and this too is showing signs of strain, particularly in response to recent political events on the subcontinent.... The system of contract labor to the South African gold fields was designed and carried out precisely according to the needs of a highly capitalized extractive industry of the type involved. Aircraft are chartered to the areas of supply, a medical inspection is carried out, and recruits are batched and labelled with names and destinations attached to their wrists. On arrival at the Witwatersrand, they are lectured in a common denominator patois on matters of safety, mining terminology, and so on, and are housed in single-sex compounds (see *van Onselen* and *Gordon*, below). The latest version of this, outside Johannesburg, comprises a modern set of high-rise buildings, with strategically located gates, electronically controlled from a defensible strongpoint and capable of being brought into operation if unrest reached alarming proportions. . . .

The owners of the South African gold mines, if not the South African government, are now firm converts to a policy of labor stabilization and urban residence that the Belgian Congolese authorities adopted 40 years ago. Though the Belgians have often been praised for their progressive policies on this issue, in point of fact the devastation that was wrought on the rural populations during the pacification period was so great that the Belgians were left with little alternative but to provide the means of subsistence around the areas of employment. In other parts of Africa, migrant labor was a useful source of labor supply, and its use left the rural areas just sufficiently viable to support the reproduction of labor power and the minimal welfare needs of returning laborers. . . .

The Rural Proletariat

. . . Despite the absence of large numbers of plantation workers in Africa there has recently been a largely undocumented growth of a rural labor force working wholly or largely for wages. In Kenya, for example, the indigenous takeover of the so-called white highlands after independence did not foster a return to smaller units of production. If anything the commercialization of agriculture, often undertaken by Kenyans prominent in business and industry, has produced a further stage in the growth of capitalist social relations – namely, an absentee landlord, employing an on-the-site manager who in turn supervises the farm labor. This pattern is as yet fairly rare in Africa, outside Southern Africa, at least on a large farm basis . . . and peasant proprietorship is, in my view, becoming the dominant agricultural mode of production, at the same time the term ''peasant'' may conceal vast differences in wealth, incomes, and power in the countryside. Many of the richer peasants and farmers are fast moving into the position of becoming small employers of rural labor, and it is in this area, rather than in plantations that rural proletarianization will grow.

The Unskilled Urban Worker

. . . Once the labor history of the continent is approached from below rather than from above case after case of action undertaken to defend class interests appears. Some authors have concentrated on describing early manifestations of strike action. Railwaymen and dockers were usually at the forefront of such events. More often than not, strikes in the early years of colonial rule were short-lived affairs generated in the heat of the moment; and, though frequently involving large numbers of workers across several occupational ranges, they left little in the way of an organizational imprint. For the most part the degree of class consciousness involved has simply been inferred from the nature of class action. Yet the social universe that was comprehended was often the workplace for a localized employer–employee relationship; rarely did workers express, in the early period of colonial rule, a national, let alone an international, solidarity. Other mitigating factors included a fairly sharp division of status between the unskilled workers and the members of a more respectable white-collar salariat, and the persistence in many areas of ethnic forms of identity and interaction. The degree to which ethnicity replaced or undercut forms of social interaction based on class lines is still contentious though recent works show that the work relationship was a far more determinate experience than a picture of African societies divided rigidly along ethnic lines of competition can possibly allow for (cf. Epstein, 1958). . . .

The chain of proletarianization has been discussed in relation to the growth of class consciousness and in relation to class action. The third necessary component is that of organization. It is clear that strike action has to have a degree of organization behind it, but it is less clear that workers were able prior to 1945 to organize trade unions to defend or promote their interests in a sustained fashion. Archival and newspaper evidence reveals the existence of many worker organizations in West Africa, some of them, to be sure, being moribund or ineffective for much of their existence. In South Africa the Industrial and Commercial Union, organized in the interwar period, mobilized large numbers of African workers until its demise.

After 1945 the pace of proletarianization was considerably advanced. Absolute numbers of workers who were engaged in full-time employment increased considerably, while the struggles that workers were engaged in to improve their pay or conditions became enmeshed in a more general anticolonial movement. . . . In so far as the unions were able to mobilize a popular base in the postwar period outside the confines of their membership, this base was not a sufficiently strong one to challenge the basis of legitimacy that the parties laid claim to. Proletarianization had not proceeded so totally as to allow the proletariat to act as the 'general representatives' of the society at large. On the other hand the trade unions had just sufficient organizational coherence and popularity not to be ignored by the nationalist politicians.

In a sense, the period from 1945 until the independence of most black African territories was one in which a temporary and often fitful class alliance was forged between the indigenous bourgeoisies and the organized working class. This co-operation rarely penetrated to levels below that of formalized structures (parties and unions) that organized each class, except on occasions like election days and rallies when the politicians needed a suitable display of mass support or acquiescence to use in their negotiations with the colonial authorities and in their construction of a neocolonial state. None the less a substratum of worker radicalism, particularly at the rank-and-file level, survived throughout this period and was to dramatically resurrect itself in the postcolonial period. (See *Sandbrook and Arn, Crisp*, below.)

Managers, Professionals, and Bureaucrats

In this category I include members of the civil service in senior staff positions, those who work in private industry or public corporations on the managerial side, and those who are employed on the public purse. Though not normally discussed in descriptions of African labor issues, this group does merit some comment in its own right, for three reasons. First, civil servants, in particular, are often well organized, especially in Francophone African countries. In Dahomey, for example, civil servants were able to effect upward salary increases during successive military and civilian regimes which amounted at one point to two-thirds of the national budget. Second, the salariat are often in a situation where their skills can be bought or sold internationally. Their reference groups tend, therefore, to be located outside the countries they live in. If successful, such pay claims serve to further widen the normally high wage differentials. They may then produce a demonstration effect downwards in the form of a felt sense of relative deprivation by other workers in the society, a deprivation that it may not be easy to satisfy within the framework of a postcolonial state. Third, the social and political role of the group identified can be seen as parasitical on other segments of the society and instrumental in serving the ends of neoimperialism either as direct employees of the state or as auxiliaries of the foreign powers and interests that dominate most African countries. The group concerned are often trained in metropolitan institutions imbued with Western tastes and prejudices, or in local institutions heavily penetrated by external influences. . . .

Other Urban Migrants

If a common thread of organizational endeavour, class consciousness and class action can be traced throughout the colonial period in the case of wage laborers, the same cannot be said for other dispossessed segments of the urban social structure. Many Africans migrating to the cities found themselves without jobs, or unable to get those they aspired to. Some accommodated themselves to a socially disapproved existence as pimps, touts, prostitutes, or thieves, living often at the margins of subsistence or preying, like parasites, at what few pickings a capital city of an impoverished country can offer. Others swelled the ranks of those who staff the industries, small trades and services that blanket the landscape of any African city. (See *Gerry*, below.) This sector of the urban economy, described often nowadays as the "informal sector", in fact accounts for a considerable degree of urban employment. . . . The conditions of employment can be extremely harsh. For three or four years apprentices are bound to their masters in a condition resembling that of servitude. A space on the workshop floor is living accommoderation, and pocket money barely covers the means of survival, while the Eldorado to the apprentice, namely a workshop of his own, is difficult to finance and may indeed never materialize.

Finally, there exist a group of genuinely unemployed workers, "job applicants" by self-description, but in fact a lumpenproletariat proper. The most dramatic growth of an urban lumpenproletariat occurred in the areas of white settlement – where land-grabbing and the break-up of rural, particularly pastoral, economies had occurred most ruthlessly. In Kenya, influx control measures in the form of the notorious *kipande* (work certificate) provided much of the incendiary material that fueled the Mau Mau rebellion. The pass system in South Africa, indeed the whole construction of apartheid as a systematic ideology, can also be considered as an attempt to meet the dilemma that white settlement and conquest generated. For the white South African regime to turn back the flow of urban migrants, let alone resettle those who have been urbanized for generations, it has to revitalize rural economies which previous white regimes systematically succeeded in underdeveloping and emasculating. Yet the chains of proletarianization have gone too far to be reversed. . . .

It may be possible to effect a degree of political collaboration across several segments of the urban poor – the unskilled wage labourers, the unemployed, those employed in the informal sector, petty traders, and the like. Some descriptive evidence of such links having been forged in the past are provided in descriptions of strike action in Sekondi-Takoradi in 1961 and in Lagos in 1971 (Jeffries and Peace in Sandbrook, 1975b). What they represent is a form of urban populism: the evolution of a set of demands and grievances common to the urban dispossessed, but articulated by its most active elements. . . .

Part II

Gender, Production and Politics

Introduction

Our opening section concentrates on men, yet the effects of colonialism and capitalism on women have been far-reaching and raise important questions of analysis, neglected by all but a few writers until recently. *Mackintosh* points out that analyses of domestic or household-based production have taken for granted, and thereby ignored, "the work of caring for children, washing, cooking, cleaning". It is not sufficient to examine how production within the household (agricultural production as well as domestic tasks) reproduces cheap labour power; we also have to understand the relation of domestic tasks to other activities, and the ways in which domestic responsibilities restrict women from earning money (cf. Meillassoux, 1975). Whereas the sexual allocation of domestic tasks is rigidly defined the sexual division of agricultural and other tasks is more flexible. These vary markedly as among African societies, and have changed over time, as a result of the pressures of migration on labour resources and the opening of new ways of making money; for example, by producing cash crops.

Hafkin and Bay, and *Dinan*, discuss the effects of colonialism on the autonomy and status of women. Hafkin and Bay stress the ways in which colonialism and capitalism have restricted the opportunities open to women and increased their dependence on men. Women have participated in cash cropping, wage labour (including "domestic service") and in commerce, generally on relatively unfavourable terms and for meagre returns (Little, 1973; Bryceson, 1980; Vail, 1980; Schwarz, 1972; Kane in Vidal, 1977; Cock, 1980; Nelson, 1981). Many women depend for their own, independent incomes on producing, and selling, food and other commodities, even when their mobility is restricted by the Muslim practice of seclusion (Boserup, 1970; Hill, 1969; Vidal, 1977; Hafkin, 1975; Wipper, 1975/6). Similarly, the political influence and organizations of women have been limited and subordinated, often, to male institutions and ideology (Wipper, 1971, 1975; Lewis in Hafkin, 1975). Yet, as *Dinan* shows, to regard the impact of colonialism and capitalism as entirely and uniformly regressive, is to discount women's ability to resist a loss of status and to

41

create new forms of activity which allow them some autonomy (see Obbo, 1980; Bujra in Vidal, 1977; Murray, 1977).

Our fourth exact is a rare autobiographical account by a woman political organizer, in colonial Zambia. It was collected and translated by the anthropologist Peter Harries-Jones, assisted by George Nsofu and John Ngwisha, and "is remarkable, not only for what it says, but for the way Foster Mubanga says it. Written originally in Copperbelt Bemba (a lingua franca among urban Zambians), and by a person with only primary education, its grammar and meaning had to be intuited at various places in the original version. But the language retains its own vivid style, even in translation. It is comprehensive in its recall of days, events and personalities, and imbued with a fervour that draws inspiration from constant allusion to Christian symbolisms of sacrifice" (Harries-Jones, 1975: 18). It illustrates both the scope for women's political activity and cultural and institutional constraints on it. Future research will probably show that women were far more routinely involved in nationalist and other political activities than is currently recognized, as well as being at the centre of several better-known events, such as the 1929 Aba Women's War (Van Allen in Hafkin, 1975; Ifeka-Moller in Ardener, 1975) or the struggles of Afrikaner women textile workers in the thirties (Webster, 1978). Researchers need to relate these activities to the less overtly political involvement of women in spirit cults, witchcraft accusations, divorce cases and various ways of disciplining men, which seem analogous in many ways to the "hidden" forms of protest by workers, and by peasants, discussed respectively by *Cohen* and *Thoden van Velzen*, below (see Ardener, 1973; Berger in Hafkin, 1975; Vidal, 1977).

Some, but not all, radical nationalist parties have encouraged more direct forms of political participation by women (compare Rivière, 1977 on Guinea with Brain in Hafkin, 1975 and Mbilinyi, 1973 on Tanzania). The most active have been armed national liberation movements (Urdang, 1979), yet despite the political and military activities of women during the wars, and the clear opposition to male dominance shown by party leaderships (e.g. Machel, 1975) it has, as *Isaacman* argues, proved difficult to defend their gains after the war.

We have not tried to cover fully many of the aspects of the sociology of sex and gender, such as family life, marriage, sexual relations or prostitution (a topic curiously attractive to Africanists). Our excerpts, and *Murray*, above, do however show their significance for the themes of participation in economic and political activity on which we have focused. Novels (Farrah, 1970; Beti, 1971; Tlali, 1979) are still among the best introductions to these aspects, as are biographies, notably that of the Nigerian Muslim, *Baba of Karo* (Smith, 1954). Academic sources include Little, 1973; and Oppong, 1973.

Women, Production and Capitalism

Nancy Hafkin and Edna Bay, *Colonialism and Women's Roles* (1975)

African women have varying degrees of economic independence, often despite social orders that place them under the authority of husbands or fathers. Wives and husbands in Africa usually have separate incomes, with clearly defined financial obligations to their children, their spouse, and their spouse's lineage. Married women generally have the right to own and acquire property that is separate from that of their husbands, and in many areas men and women are guaranteed equal rights to land use. Business transactions and earnings beyond marital obligations are considered a spouse's private affair. Women are said to lend money to husbands at rates only slightly less usurious than those offered to others, among the Ga of Accra.

Women typically develop economic skills well before marriage, though a husband may provide trade capital or fees for schooling to a new wife or fiancée. The few women who have gained access to Western education have been channeled by and large into the ''feminine'' professions – teaching clerical work, nursing, and midwifery. Outside the so-called modern sector, women engage in a variety of occupations: they prepare farm products or cooked foods for market; raise surplus crops for sale; produce craftwork; and trade farm produce, prepared foods, or manufactured goods.

Retail trade appears to be the most widespread of women's occupations, in West Africa in particular. . . . Records of women's entrepreneurial activities go far back into the precolonial past; thus women traders in the Senegambia region, in collaboration with European merchants, became women of wealth and prestige, intermediaries providing access to African commercial networks.

The independence of trading women, coupled with their marketplace outspokenness, has led many Western observers, past and present, to assume egalitarian sentiments in African societies. To the contrary, most African women live in societies with strong biases toward male superiority. In historical Dahomey, the formidable women soldiers boasted of their victories by singing ''We marched against Attahpahms as against men. We came and found them women''. Market women's groups have occasionally applied their leverage to the betterment of economic or political opportunities. More often, though, women have found it difficult to define and seek common goals. The internalization of antifemale attitudes may be a factor in women's lack of a sense of economic power or political potential. In Africa, the economic independence of women is less a mark of privilege than a matter of necessity; women take responsibility for their economic well-being because they must. We should not be surprised, then, to see independent Ga trading women emulating Western-style nuclear-family marriage and financial dependence on a husband.

In many African societies, women's and men's spheres have been separate. However the perimeters of the respective spheres do not remain constant, but vary according to ethnic group, geographical setting, social class, and historical era. Women frequently act collectively within their sphere, either through voluntary associations or through institutions paralleling those of men. But this apparent structural complementarity does not necessarily imply equality between the sexes. The male sphere was often accorded particular advantages, even in the precolonial period. Though women had a substantial measure of economic independence and a voice in political affairs in many parts of the continent, they were not dominant, as some have said, and they were not equal.

Even in the case of the dual-sex political system of the Igbo, which appears closest to "separate but equal", the basic framework is one of patriarchy. The process of acquisition of status operated the same way for women as for men. In striking contrast to American society, Igbo women's public status was achieved not from their husbands but from their own acquisition of titles. Though men and women both attained public status in the same way, men's greater access to the resources necessary for gaining titles and status gave them an advantage over women. Thus Igbo society had a democratic ideology, but not an egalitarian one.

In addition to unequal access to resources, there were other ways in which African societies restricted women from attaining equal status with men. Numerous societies had cultural restrictions that kept women subordinate. . . . Many societies had menstrual taboos, keeping women apart in menstrual huts. Some secret societies were open only to postmenopausal women, and other male societies were designed to ensure women's submission. Other rites of passage can be seen as culturally legitimated ways of suppressing women.

Western observers, frequently unaware of the prerogatives of women in many African societies, saw the advent of European colonialism as a positive event for African women. The light of Western Christianity and education would lift them from the toil of agricultural labor, the burden of polygamy and forced marriages, and the pain of clitoridectomy to a richer and more fulfilling life. But on the contrary, colonialism actually had a retarding effect on African women; they experienced a substantial loss in their economic and political status. Boserup (1970) described how Europeans decided that men's cultivation was superior to women's and set out to replace them, even in areas where women had introduced cash-cropping: "Virtually all Europeans shared the opinion that men are superior to women in the art of farming; and it seemed to follow that for the development of agriculture male farming ought to be promoted to replace female farming. Many Europeans did all they could to achieve this." Similarly when Ga women turned enthusiastically to petty trading with the introduction of a money economy, several researchers regarded their position as enviable. But petty trading was precarious, and most women managed only a marginal subsistence from it. Women remained in this sector while men alone were gaining access to new job opportunities in the modern sector.

African women lost political as well as economic status under colonialism. Europeans failed to see that African women had political roles and institutions in their societies, particularly in the case of the British system of "indirect rule", under which women's institutions somehow disappeared. The traditional principles of dispersed and shared political authority had no place in the colonial system.

African women did not accept their loss of status passively. The most dramatic example of their response came in the 1929 "Women's War". Stimulated by what they perceived to be a move to tax their property, Igbo women organized through their *Mikiri* network, attacked the Warrant Chief they suspected of carrying out the taxation scheme, and massed in protest at the colonial District Office. The British administration met the women's protest with police and soldiers, followed by retaliatory punitive expeditions. . . . When in western Kenya men went off as contract labor to the White Highlands, women were forced not only to support themselves, their children, and frequently the men (whose migrant-labor wages were below subsistence), but also to meet colonial demands for sustained and sometimes increased agricultural production. The women responded with agricultural innovation and experimentation: they assumed more of the burden of agricultural labor; introduced labor-saving crops such as maize, cassava, and groundnuts; adopted new implements; and made trade and marketing a regular part of their lives.

In most newly independent African countries, the process of deterioration of status that beset women under colonialism has continued. For Ga women the deterioration has accelerated. As the male-dominated modern commercial sector has grown, increased importation of manufactured products has reduced co-operation among women and between spouses. Trade capital has been increasingly difficult to amass, and the result of Western education has been a reduction in the scale of business among traders. The deteriorating economic situation of small traders has left Accra women fighting to hold onto their economic independence.

The decline in women's status has continued even in some of the most progressive African countries. Women in the *Ujamaa* villages that were to form the nucleus of socialist development in Tanzania are sometimes worse off than they have been in traditional society. On rural development projects, women were expected to put in the same amount of time doing farm labor that men were; but women were also expected to continue with their domestic labor, and thus had a double burden. . . . In the liberation movements that developed in the 1960s in Portuguese-controlled areas of Africa, however, women made important contributions, and the new regimes in Mozambique and Guinea-Bissau have been cited by many observers as models to be emulated in their treatment of women. Male dominance and female subordination are seen as inequities that arose from colonialism and its resulting class stratification, and the Mozambique government's commitment to the reconstruction of society makes equality for women a necessary part of social and economic change.

Maureen Mackintosh, *Domestic Labour: Production and Reproduction*
(1979)

Marxist economists studying domestic labour under capitalism have tended to take the work done within the household as an unproblematic whole. Marxist anthropologists have tended to do the same thing when studying societies where a wide range of production is household-based and not produced for the purpose of exchange. A number of economic anthropologists have variously tried to define a mode of production whose defining characteristic is that production is carried out within the household. Universally, these attempts, while admitting the existence of a sexual division of labour in production within the household, do not integrate this division of labour into the analysis of the mode of production as a whole, but merely comment upon it in a descriptive way. . . .

In Meillassoux (1975) one can trace the same absence of investigation of the division of work within the household. Production, for Meillassoux, is agricultural production, and the relations of production are the relations of production in agriculture. The relations of reproduction on the other hand are purely relations of marriage and kinship, the relations of men to their progeny. The work of caring for children, washing, cooking, cleaning – the work which feminists see as fundamental to an understanding of the whole sexual division of labour in capitalist society – has vanished.

The Senegalese village which I shall now discuss is one where, until the arrival in 1973 on part of its land of a foreign-owned plantation, all the production done within the village boundaries was household-based. That is to say, for the agricultural production which produced both the main subsistence (non-marketed) crop and the cash crops which were the main source of money income in the village, the household was the unit of decision-making and of effective land appropriation. A large majority of the agricultural labour time spent on the fields of a household was drawn from within that household. Leaving aside the cattle herding, artisan work and retail selling, I shall examine the agricultural and non-agricultural work for similarities and differences in its organization. The non-agricultural activities then include the following: food preparation, cleaning, washing, care of children, wood and other gathering activities, care of the sick, physical maintenance of the house and its fencing.

Men and women engage in both agricultural and non-agricultural activities in this village. Men do the bulk of the agricultural labour but some women have fields of their own and there are some agricultural tasks on the men's fields which are typically done by women. In the non-agricultural sphere, men do the building, repair and maintenance of the house; women do all the other tasks.

The division of labour between the sexes is, however, much more rigid in the non-agricultural sphere. There are tasks where men and women work side by side in agriculture; there are none in the non-agricultural sphere. Technical change in agriculture – the introduction of donkey- or horse-drawn equipment – has eroded the women's role in agricultural production since the women do not use the equipment. Men have taken over tasks that used to be done by both men and women, and even sometimes tasks that were generally done by women alone. Furthermore, in agriculture, young male labour is quite frequently used to replace female labour, without there being a stigma attached. The rigidity of the sexual division of labour in agriculture is most marked in the subsistence crop (millet) and it is least marked in the newest cash crop (wet season vegetables) where there is considerable fluidity of definition of the sexual division of tasks.

No such fluidity exists in the non-agricultural sphere. Men construct and maintain the physical buildings and walls. All other tasks of caring for and maintenance of the people in the household are done by the women of that household. Men provide the subsistence food, millet, either by growing it or occasionally buying it for cash when the crop is finished. Once provided, it is under the control of a woman in the household. Otherwise, the provision of food is the sphere of the women. They may gather or cultivate plants to eat with the millet; if additions to the millet – oil or tomato, for example – are bought, the women will do the buying, even if the men have sometimes provided the cash. Food preparation is done by the women exclusively, and all members of a household eat from a common pot. The physical caring for other human beings is entirely a woman's task, including washing clothes and caring for the sick. This division of labour according to gender is not undergoing any process of change. . . .

The non-agricultural tasks are extremely time-consuming. The following is a description of a day's work of a young woman who does all the tasks for the household in which she lives. She gets up at around 5 a.m.: that is, well before it is light. She pounds millet for perhaps one hour. Then she goes to the well for water (which may mean a long wait) and prepares breakfast, which consists of millet couscous largely prepared the day before. The next stage is preparing the ingredients for lunch, which may be millet porridge or rice, and may involve gathering or going to the village shop. The couscous for supper and the next day's breakfast is prepared during the afternoon. If her mother-in-law is working at the plantation she takes food to her. In the evening she pounds millet again. She goes to bed at around 9 p.m. During the day, usually in the morning, she does the washing as necessary for six adults and a child, and she has a one-year-old-child constantly with her. She herself is sixteen years old.

A young woman doing all the non-agricultural labour for a household therefore spends her whole working day upon it. She does not have a field of her own, and does little agricultural work, though in the rainy season she takes food to the people in the fields. Later, as she becomes older and has daughters to help her with the cooking and washing and child care, she may take on more agricultural labour.

The rigidity of the sexual division of non-agricultural work has become even more evident since the arrival of the plantation, offering wage work during six months of the year to both men and women. The participation rate of the women as well as the men in the plantation labour force is extremely high, there being no feeling among the men that the women should not do this work. The working day on the plantation is normally from 7.30 in the morning to mid- to late afternoon, though packers often work more irregular hours in shifts. For the men, this plantation work is an alternative to other activities during the plantation season, which is the dry season in Senegal when they do not work on their own crops. . . . The women inevitably have simply added their plantation work to their non-agricultural tasks which they undertake all the year round, thereby stretching their physical endurance almost to breaking point.

This, for example, is a working day of a woman, doing the non-agricultural work for a household all on her own, and also working at the plantation. She gets up at least an hour earlier than the young woman just described, to pound her millet, fetch water and make breakfast for the household. She prepares and leaves something for lunch, perhaps couscous to be heated, for the children, which has been partly prepared the night before. She leaves the children with an old woman in the compound and goes to work at about 7 a.m. She returns from work around 4 or 5 p.m., and goes to the well or the plantation tap for water on her way home. Once home, she prepares the couscous for supper and for the next day, and pounds the millet again. When there is washing to be done she does it at night. She always goes to bed later than when she is not working at the plantation, and when she is washing perhaps as late as 11 p.m. or midnight. She is up again the next day at 4 a.m.

Not only do men never do any of this work, but young boys also do none, despite the fact that they are in the household, and do not begin to work on the plantation at as young an age as the girls. As the woman just described explained, ''I have only sons, so there is no one to help me''.

There are a number of ways in which women try to cushion the appalling strain of this double day. One is by simply not working as regularly as the men. To the extent that it is possible, women shift the way in which their work is spread over the year, but the very nature of their work, daily maintenance of a household, means that there is very little they can do in this respect. Therefore they inevitably need days off when their household work piles up or a child is ill. Employers take advantage of these constraints on women to treat their female employees differently from the men they employ. The men's jobs tend to be stabilised, to last all season, and they are paid at least the minimum wage. The women's jobs tend to pay less, the women are treated as an interchangeable mass of workers, frequently hired at the gate each day, and the management make far less effort to stabilize the work force. Thus the rigidity of the sexual division of labour in domestic tasks is visibly the source of women's greater oppression within the sphere of wage work.

The other way in which women cushion the strain of doing two days' work in one is through the use of an already existing division of labour among women in the household. Women do non-agricultural household labour only if their status in the household is that of wife or daughter. Nor do all wives do this work. A girl starts to help her mother with her household work when she is quite young; by ten she is doing quite a lot of cooking and fetching water, but is not yet strong enough, for example, to get the washing clean. By thirteen, two years before she is likely to marry, a girl may be doing virtually all her mother's work in the home. Once she marries and leaves her parental home, a young woman works for her mother no more. Instead, if she is the first wife of a young man, she is likely to take on all her husband's mother's household work. This is the main way in which an older woman is finally relieved of the burden of housework. An older, active woman with a daughter-in-law at home can go to work on the plantation without exhausting herself in the way that the younger women do.

If a woman is the second wife of her husband, the situation is different. In this case the first wife will already be doing the work in the household, and the second wife will share the work. Only if a woman has just had a child will she have a break from the work. . . . All that has been said above, however, refers chiefly to cooking and does not extend to child care, which is the individual mother's responsibility. Only older daughters can be relied upon to look after younger children when necessary. Very young children are the strongest constraint preventing women from going out to work for a wage. A woman, if she is prepared to work very long hours indeed, can reorganize cooking, cook in the morning for lunch time and do her washing at night; but if she has no one to look after a young child she is tied. . . .

When the economy becomes much more monetized than the village economy I was describing above there comes to exist what is almost a separate sphere of exchange in the village: that of petty selling between women. This selling is either of vegetables and fish bought in small-quantity lots and broken down for resale, or partially prepared food (couscous only needing final steaming), or small cooked foods (fried doughnuts for example, or grilled peanuts). There is an enormous amount of this petty selling, and it is very important to the way in which women succeed in providing for their families. Its proceeds supply the small sums of money of which women are in constant need, in order to buy small quantities of relish to add to the staple foods, or to take a child to the dispensary. Women may even sell some of their crops from their fields in this small-scale way, though if they have many crops they will sell them wholesale (see also Hill, 1969).

Men never go in for this small-scale petty selling. They sell their crops wholesale, they buy millet when they have to do so in as large lots as possible and leave it to the women to break it down. If they pay money for minor ingredients to the meals they give the cash to the women to shop, but they would never have a woman buy a sack of grain for them. It is the sexual division of the non-agricultural tasks in the household which creates these two separate types of exchange and the sex-typing of the petty selling. Women also grow crops, but men do not cook food or care for children, and so they also do not become involved in this petty exchange economy. . . .

What then are the relations under which domestic labour is performed, the relations which constitute the unit of domestic production? This raises the issue of reproduction, in the various senses in which that word is used in the literature, since the feature of domestic labour from which we began is that it is all, or almost all, done by women, and it consists of the production of essentially identical types of use values in very different societies. In an earlier commentary (1977) on Meillassoux's work I argued that Meillassoux, in common with other writers who have tried to formulate modes of production for this type of society, detached the relations governing the production of people and their distribution through the society – the relations of kinship, marriage and filiation – from all basis in social production and thereby emptied them of content. Meillassoux admits the subordination of women as part of the content of the kin relations that he describes, but he sees the maintenance of this subordination as unproblematic. I went on to argue that we need to distinguish the social relations of human reproduction from the ways in which the reproduction of the mode of production as a whole is ensured or enforced. This formulation, however, offers no way out of the problem just stated. No amount of reformulation of definitions will help, in the absence of a theory of how women's subordination is reproduced through her participation (or absence of participation) in social production.

It is this theory which an analysis of domestic labour should help us to work towards. The institution of the household mediates two sets of social relations, both of which have economic content in the sense that they are based in production activities, and is itself an economic institution. The first set of relations is those which reproduce the subordination of women and the alienation from her of the control of her body, her progeny and the products of her domestic work. The second set of relations is those governing the performance of social labour other than domestic labour, relations which may be more or less oppressive or exploitative.

In the household-based economy, the household is the institution which contains within itself both of these sets of relations. But even in this case one can see that there are two mutually imbricated sets of social relations present, the division between them coming to the surface in the differences between domestic labour and other labour. On the one hand, one has the set of relations which involves the marriage, filiation and residence rules, the performance and control of domestic labour, and the resultant exclusion of women from certain roles in the rest of social production. These relations are those that constitute the household and control its membership. On the other hand, one has the relations involved in the performance and control of agricultural labour. This second set of relations is the one that has been the subject of the debate concerning the lineage mode of production, and the debate has centred on the control by the older men of the younger. These two sets of social relations are mutually determining, and one set cannot continue to exist without the other. In a household-based system, the control by male elders of the whole system involves the maintenance of the subordination both of women to men and of younger men to male elders. To threaten the subordination of women would be to threaten the stability of the household and therefore of the system as a whole. . . .

Carmel Dinan, *Work, Marriage and Autonomy* (Vidal, 1977)

Has the condition of African women been improved or worsened by modernization and a movement to the cities? Two schools of thought have emerged on this issue. The "Optimists" feel that urban living has improved women's position; that the city offers them wider occupational options and hence greater scope for financial independence; higher standards of living; greater freedom to assert their economic and sexual independence from husbands, or, given the favourable sex imbalance of the cities, greater scope for selectivity should they decide on marital or quasi-marital partners; and, overall, greater possibilities for personal emancipation from male-dominated traditional family systems.

The "Pessimists" hold that the urban milieu has eroded the traditionally powerful position of African women and that urbanization has introduced new positions of subjection and dependence for them; that unequal educational and economic opportunities result in the preferential employment of men and that the majority of women have few real occupational options apart from petty trading, formal or informal prostitution and illicit brewing; that urban feminine roles have crystallized in sexual and domestic areas in contrast to the important "public" roles they played in traditional society; that urban women generally, are regarded as unmarriageable because of the negative male evaluation of city women as being sexually loose; that unmarried women are regarded by men as prostitutes whether true or not and that the general stereotype of city women is that they are superficial, pleasure-seeking and work-shy.

The protagonists of the "pessimistic" line of argument tend to take as their basis for comparison the status of women in traditional society where, they say, women enjoyed a measure of economic, legal and political equality with men; that the division of labour in precolonial subsistence economies placed the main burden of food production on women; that this resulted in a complementary rather than subordinate position for women *vis-à-vis* men as each had equal need of the other; that their economic status in such economies was high as women could maintain control over their own self-acquired property; that women had their own political associations where they could promote their own specific interests as opposed to those of men and could act collectively against them when necessary; that in some societies women actually held high political office with powers to enthrone or dethrone a chief, as in Ghana, and that they played an active military role.

The high status of women in these societies became progressively modified primarily by external factors, the most important being the advent of the colonial era. Some writers argue that the ideological infiltration of Western values and norms into indigenous cultures was even more important than actual conquest in this down-grading process. Western colonialists were apparently imbued with Victorian ideas and assumptions about ''proper'' male and female roles; their definition concentrated largely on domestic and social rather than on economic and political roles.

Such colonial attitudes of male supremacy are thought by the ''Pessimists'' to have been further reinforced by Christian missionaries, who, in their educational endeavours, placed greater emphasis on turning out Christian wives and mothers than on equipping a woman for an economic or civic role. The women's associations – the locus of their political power – were also undermined by conversion to Christianity as membership required avoidance of the pagan rituals which were a basic requirement in membership of these associations.

European technical advisors also apparently carried this narrow definition of the female role with its assumption that agricultural work was not naturally a woman's job. This resulted in women being excluded from lucrative cash-crop agriculture despite their traditional heavy involvement in subsistence production, food processing and the retailing of such products. The redistribution of tasks resulting from the introduction of improved agricultural techniques worked to the women's disadvantage: with men monopolizing the modern agricultural machinery, the productivity gap between men and women widened, with a resultant decline in women's relative status within agriculture. In the later era of development aid they were ignored by development planners, under-utilized in development programmes and denied the opportunity to acquire the skills which would have enabled them to enjoy the benefits of modernization. . . .

The "pessimistic" line of argument is persuasive up to a degree, but there would seem to be a tendency, on the part of some writers, to pursue this line even when faced with empirical evidence which points to the opposite direction. Alf Schwarz (1972), reporting on his research amongst female Zaïrian factory workers, notes that they themselves perceived salaried work as being their "salvation". He describes their praise for it and records that they reported that work enabled them to be financially independent; that it afforded them self-respect and that their status had been elevated to the point where they felt that they could be treated like a man. Nevertheless, despite such strong evidence from the women themselves that work enabled them to maintain their self-respect and independence, Schwarz concluded that the women were suffering from a false consciousness; that they were deluded and indulging in self-deception; that they were living in a fantasy world, attempting to dismiss from their consciousness their feelings of disgrace and exclusion; that their stand was an elaborate pretence, gross wishful thinking which struggled to give meaning to an otherwise degrading existence. Unless Schwarz's views are derived from unquoted data, it is unclear how he arrives at such a "pessimistic" conclusion about the women he was studying.

The notion propounded by Western feminists that Third World women have been subordinated, humiliated and dominated is one not always subscribed to by African writers. It is, moreover, a notion that they resent, implying, as it does, that African women are passive, submissive creatures, incapable of looking after their own interests. . . . Thus a Nigerian journalist at the International Women's Year Conference in Mexico City wrote: "It is presumptuous for anyone to presume that women of the Third World are unable to articulate their own outrage at any issue that concerns them. As a member of the Third World, I repudiate this patronising attitude and particularly the underlining intellectual imperialism."

. . . A useful way, it is suggested, of approaching the problem is to conceptualize women as social actors using strategies in structured ways to achieve desired goals. . . . In this model, the goals that women set themselves are defined by their position within the overall social system and by the resources that they themselves possess. The strategies they use involve attempts to maximize these resources by manipulating the opportunities that they perceive in their environment. Such a model would limit itself to a description of the social environment within which the women operate; it would pay particular attention to the constraints and incentives in their economic, occupational, political and social worlds. It would also involve an elaboration of the goals of the women and the choices they must make to maximize their chances of attaining them. It would, finally, include a description of the actual strategies being used by the women.

Such an approach has the advantage of placing the emphasis on the women's own perception of their situation: it sets aside any ethnocentric notions of "proper" women's roles. It also credits women with being, like men, purposeful social actors actively attempting to control their own social environment and with maximizing their own resources within that environment.

This, therefore, is the model chosen for the present analysis of the professional "single" women of Accra, Ghana. . . . Has the process of urbanization improved or worsened the position of this important, albeit privileged, category of urban women?

1. One obvious focus of interest for these women is their *careers*. Apart from the intrinsic satisfaction that the women obtain from their professional work, they enjoy steady employment and high, secure incomes; they also control the allocation of their own economic resources. Thus the city affords these women greater options than did a rural economy. It offers them a real opportunity to be financially autonomous of husbands and kin; it enables them to retain their single status; to maintain themselves if inadequately provided for in marriage; and to break away from an unsatisfactory union if they so determine.

2. Another area where the city seems to offer the women increased options is on the question of *marriage and motherhood*. In traditional Ghanaian society, motherhood and marriage were the prescribed roles for women; they also had little choice to decide whom their husbands would be. In the surveyed area of Accra, however, as many as 30 per cent of the women were not complying with this norm. This was not, as the "Pessimists" would claim because urban women cannot get husbands, but because they actively choose to remain single. For all these women, marriage offers were at some point considered but turned down as the ideal partner did not present himself or their own carefully-laid career plans precluded marriage at that point in their lives.

Neither does the single state preclude boyfriends or a sexual life. Modern methods of contraception available in the city enable them to lead sexually active lives without fears of motherhood.

When these women eventually decide to marry, the marriage will be based on their free consent; they will insist on legal, statutory marriage which is monogamous and will give them maintenance rights for their children; as widows they will be entitled to share in the inheritance of their husbands' property. Their strong economic position also gives them a greater chance of commanding an egalitarian relationship with their husbands. They will also enjoy considerable choice in the area of reproduction: they will be able to decide on the number and spacing of their children. And, finally, if the marriage proves unsatisfactory, they can initiate proceedings for a divorce.

3. A third major area of broadened options for the women concerns their *relationshisps with kin*. Whilst geographically separated from most members of their extended families, they are able to avoid close scrutiny of their activities and to enjoy more day-to-day freedom. Their own economic strength, on the other hand, enables them to select a power-base in whatever limited but strategic segment of their lineage that they choose.

4. A last major area of increased freedom lies in the *life-styles* they choose to adopt. Living in a city involves a considerable increase in their freedom of movement and a greatly expanded social world. Traditionally, social life was rigidly dichotomized by sex but this rigid segregation of the sexes breaks down in the city and women enjoy the same social round as their men friends, accompanying them to hotels, parties, and beer bars. This has brought about radical changes in the relations between the sexes, the traditional distance which characterized relations between women and non-kin males being no longer appropriate. As "single" women they are treated as social equals.

The range of associational options available to them has also increased. They can still belong to exclusively female associations like their own professional women's groups, but they can also join unsegregated clubs. There is too a wider range of benevolent, religious and educational organizations open to them than was available in traditional society. Urban living represents a real improvement in the life-styles , freedom and options available to these women; such choices did not exist in traditional Ghanaian society and are only available in an urban environment.

These professional Accra women, therefore, rather than being passive, submissive creatures subjugated by men, have developed a highly self-interested orientation and a considerable measure of independence from them. They are reluctant to marry them, preferring to concentrate on their own economic and social advancement. At the same time, they orient their lives in the direction of their own kinship groups, in which they anticipate most emotional satisfaction, support, and personal security.

The prevailing ideologies and social structures in Ghana may actually facilitate a positive approach by women in relation to their economic role. A strong ideology exists that stresses the economic role of women. The structural supports of equality of economic opportunity, equal status in law, maternity leave, etc., also facilitate long-term career amibitions for women.

Such factors undoubtedly influence the women's own self-image.

They have a real sense of themselves as being the decisive agents in the shaping of their own social and economic environment. They are highly active, resilient strategists choosing *their* own ways of promoting *their* own interests based on *their* own rational assessment of *their* own social, economic and political resources. They are satisfied with the existing channels for economic self-realization and are confident that they can be financially self-sufficient and, to this extent, have better control of their own destinies.

The women, however, could in no way be considered feminist. Although they are aware of the sexual inequalities of their society, there is no evidence to support any theory of a developing feminism amongst them. On the contrary, they accept that in many spheres they are subordinate to men. They choose rather to acknowledge this male superordination, but to manipulate it in their own interests. In this sense, they can more properly be considered as pragmatists than feminists.

Women, Nationalism and Revolution

Foster Mubanga, *Freedom and Labour: Women and the Nationalist Movement*
(Harries-Jones, 1975)

[Foster Mubanga began her political activity in 1957, organizing a beer-hall boycott, for which she was put on probation, though other women involved were jailed. Her activity then lapsed – "after this there were no more meetings for women; it was only the men who met" – until the split in the nationalist party, the African National Congress, and the formation of the more militant United National Independence Party, led by (Dr) Kenneth Kaunda, now President of Zambia.]

At this time I was constituency vice-chairman of the Women's Brigade. Two officials came and talked to us women too, and asked us individually: "Among you women, who is willing to volunteer to work for the organization without pay." All the women were quiet and so they asked us a second time: "Talk to your men and say UNIP wants volunteers in the office as full-time workers." But when we met for the second time, most of the women flatly refused. Though some women were willing, their husbands refused and said that they would not allow their wives to work together with other men. "Let them look for other women." Other women refused on the grounds that they had children and they would not be able to find time to cook. "It could happen that I would be thrown into prison, leaving my children to suffer for something they do not know about." I turned the matter over in my heart and asked myself what would happen if everyone refused to work for the country – how would we become free? To suffer for your brethren is a good thing, because you can be received by Jesus; working for your brother is working for God. Jesus suffered when he died for us, and so suffering would be in the name of God.

On the following day it was the same as before. The women still refused. When they asked me, I agreed to take up the post and said that if it was the will of God, I will be the agent of my friends. But I could not agree on my own because I have got my man.

My husband said he would not stop me if I had agreed to work for the organization. "If she has volunteered to work, let her work as the agent of the people. Let her work, I cannot stop her. It will be lucky for us when our country is in our own hands. But there are so many people,

how is it that it has fallen on her to work for the organization? She must
have been chosen by God and the people.'' Then they said: ''Go and
call this man so we can hear him swear to his words.'' They arranged for
him and me to meet at the Branch Office in the afternoon. . . .

They began talking to my husband and said: ''Brave man, you have
been called here so you can tell us the truth about what you have said to
one of our friends whom we sent to you. Your wife has volunteered to
serve the country.'' He said: ''What I said yesterday to your messenger
still stands. My wife has been chosen by God to suffer for the country
together with me.''

They spoke to him again: ''You must realize that if you permit your
wife to suffer for the country, you are taking a burden on your own
shoulders. All the difficulties your wife will bear will also be yours.''
They explained to him that his wife will not only work around here.
''Your wife may be called to work in countries far away. Secondly, she
might stay away from you for weeks.''

My husband agreed to all they asked of him and he vowed to keep his
word under all the difficulties which were going to face him and his wife.
''Even if they send my wife to sleep in villages far away from here in the
bush, when she returns, she will still be my wife.''

They mentioned another thing to him: ''In these difficulties your
friends and their wives will come over to fool you, and say that you are a
fool, and that you are no man. They will say: 'Only a dead man would
allow his wife to sleep from place to place and work alone among men.'
All these things your friends will tell you, but don't listen. You must not
listen. You will hear rumours that so and so plays with your wife. All this
will happen to you.''

I received word from Lusaka through the Regional Office. The
message said: ''Mama Foster Mubanga, we have received your name.
You wish to volunteer to work for the country. You will suffer very
much. You will be despised by people. You will not be respected. People
will always swear at you. They will engage in backbiting and imagine
many things about you. . . .''

The problems and the difficulties which I had accepted would come
my way, started when I began walking out of town into the surrounding
areas to form branches. The male officials with whom I used to travel
gave me a lot of encouragement. I used to leave town to walk to the
pump station with my three children. The first-born, Rosemary, was
still young, and was a sub-B (in school). She used to remain at home. I
used to walk with the other two, carrying one with my hands, and one on
my back, wherever I went. I met a lot of problems with my children: we
walked on foot in the sun; hungry, because at the place where we had
meetings the people did not give us food, and we had to beg for water.

Leading people is hard work, and we must thank God for giving us Dr. K. Kaunda to unite us in the same way that Jesus used to pray to his father, saying: "Father I pray to thee so that those whom you have given me can be united, with one shepherd over everyone." It was the same for us wherever we went. We were suffering, walking on foot, hungry in the hot sun; and if it was raining, it was all the worse. We found many difficulties during our travels, and on our return my children would not eat anything because their normal mealtime was passed. So they just went to bed, and the child I left at home I found asleep on the verandah, hungry and exhausted. You know, when you are used to having two meals a day, it is very difficult for the intestines to get used to eating three times a week.

I used to suffer together with my children because I had not a penny with which to go out and buy food. When we started work, they had promised to help us with a few pennies, but I never saw this money. This sum was in writing, that's all.

In spite of all this, I went ahead. At the time when I founded these bush branches, the branch treasurer of the men came to a sensible decision: "It's wasting a lot of time visiting people in the bush. We should buy two bicycles, a lady's and a man's." They bought these and my troubles lessened because I had a bicycle, even though it was not mine but the organization's. Yet though they bought these bicycles, friends, this man took it away, and that man took it away. My difficulties did not cease. We used to go on bicycles to the branches in the bush, and I suffered greatly, carrying one child on my back and one child on my (bicycle) frame. There was no rest. We travelled like the devil and my husband used to suffer greatly from hunger the whole day. He used to return at 12 o'clock and found nothing to eat. At home there was silence.

The neighbours did not call him over at all to eat. They used to laugh at him and say: "He's had it now. Never mind, he loves the organization. Hunger will teach him to be more clever. They brought this upon themselves." Also, when my daughter Rosemary returned home from school and saw the neighbours eating, she went away and sat on the verandah. When she was overwhelmed by hunger, she went off to sleep on the verandah.

When I came home and woke up little Rose and asked if she was ill, she replied: "No, it was the hunger." I made the fire, and if I had not prepared relish the previous night, I went out asking for some dried fish at the houses where it was sold. The neighbours, pulling their faces, mocked, saying: "You will eat a diviner's meal. The world is large – you could die without enjoying anything. You are worrying your children who know nothing (of your reasons)." I did not care although they were backbiting me. I used to say to myself that it did not matter even if they said all these things. However, these things used to trouble my heart, and my heart suffered as did my body. These were the difficulties I encountered, I, your friend.

And so, brethren, it came to the time when we heard from Kaunda that there will be registration to determine the number of voters. This was a big job for us, teaching the women individually how to write their names. It was not only the women, we had to teach the men too. You know, it was very difficult to teach an old person who had never been to school to write his name. They used to hold the pencils with stiff fingers or as if these had been cut off. Indeed, they wrote as they were cooking mealie porridge. . . . We worked very, very hard so that we could win the election. This being the first election, we must not lose, and we were adamant that we should fight for the country. We fought until we won some seats, some lower roll seats (largely African voters) and some upper roll seats (largely non-Africans). . . .

After the 1962 election we heard an announcement on the radio: ''Here is the latest news from Lusaka. Mr. Kaunda has approached the leader of ANC so that they can combine the votes and form a government.'' They combined the seats. Theirs were seven and ours were 14, which made 21 seats, and so we formed a coalition government. The following day this was in the *Northern News*, and it said: ''Black Government''. The foreign Europeans who jeered at us saying that we had lost, read the top front page of the newspaper where the headlines said ''Black Government''. Now their women, who used to swing their hips all the time, drooped, and walked along in the same way as you see a hen walk when hit by a stick – with its tail feathers hanging down. Theat's how they were; from then on there were no proud foreigners. If you saw a European walk towards you, you looked away, hoping that you would run into him; and you would see him go round you in the same way we do when meeting in-laws. That's how they walked. No Africans feared foreigners – they began fearing us. We wanted to push them on the streets so that they could speak back, but they used to fear us like you would fear a venomous snake.

When we came to the second [1964] election, I suffered very much, moving from branch to branch, informing our people whom to vote for, and about our candidates. At this time I had another baby on my hands, and he suffered together with me, because he used to eat irregularly, and I also became skinny for lack of food and from walking in the sun. But still people used to say: ''That will teach her a lesson. Why did she agree to take it up when she had a child on her hands? Let her become thin, as thin as a tree and if she is not careful her children will die. Her children's lips are becoming dry from hunger and they are exhausted and always sleep on the verandah.''

When the neighbours prepared food, my children went away from the neighbours' houses, and after eating, they called them back to play. When I returned they (the children) told me how their friends used to lay it on thick and this used to make me cry. I thought: ''What had made me so drunk as to get into this world and to subject my children to so much suffering. How does God not see the poor and their suffering? He should subdue the mouths of our enemies so that we can get this country, so that it comes about that our second father, Kaunda, will take us out of the bondage of our enemies.'' I used to cry a great deal, but even though I cried, I always knew what I wanted to do for my country.

Allen Isaacman, *A Luta Continua: Women and Liberation in Mozambique* (1978)

The process of emancipating women and incorporating them into the new society remains at an early stage of development. At a Conference of the Organization of Mozambican Women (OMM) held in 1976, President Machel underscored the urgency of this task. ''The participation of Mozambican women in all sectors is an essential condition for the triumph of our Revolution. It is the essential condition for the advancement of the new society which we wish to create.''

Despite such government directives opposition to the principles of women's equality is deeply imbedded in the Mozambican past. Exploitation manifested itself in a myriad of ways. Allowing for slight regional and ethnic variations, the heavy workload of peasant women, the sexual division of labor, and the absence of political power among women reflected their subordinate status throughout precolonial Mozambique. Numerous traditions and customs, including bride price, forced marriages, polygamy, fertility requirements, and the ease of male divorce, reinforced and legitimated the exploitation of women. The colonial regime encouraged these exploitative relationships and imposed a new set of abuses, such as forced labor, appropriation of peasant land, coerced recruitment of males, which further eroded the position of women and left them extremely vulnerable.

With the defeat of the colonial regime, strong pressures emerged to reconstitute ''traditional'' sexual relations. Many fathers and husbands, humiliated under colonialism, saw independence as an opportunity to reassert their authority over the household. A number of males resorted to intimidation and violence in an effort to retain their primacy, husbands publicly chastizing their wives, beating them, and locking them in their homes. Many fathers also resisted FRELIMO's directives requiring that girls, as well as boys, be sent to school and forbidding the practice of bride price.

Opposition to women's equality extended beyond aggrieved husbands. Many rural elders, both men and women, sought a return to the "ways of the ancestors". Their objectives logically implied revivifying the complex of customs and traditions, which in part had resulted in the subjugation of women. Wives of the chiefs were also against any reforms which would alter existing societal relationships and challenge the privileged position of their family. Among the small number of women who had gained relatively prestigious jobs as civil servants, bank clerks, and secretaries, most opposed any alliance with illiterate peasants whom they considered to be distinctly inferior.

Against the backdrop of anxiety and hostility, the government initiated a major educational and action campaign under the direction of the Organization of Mozambican Women, itself reorganized and strengthened in 1976. At the national level job, wage, and other forms of discrimination in the public sphere were explicitly forbidden. At the same time newspaper accounts, magazines, articles, pamphlets, and daily radio broadcasts denounced the evils of sexism. Letters to the editors from ordinary women and men describing their efforts to combat exploitation received prominence in the newspapers. . . . The media campaign particularly stressed the abuses of bride price and polygamy which dehumanized women and "insured that their principal role was to serve men – their fathers, brothers and husbands". African prostitution, which had run rampant in the cities as a result of the presence of a large Portuguese army, also came under heavy attack as a decadent vestige of the "colonial capitalist system".

A fundamental dimension of the restructuring of the OMM was its transformation into a grassroots movement capable of mobilizing millions of rural Mozambicans. In the first instance, organizing women who lived in communal villages, co-operatives, and state farms received the highest priority. Three considerations dictated this decision. The absence of transportation and trained OMM organizers limited the initial scale of operations to select locations which were heavily populated. The communal villages, co-operatives, and state farms premised upon equality, collective action, and new economic relationships, also provided unprecedented "space" and opportunities for women to gain the freedom long denied them. Moreover, the OMM could draw upon other grassroot and government structures which already existed in these new rural structures.

The rural campaign began in earnest in the second half of 1977. Sarafi

Amati, head of the OMM for the Province of Gaza, has described the process of mobilizing thousands of women living in the regions. Small groups of OMM representatives, initially visited the local communities where they met with elected representatives and members of the grassroots dynamizing groups. To advance the cause of women's liberation, they contended, the political consciousness of both women and men had to be altered. With the help of the dynamizing groups they organized a series of public meetings as well as weekly study groups for women. Both often developed into heated debates touching basic and extremely sensitive issues. Peasant women were encouraged to describe familial relationships and the abuses which they had suffered. Following these personal exposés, all the participants tried to identify collectively the underlying causes of the exploitation and how they could be remedied. After several weeks of discussion, four themes prevailed: (1) Traditional institutions, especially bride price and polygamy, dehumanized women as did exploitative colonial practices; (2) Concerted efforts had to be undertaken to ensure that girls had opportunities similar to those offered to boys in all aspects of their development; (3) Women had a right and, indeed, a responsibility to assume all the positions which men held; and (4) A local branch of the OMM should be organized and new members recruited. Meetings such as these which took place in select rural areas of Mozambique produced similar calls for action.

One of the most contentious issues which the OMM has had to overcome is the claim, accepted by both men and women, that physical differences between the sexes preclude equality. To counter these claims, organizers pointed to the heroic efforts of women's military brigades during the struggle for independence and cited examples of well-known cases of women who had assumed important positions in communal villages or co-operatives. The most successful tactic, however, was to encourage peasant women to join them working side by side with men in the most arduous tasks.

While such actions as well as the study groups and public discussions heightened the consciousness of many women, many males felt extremely threatened. In several instances, they prevented their wives from attending OMM meetings, dragged them out of study groups, and threatened to leave them. These men were brought before dynamizing groups for disciplinary action and additional education. In most cases, after intensive discussion and public criticism, extending over several public meetings, the men agreed that they had erred. To demonstrate the gravity with which it viewed such actions the government prohibited these recalcitrant individuals, as well as those who continued to practise polygamy and bride price from holding positions in the state administration and ruled them ineligible for any candidacy in the national elections.

Although the major efforts of the OMM have been made in targeted rural locations, a concerted effort began early in 1978 to mobilize women working in factories and living in urban centers. In an effort to create new job opportunities the OMM, in conjunction with the government, has helped to organize more than fifty day-care centers, primarily in Maputo, and projected plans call for a national network of creches in the near future. The OMM has also participated in programs with local dynamizing groups, the Mozambican Youth Movement (OJM), and the Ministry of Education, to encourage women to attend literacy classes to ease the culture shock which new city dwellers often face, to re-educate former prostitutes, and to introduce concepts of sexual equality in all primary and secondary schools.

Although the OMM has recently scored impressive gains and the government remains an ardent defender of women's rights, for many equality still remains a hope of the future. While thousands of women have joined the OMM during the past year, the lack of a sufficient number of highly qualified organizers, transportation difficulties, and the dispersed residential patterns in many parts of rural Mozambique, have necessarily limited the movement's impact. In many remote regions OMM cadres have not had sustained interaction with the local population. Often these are areas in which other critical social and economic transformations have not as yet taken place, and "traditional" institutions remain potent. Even where the OMM, dynamizing groups, and the state have co-ordinated their efforts and discrimination has been eliminated in the public sphere, traditional sex roles often prevail within the private domain. Although not as prevalent as in the past, it is, nevertheless, common for men to refuse to do such "women's work" as pounding mealie, washing clothing, and cooking. Moreover, until a new system of family law, now under consideration, is codified, women and children will continue to be dependent on a colonial legal system which afforded them little or no protection. These difficulties notwithstanding, the prevailing sentiment among women with whom I talked was that their objective conditions had already improved and that full equality will be achieved in the next generation. Recent elections in which 28 per cent of the deputies elected to the local assemblies were women confirms their faith.

Part III

Peasants, Poverty and Patrons

Introduction

During the twentieth century, most rural producers in West and East Africa have been transformed into peasant smallholders, producing food and other crops for their own consumption and for sale. They cultivate their own land with their own, family and wage labour, but often also buy food and sell labour-power (see, in general, Shanin, 1972; Cooper, 1981; and for case studies Howard, 1980; Klein, 1980). They live in unequal communities but, *Williams* argues, neither inequalities nor commodity production, nor even the appearance of wage labour, transform them into rural capitalists and rural proletarians (but cf. Cliffe, 1976, in Gutkind, 1976). In southern Africa land and labour legislation, created a large rural proletariat of farmworkers and tenant and migrant labourers (cf. *Marks and Trapido* above; Morris, 1976).

The extent of prosperity and poverty among peasant communities, and within them, varies considerably, depending on people's access to land and to non-farm earnings, what they can grow and on what terms they can sell it (Hill, 1972). Inequalities within peasant communities are shaped and even generated by their relations to classes based outside their communities and, in particular, to state agencies (*van Velzen*, below; Feldman in Oxaal, 1975; Kitching, 1980; Raikes, 1978; Lonsdale in Samuel, 1981). Government marketing boards reduce peasant incomes and, in southern Africa and Kenya, subsidize capitalist farming (Leys, 1975; Morris, 1976; F. Wilson, 1971). Capitalist firms and government boards may dictate the conditions on which peasants can cultivate or sell export or industrial crops (Bernstein, 1979; Cowen, Williams, in Heyer, 1981). The major concern of most peasant men and women is to produce and earn enough, from farming, wage labour and other occupations, to meet their subsistence needs and social obligations; all too often the burden of state intervention is to render this almost impossible (Adams, 1978, in Heyer, 1981).

Hill describes the reasons for general poverty in northern Hausaland where farmers have to import food and provide for the long dry season (cf. Copans, 1975; Bondestam, 1974; Watts, 1980; Shepherd in Heyer, 1981, on droughts and famines). The decline in crafts and long-distance

67

trade based in rural areas and increased dependence on cash expenditure to buy necessities at rapidly inflating prices intensify rural poverty and indebtedness, and increase the need for dry-season labour migration (Hill, 1977).

Van Velzen shows how government officials control rural communities with the collaboration of local notables who turn state resources to their private advantage, even where this is contrary to state policy. Poorer farmers are excluded from access to local resources and government decisions. Rather than challenge government power, peasants tended to evade unpopular policies (cf. *Cohen* on workers, below), to take personal action against unpopular people and to use government resources for their own purposes. Government activities tend to worsen inequalities and factional conflict; they rarely improve rural incomes or agricultural output (Heyer, 1981; cf. Derman, 1972; Beckman, 1976; Leonard, 1977).

Jeffries (1978a) argues that radical scholars have exaggerated the political radicalism of peasants. In the excerpt below he draws on Lamb (1974) to explain how Kikuyu peasants in Kenya deferred to the values of individual advancement and the realities of institutional power, and on D. O'Brien (1977) to show how the established organization of the Mouride brotherhood enabled its leaders to force the government to improve crop prices (see also Copans, 1980). However, peasants have rebelled against government agents and authority where they have lacked the means to maintain their way of life, as the excerpts in *van Velzen* show.

Poverty and Inequality

Polly Hill, *"Causes" of General Poverty in Rural Hausaland* (1972)

(i) The brevity of the farming-season.

(ii) The unreliability of the climate, especially as concerns annual variations in the dates of planting rains, and erratic distribution of rainfall within the farming-season.

(iii) The under-utilization of labour resources during the farming-season resulting from:

> (a) the inability of many poor farmers to farm on a scale which matches their labour resources;
>
> (b) the rudimentary nature of the system of farm-labour employment;
>
> (c) the Muslim seclusion of women.

(iv) The dire shortage of working-capital, which severely limits the scale and productiveness of farming, especially where permanent cultivation of manured farmland is the preferred agronomic system.

(v) The shortage of cattle manure derived from Fulani-owned herds.

(vi) The dearth of remunerative non-farming occupations during the long dry season, this being connected with the declining demand for craft goods and with the decreased opportunities for rurally-based long-distance trade (*fatauci*).

(vii) The inability of many poorer men to finance migration for farming

(viii) The ''balance of payments'' difficulties from which village communities are apt to suffer, owing to the small range of produce and craft goods which is sold ''abroad'', the obstacles to increasing groundnut production, and the need to ''import'' many types of goods, including grain.

(ix) The burden of assisting in the maintenance of many poverty-stricken people, which is borne by the community generally.

(i) *The short farming-season* The brevity of the single farming-season (especially in *northern* Hausaland) results in under-utilization of labour resources, as it does in the northern savannah generally – except possibly where fertile *fadama* [marshland] is extensive. Given the small range of basic crops, *all of which are harvested within a short period*, economic life in the savannah is much riskier, in terms of the consequences of variations in crop size, than in the southern forests, where most farmers subsist on a greater variety of crops which are harvested at different seasons. Then, far more capital is tied up in crop-storage in the savannah, which is much longer term than in the south. The risks of mortgaging the future by unfortunately-timed crop-selling would thus be great in rural Hausaland, even if individual farmers did not nowadays stand so solitarily, unsupported by the farming services of their wives or by corporate lineages.

(ii) *The unreliability of the climate* The dates of the first planting rains, and (accordingly) of the millet . . . harvest, are so variable that grain requirements between one harvest and the next may vary by (say) 20%, making long-term planning difficult. Considerable quantities of seed may be lost in abortive sowing . . . In 1967 most Batagarawa men were very idle for about two months, while waiting for the rains which fell as late as 15 June. General uncertainty lasts throughout the farming-season, when the rain does not fall regularly, but in fits and starts, lengthy periods of drought often occurring within the rainy season. Such uncertainties aggravate seasonal price fluctuations, which may be more pronounced in northern than in southern Hausaland – famines . . . were always worst in the north.

(iii) (a) *The under-utilization of labour resources* Our analysis of the causes of extreme rural poverty, which is summed up in the concept of "too poor to farm", suggests that some degree of destitution is likely to occur in most communities where permanent cultivation . . . is the preferred agronomic system, and where poorer farmers have few opportunities of significantly supplementing their income either by growing special crops (other than grains or groundnuts), or by pursuing remunerative non-farming occupations. Young fatherless men, and older men who lack the services of working-sons, are certain to exist in all communities – though they will be more at risk in some than in others. Our analysis of the general obstacles which hamper poor men in their struggle against poverty, is likely to be of wide application where most farmers gain their livelihood mainly by growing basic crops: "With abundant land and reasonable fertility, a very considerable proportion of farming households fail to produce crops sufficient to build up reserves of the food staple to meet their regular subsistence needs" – L. C. Giles on Zaria farmers, cited by Forde (1946, p. 168).

(iii) (b) *The farm-labouring system* . . . The *gandu*[1] system provides the married sons of richer farmers (as likewise the slaves in former times) with the opportunity of establishing themselves as private farmers within the framework of the security provided by their father's farming. The fathers (and slave-owners) not only give their sons *gayauni* [a private plot], but by maintaining them from the proceeds of the *gandu* farms, by providing seed and tools, by meeting their marriage expenses and so forth, they effectively invest capital in their sons to enable them to develop their farming – and, consequently, their non-farming occupations. Even with the best-organized *gandaye* it is impossible, owing to the unpredictability of the weather, to plan the various agricultural operations in advance, so as to ensure that team-work is regularly performed for five (or so) days a week throughout the farming-season. When the fathers do not require the services of their sons, the latter are not idle, but can fall back on their private farming and other occupations – as could the slaves in former times. The sons resemble a permanently-hired labour-force in that they are always instantly available for farmwork as required – but at the same time they are men who regularly supplement their own earnings.

It seems likely that in West African conditions large-scale farming by rurally-based farmers (farmers resident in cities may be differently situated) depends on the presence either of stranger–labourers who return home during the dry season, or of fully-resident labourers (whether strangers or local men) who are partly occupied in cultivating their own farms in order to supplement their food supplies. There seems to be no example in the literature of the emergence of a "class" of landless, permanently-resident labourers, as a consequence of the development of a basic export crop. . . . Thus, the rapid development of cocoa-growing in southern Ghana seventy years ago – see Hill (1963) – was greatly dependent on stranger-labourers who were usually rewarded with a one-third share . . . of the cocoa crop and who were always allocated portions of farmland on which they grew food crops; although daily-paid labourers were sometimes also employed, they were stop-gaps only – their work, unlike that of the labourers, requiring constant supervision.

There are at least four reasons why it is beyond the power of Hausa farmers to offer such attractive conditions to resident labourers. First, they lack lineage (or family) land, portions of which are commonly made available to cocoa-labourers; secondly, they cannot buy large tracts of

---

[1] *Gandu* (plural *gandaye*): "a voluntary, mutually advantageous agreement between father and married son under which the son works in a subordinate capacity on his father's farms in return for a great variety of benefits, including a share of the food supplies" (Hill, 1972: 38).

uncultivated land (in the manner of the migrant cocoa-farmers of southern Ghana); thirdly, farming is only possible during the single short rainy season, whereas in the southern forests cultivation of one crop or another is possible for many months; fourthly, labourers would require finance for seed and manure, unless they were content to cultivate bush-farms only – planting material for perennials such as plantain and cocoyam and also for cassava, may be made freely available in the southern forests.

While a "labouring-class" may exist in Hausa cities, where regular employment is on offer throughout the year, it is difficult to see how a "class of resident landless labourers" could ever emerge in the countryside, except possibly where dry-season crops are grown or where there were special opportunities of non-farming employment. However regular his employment during the short farming-season, a landless labourer's earning would always be insufficient for the maintenance of himself and his family during the long dry season, for poor men lack finance to pursue the more remunerative trading occupations. . . .

(iii) (c) *Wife-seclusion*   Presumably Muslim wife-seclusion is becoming increasingly strict throughout rural (Nigerian) Hausaland. However, for present limited purposes there is no need to speculate about the proportion of wives who still enjoy any day-to-day freedom of movement (perhaps because they live in dispersed settlements, or are required to carry water), the likelihood being that, in any case, Nigerian Muslim Hausa women (unlike many of their sisters in the Niger Republic) undertake little cultivation proper, though they may have responsibility for special tasks such as cotton picking. . . .

The Nigerian Hausa thus stand in great contrast to many other peoples – including their neighbours the Kanuri of Bornu, with whom – R. Cohen [1960] the number of wives a farmer has available for work is a "major factor in crop production". Perhaps it is usually only in certain forest-dwelling societies, such as the Akan of Ghana, that women do most of the food farming. Yet, according to Haswell's excellent study (1953) of . . . a savannah village in the Gambia, the men farmers' efforts at cultivating late millet were so "pitifully inadequate" (p. 25) that they were wholly dependent on the women's cultivation of rice, which work was maintained at a "high pitch of activity" throughout the period May to January.

(iv) and (v) *Capital shortage and permanent cultivation*   The shortage of working-capital in Batagarawa is associated with the general level of poverty; with the failure of "farming-businesses" (*gandaye*) to survive the shock of the death of the *gandu* head; with the fact that there are few other types of business enterprise which enable an individual to build up capital during the course of his working-life (most traders being younger men – p. 186); with the lack of durable equipment; with high levels of celebratory expenditure; and so forth. Such factors are likely to have general relevance to many Hausa communities where the farmers mainly grow basic crops, and where few men are engaged in hereditary crafts.

It has been concluded that irrespective of population density, permanent cultivation . . . of manured farmland is often the preferred agronomic system: there is much general evidence in favour of this hypothesis, and it is our presumption that where, as in Batagarawa, the incidence of farm-selling is high, the bulk of basic produce is grown on permanently cultivated farmland.

As noted by Netting (1968) in his valuable examination of the cultural ecology of the Kofyar of the Jos plateau, whose primary dependence is on staple crops grown on permanently cultivated farms, land cannot be viewed as a really valuable resource unless it is being kept in production by its owner – this involving the expenditure of working-capital. Most richer farmers in Batagarawa buy some types of manure, such as compound sweepings and imported fertilizers, and are able to attract visiting Fulani to herd their cattle on their farms after harvest, if they are not themselves cattle-owners.

But whereas a farmer with sufficient working-capital is always in a position to increase his supplies of manure, his increased production may be at the expense of that of poorer farmers in his own community. This is the situation in Batagarawa, where no one except a single member of the ruling-class is reported as "importing" compound sweepings; where supplies of imported fertilizers are limited . . . ; where there is much competition for the dung provided by locally-based Fulani-owned herds . . . and where the Hausa farmers themselves own no more than about 100 cattle. The situation could presumably be alleviated by rearing (and penning) more sheep and goats and the manurial contribution of the donkey should not be neglected; but whether the limited grazing would support more cattle is not known.

(vi) *The decline of craftwork and rurally-based "fatauci"* . . . A few rural crafts . . . continue to flourish – an example is smithing, for traditional-type farm-tools . . . have not been replaced by manufactured tools, and blacksmiths are learning to repair imported ploughs and to make spare parts . . . ; but many skilled craftsmen, such as weavers and dyers, are suffering from the competition from manufactured goods, and in many hamlets, . . . few crafts are pursued. However, there are presumably still many rural communities which continue to specialize in certain crafts, including weaving, mat-making and potting: dry-season idleness will be a less serious problem there than it is in Batagarawa.

The idea that rurally-based *fatauci* . . . is decreasing in importance, chiefly as a result of switching from donkey-caravans to lorries, but also owing to the decline in craftwork, requires investigation. Whereas most caravan-donkeys were owned by farmer-traders resident in the countryside, nearly all lorries are owned by rich men in cities, where the only large lorry-parks are situated. Certainly *fatauci* provides few men in Batagarawa and neighbouring hamlets with lucrative dry-season opportunities, such as existed in former times – it is much cheaper to transport natron (natural potash) by lorry than by donkey-caravan.

(vii) *Migration for farming* Although it might be thought that poor farmers are always able to escape from their poverty by migrating as farmers to localities where fertile farmland, which does not require manuring, may be freely cultivated in the neighbourhood of their farmsteads, our findings in Batagarawa . . . suggest that most of those who are "too poor to farm" in the home village, are also "too poor to migrate for farming", unless they have relatives or friends in the reception area who are prepared to maintain them. As many of the vacant lands to which Batagarawa people migrated in former times lie not far to the west and are not "full up", it may be that the concept of "too poor to migrate for farming" commonly applies even more strongly in less favourably situated localities [this point was confirmed by Hill, 1977]. It is possible that young fatherless men without working-sons (who are particularly likely to be poor), seldom migrate for farming, except to join relatives.

(viii) *"Balance of payments" difficulties of rural communities considered as "island economies"* The exceedingly rough estimates of Batagarawa's "imports" and "exports" which follow should not even be regarded as indicative of the orders of magnitude involved (which anyway vary greatly from year to year), but rather as realistic hypothetical figures.

On a number of heroic assumptions, Batagarawa's groundnut exports . . . have been very roughly estimated at 100 tons in 1968, worth (say) £2500 to the farmers – production by the *masu sarauta* [members of the ruling class] is excluded. A few local traders export cowpeas and there is a little "external trade" in such produce as sweet potatoes, cassava, fruit and small vegetables – as well as in tobacco. A few farmers "export" small quantities of grain, which they sell in local markets such as Abukur, but our presumption is that "net imports" of grain (see below) are always substantial. Most craftsmen and traders (other than firewood-sellers) nowadays mainly rely on local demand and do not "export" their goods – though some blacksmith's tools are sold "abroad", as also small quantities of embroidered caps, mats and other "free goods". Excluding the *masu sarauta*, it may be that Batagarawa's total annual "exports" do not exceed some £3500 or (say) £10 per adult man.

Again excluding the *masu sarauta*, what might the value of grain "imports" be? The total area of manured farmland is some 1200 acres, of which some 500 acres is estimated to be under groundnuts. As little early millet . . . is grown on bush-farmland, and as the total area of bush-farmland which is under cultivation at any time is likely . . . to be much smaller than the area of manured farmland, it may be that the equivalent of some 1000 acres of farmland is under grain. Then, if yields average a quarter of a ton an acre (a high figure), and if . . . average annual grain prices are arbitrarily set at . . . £28 per ton), [1967 prices] the gross value of 250 tons of grain would be some £7000. If grain requirements . . . were put as high as 2 lb. per head per day, then a total of about 400 tons would be required annually, necessitating net "imports" of 150 tons, at a value of (say) £4000 – a rate of "import" which, with groundnut exports at £2500, could not be financed. Although in an exceptional year like 1968 (when grain prices were much lower relative to groundnut prices than is here assumed), grain consumption might have been as high as 2 lb. per head, it is clearly not beyond the bounds of possibility that consumption rates might often be much lower. Certainly, the shortage of "foreign exchange" for other purposes is likely, always, to be acute.

Clearly, Batagarawa's "capacity to import" manufactures often varies greatly from year to year. Many of these goods are very expensive, having passed through a long chain of traders, and being packed in small quantities, such as tiny packets of detergents. Apart from cloth, which is "imported" in huge quantities, at competitive prices, and some other manufactures, like kerosene, which is handled in large tins, Batagarawa's "terms of trade" tend to be markedly unfavourable. In so far as these imports are not manufactured in the northern states, heavy transport costs from the distant seaboard enhance prices. The very high price of kola-nuts . . ., especially at certain seasons, is also a serious drain on the "balance of payments".

In many West African communities, for instance in southern Ghana and Yorubaland, women trade largely with the outside world, often travelling long distances in lorries. But Muslim attitudes preclude most Hausa women from "exporting" in this way: the dozen (or so) older women in Batagarawa who trade in Katsina market, are most of them wives of poorer farmers, for husbands are put to shame when their wives do this work.

As far as the "invisibles" in the "balance of payments", . . . remittances from . . . migrants are likely to remain at a lower level than with many other West African ethnic groups, as migration . . . is often more permanent.

While many of these "balance of payments" difficulties will obviously affect Hausa rural communities generally, some communities are certain to be much more favourably situated than others. Large exports of both grains and groundnuts may be achieved by communities which are well supplied with cattle manure; communities with much rich *fadama* land, or with access to irrigable farmland on river banks, may derive a large income from special, highly-priced crops, such as vegetables, onions, wheat; there may (as already noted) be some communities where traditional craftwork for export continues to flourish on a large scale. On the other hand, there are some localities, such as northern Sokoto, where high population densities combined with low soil fertilities have produced a situation such that local communities could not survive there at all were it not for the high incidence of dry-season migration.

(ix) *The burden of poverty*   Some measure of "exploitation" of the poor by the rich is inevitable in every community where economic inequality is pronounced: thus, profits from grain storage would be lower if there were none who were "too poor to farm" and farm-labour employment would be a less advantageous stop-gap. But, on the other hand, the richer members of the community are obliged to give food, clothing and money to the under-employed: to provide partial maintenance for those who, for financial reasons, they are unable to set to work. Rich merchants in cities do not carry the burden of maintaining unemployed labourers generally, many of whom are strangers cared for by their "countrymen" in the city. *Village responsibilities for providing social security are much wider and inhibit capital growth.*

Gavin Williams, *Taking the Part of Peasants* (Gutkind, 1976)

Peasants and Inequalities

Numerous studies in different societies have established varied but significant inequalities among peasants in access to the whole range of sources of income. Wealthier farmers not only own more land than others, but usually command more family labor and more and better tools with which to cultivate it. They are more likely to employ hired labor and can do so at lower average costs than poorer farmers. Their farm production is better organized and is more likely to take place at the best time of year. They grow more food crops per family member or per working man than others and are more likely to diversify production into one or more lucrative cash crops. They are more likely than others to purchase land or to rent land, and they do so on better terms than poorer farmers. Income inequalities from nonfarm employment – trading, money-lending, manufactures, and salaries – are usually even greater than inequalities from agricultural production. Wealthier farmers can market their crop more cheaply and expeditiously and may be in a position to store grain for profitable resale to the less fortunate. They are likely to be recognized by the authorities and by other farmers as the proper representatives of their communities, and they have far greater access than others to credit, extension services, sprays, and fertilizers.

Inequalities are not sufficient evidence for the fundamentally capitalist tendencies of the development of the peasant economy. Class relations, not inequality as such, define production as capitalist. With the expansion of commodity production, and the availability of opportunities for wage employment outside the peasant household, labor-time itself acquires a cash value. Conventional arrangements for the mobilization of labor break down, and neighbors and strangers are employed for wages to supplement family labor. For their part, the employees may supplement the products and incomes from their own farms by wage employment. Thus we are no longer dealing with Chayanov's ideal peasant-farm, from which the very principle of wage labor is excluded. Nor are we dealing with Marx's and Weber's free wage capitalism in which the producer has no access to his own means of production.

Employment for wages, both within and outside the rural economy, may provide a source of cash income and of savings which are then reinvested in the establishment of peasant holdings. Migrant workers may be able to earn cash incomes in periods when their labor is not re-quired on their home farms. Migrant cocoa farmers in Western Nigeria finance the purchase of land and the hiring of labor to establish their own farms with savings from wage employment on others' farms. During a specific period in their life-cycle, young men are faced with demands for cash income to pay both for daily necessities and for such investments as a dowry (the main means of acquiring farm labor) and the land on which to establish their own cash crops. Young men who have completed periods of apprenticeship as craftsmen earn wages to purchase the equipment necessary for their business. Thus the use of wage labor does not necessarily presuppose the existence of a landless proletariat or even of allotment-holders tied for a lifetime to wage employment because of the lack of other sources of income. Aggregate figures for contemporary Tanzania, reveal few proletarians outside plantations and state farms. This is not incompatible with periods of wage employment by peasants, especially younger men. Wage employment, like inequality, may be integrated into peasant production.

Undoubtedly there are cumulative advantages accruing to the better-off in a rural economy as in any other. Nevertheless, peasants survive the development of capitalism and the expansion of commodity relations because of their ability to deliver goods to consumers at lower prices than capitalists. They have adapted production to take advantage of new opportunities and to integrate changes into the peasant economy. Peasants benefit from their knowledge of the local environment. They are able to combine the production of different crops with symbiotic ecological features and complementary requirements for labor and other inputs. They are knowledgeable about the availability and relative costs, including opportunity costs, of local resources and can adapt decisions to the requirements of particular farms and localities. Labor is provided by family members at no marginal cost, except in additional drudgery to the household, and by temporary employment of hired labor for peak periods.

Innovations can be integrated into existing patterns of production. Existing social institutions can be used to acquire cash funds, labor, and land and to regulate the provision of these resources. The introduction of new crops and methods may be combined with older, tried methods for the production of subsistence crops, thus enabling farmers to experiment with new possibilities while ensuring their own security. Unlike wage earners who rely on their employers to provide their means of subsistence, peasants must save out of their income and invest that saving in order to sustain their own source of livelihood.

The management of capitalist and state farms and of state schemes for settlements and co-operative cultivation incurs high costs for items which are not required by peasant households or met more cheaply within them. High salaries are paid to officials, managers, and technicians, and the wages are paid in advance of the sale of the product of labor. Outsiders have all too often misunderstood local conditions and sought to apply rules and examples without due regard for the advice of peasants, the availability and complementarity of local resources, and the burden of labor on the prospective returns to innovation.

Mechanized inputs, whose superior yields are held to justify more authoritarian forms of labor organization, are often too costly to justify the improved returns they bring, if any. Equipment, spare parts, and repairs must be paid for; skilled workers must be employed to operate and maintain machines; unskilled labor must be employed to prepare land for ploughing and to weed ploughed lands. Other costs may include the exclusion of intercropping of other crops, the expense of fertilizers to maintain soil fertility, and the loss of both topsoil and the cover for the land. Capitalist farmers tend to treat the land as a source of profit, which can be reinvested in other activities, so that they may have less incentive than peasants to maintain soil fertility. Wage earners do not share the peasant's commitment to his work since they do not own the product. Peasants regard state-managed settlements and co-operatives as "government farms" and consider work on these schemes as work for the government, and subsistence allowances to settlers as low wages.

Peasants have initiated a variety of co-operative activities. These have usually been undertaken for specific tasks, over specific periods, to supplement household production or to develop resources for household use. Communal systems for allocating resources have been widely used, but as a means of regulating access to resources among individual households. Plans for co-operative labor flounder when no clear relation can be established between an individual's earnings and the effort and efficiency of his work.

Co-operation imposed from above has rarely recouped its administrative costs in increased output. In some cases, the more powerful members of a community have turned it to private advantage. It has rarely enhanced the well-being of its members. Usually it has subjected peasants to outside direction and confirmed peasant suspicion of state plans. Peasants resist outsiders' plans to change the countryside not out of an obtuse conservatism, but because of a clear and comprehensible preference for a way of life which allows them the freedom to manage their own resources. They will not welcome schemes for co-operation without clear evidence that the schemes will bring material benefits and improve their way of life, rather than destroy it.

Studies of social mobility within and between generations in peasant communities have revealed tendencies which counteract "short-term spirals of relative affluence or poverty" (Hill, 1972: 152) and contain peasant social differentiation within the broad parameters of an unequal peasant society.

Accumulations of wealth in one generation are rarely passed on to the next in the form of large landholdings. A wealthy farmer tends to have several wives and many sons, none of whom inherit the whole of his property or household including the ability to command and organize the labor of its members. While larger households tend to divide, smaller households may merge. Extreme poverty within rural communities is attributed to the individual misfortunes to which poor people are always vulnerable. Lack of family labor is the most common circumstance cited in a Nigerian study. This in turn may be occasioned by illness or natural disasters. The downward spiral into extreme poverty involves the isolation of the individual from a household – and by the same token the extinction of the household (Hill, 1972).

The size of peasant households tends through division, merger, and extinction to regress to the modal size. This is not just a product of rules of inheritance and the imperative of cultural tradition. It reflects the limited advantages of expansion of scale beyond the means of the peasant household, which do not outweigh the benefits of an equitable division of household resources that is essential to co-operation in developing the household economy.

The process of merger and division also depends on the relative advantages of employment, income, and profit in the urban economy relative to farming. Poor farmers will migrate to seek opportunities elsewhere if either land or wage employment is available (but see *Hill*, above, and 1977). Wealthier men will seek to educate their children to give them access to the benefits of salaried employment or will establish themselves or their children in trade. State taxes and spending tend to transfer resources and thus opportunities out of the rural into the urban areas. Thus rich peasants may not pass on protocapitalist farming enterprises to their sons, but they can pass on access to education and to commercial opportunities, so that their sons can become bureaucrats and urban entrepreneurs. Capitalist farming can only be introduced to develop new areas of cultivation, often at the cost of pastoralists and the expansion of peasant cultivation, or by measures to eliminate peasant competition. It may be easier to leave the business of agricultural production in peasant hands, and exploit them rather than overcome peasant resistance.

Both capitalist and socialist development strategies require peasants to provide the resources necessary for the development of the urban, industrial economy. Peasant households control and manage their means of production, thus allowing them a measure of autonomy *vis-à-vis* other classes. This autonomy must be broken down if peasant production is to be adapted to the requirements of urban, industrial capital formation and state development planning. Peasants must be made dependent on external markets and power-holders for access to the resources which come to be necessary to their way of life, or they must be coerced into organizing production to meet external requirements.

The surplus value of peasant labor can be appropriated by control of the exchange relations through which the value of the product is realized. Peasants can limit the rate of exploitation to the extent that they can switch production from one crop to another and from production for exchange to direct consumption, and they can seek out alternative buyers and sellers of commodities. State marketing monopolies allow the state to determine the rate of exploitation according to its own priorities. State monopolies reflect an authoritarian belief in the virtues of state regulation of commerce and production and state direction of resources and opportunities – a belief common to colonial administrators and their successors.

In Tanzania, peasants have been resettled into villages so that the state can provide amenities, impose taxes, and supervise production more easily. But it lacks instruments for enforcing the compulsory delivery of crop quotas. Conformity with official priorities and directives and provisions of economic plans can be imposed more easily when the state controls access to land, irrigation, and other resources necessary to production. Hence the continued attractions to bureaucrats, despite repeated disasters, of settlement schemes where farmers are dependent on the state for their livelihood, isolated from their communities, and subordinated to the supervision and control of officials. Coercion needs to be supplemented by incentives. Incentives are relative and may depend on the state's ability to limit alternative sources of income. The model for all subsequent settlement schemes, the Gezira, depends on management's monopoly of irrigated land to enforce the delivery of cotton from tenants (Barnett, 1977).

Peasant Politics

The first priority of the colonial state was to establish itself as the ultimate source of legitimate power and to remove any rulers who failed to give it full recognition. The state ruled through local intermediaries. In return for their loyalty and the carrying out of administrative tasks the government supported them, not only in exercising authority, but in their claim to land rights, political jurisdiction, and favors for themselves and their clients. When government policy shifted toward institutional reform and economic development, colonial rulers and their successors used the "progressive" elements, identified by their education, wealth, and outlook to promote "modernization" among their communities. Officials formed an alliance with local community leaders based on control of access to the resources within their respective arenas: on the other hand, there was access to the patronage, credit, office, and plain graft of public institutions (including the state, the co-operatives, and the party), and, on the other hand, there was access to land, ready cash, and influence among the community. Peasants will normally adapt to the realities of institutional power and public status. Their opposition to unpopular officials and resentment toward local notables may take such forms as witchcraft accusations or campaigns for the removal of particular individuals from office, with the support of their rivals among the local elite (*van Velzen*, below). Objectionable state directives are met by various strategies, from sullen obedience and a formal show of co-operation to dumb insolence.

Peasants have resisted the exactions of the state, landlords, and capitalist farmers when such exactions have threatened to deprive them of the resources necessary to maintain their way of life, especially by denying them access to land and by imposing excessive and arbitrary taxation. In Africa, rural communities have resisted their subordination to the administration of the colonial state, and they have resisted state measures that force them into cash-crop cultivation, enforce labor service, and coerce them into wage employment. Successive Nigerian risings have opposed extortionate exactions by state agents and the extension of taxation in periods of worsening terms of trade for rural producers. Tanzanians and Nigerians resisted the imposition of agricultural regulations by colonial authorities. Peasant hostility was directed against government agents, notably court officials, agricultural officers, and the ubiquitous sanitary inspectors and against government institutions, courts, offices, even railways and schools. They also attacked local rulers, who were seen to support their masters rather than speak for their people, and they have attacked their local allies, usually wealthier farmers and traders (Beer 1975; Beer in Williams, 1976; Iliffe in Cliffe, 1973).

Conflicts within peasant communities did not arise out of the internal differentiation of peasant society. They arose out of the primary contradiction between peasants and the state, and the resistance of peasants to state exactions which threatened their way of life. Local rulers, traders, and wealthy farmers were attacked and even killed because in such conflicts they were loyal ultimately to their protectors, the state, rather than to their own communities.

Peasants' resistance has been able to redress specific grievances, such as excessive taxation or agricultural regulations. Peasants have not ended their dependence on external markets and subordination to the state, but they have imposed limitations on their own exploitation. Nor have peasants ended the domination of rural communities by a ''bloc'' of officials, traders, and farmers or intervened effectively in the routine process of resource allocation, except as clients of influential patrons.

Peasants have not usually sought to transform their society either along lines of their own choosing or on the lines willed for them by socialist intellectuals. They have sought to defend their gains within the frontiers of peasant society, but have not acted of their own accord to seize state power and thus control the instrument of their own exploitation. This is not because of their lack of imagination or their inability to acquire an appropriate political consciousness. It stems from two sources. First, peasants lack any clear evidence that a transformation of their own way of life along capitalist or socialist lines will ensure their security, improve their well-being, and extend their independence – and they find considerable evidence to the contrary. Second, not only do they lack the resources necessary to conquer the state; they even lack the means of gaining access to its administration. In particular, African peasants lack access to the literate culture through which the contemporary state is administered and legitimated. They do not command the technology with which industrial production, together with many of the exchange and marketing activities necessary to the prosperity of the rural economy, are carried out. They do not wish to withdraw from the market economy and bring into being a vision of a precapitalist community. They therefore remain committed to the institutions which are the means of their exploitation and oppression.

Peasants and Patrons

Bonno Thoden van Velzen, *Controllers in Rural Tanzania* (1972)

The subject of this analysis is the elite of administrative and party personnel which represents, or is supposed to represent, the national interest at the local level. Some are residents of Tukuyu (the capital of Rungwe district in Tanzania), while others live in a number of "outposts"; villages which have been selected as rural centers. But wherever they are stationed in the district, and whatever their internal disagreements, these controllers form a separate social grouping, occupying a clearly distinct social position *vis-à-vis* the peasantry. The reasons for this social distance are twofold: the powerful position of the controllers and the vested interests which they attempt to safeguard.

The power assets of the controllers derive from the strategic position which they occupy as *gatekeepers*. Society is conceptualized as a huge flow system; goods are extracted and manpower is mobilized to be put at the disposal of the centre. From there, part of it is redistributed again through certain channels to particular sectors of the periphery. Each channel has its check-points which are manned by gatekeepers who regulate the flow and may – to some extent – redirect the stream or shift its projected course, thereby providing privileges to certain sectors of the peasantry. The gatekeepers take their toll as the resources pass them. Controllers are contestants themselves in the struggle which takes place at the periphery about the distribution of resources. They have to defend their own "class" position and safeguard the various emoluments which are attached to it. Equally important, they cannot be indifferent towards development in rural areas because they have used their advantageous position to develop mutually profitable exchange relationships with the wealthier peasants. . . . (van Hekken, 1972).

At first glance, the adjective "exploitative" seems hardly appropriate to characterize the relationship between controllers and peasants. There is no discernible flow of goods and services from the [peasantry] to the controllers. Though some government officials receive goods (vegetables, maize or other agricultural produce, a loan of land and in a few cases a cow) in a clandestine way, their benefactors are wealthy farmers. . . . Tanzania has for many years accepted and propagated a socialist ideology. At the national level, the planning agencies of the various Ministries consciously strive to protect the interests of the

84

peasants, and the abolition of the poll tax testifies to the seriousness of their intentions. . . .

1 – The present position of the controllers in the district capital and at the outposts offers them a vast number of opportunities for the ostentatious demonstration of an elite culture and ''style of life''. In this way, symbolic divisions between controllers and peasants are being sustained and infused with new and bad blood.

2 – The controllers support the wealthier sectors of the peasantry, thereby encouraging further processes of power accumulation in the periphery. This frustrates efforts to introduce programmes for collectivized agriculture (*Ujamaa*). Moreover, such support tends to discredit the Tanzanian Party, TANU, as an instrument of the happy few. In fact, when I first came to Rungwe Districts TANU was almost a shopkeeper's party; many small retailers occupied functions such as ''ten-house-group'' leader, chairman of the Village Development Committee, etc. The rich farmer is not only overrepresented in TANU's grass-roots machinery, but also occupies most of the salaried positions in the villages. Of 143 such functions available in 1967 in five villages of Rungwe District 72 were filled by the wealthiest 20% of the population.

3 – Though a country such as Tanzania is sparsely populated in comparison with most European or Asian countries, fertile land fit for agriculture is rapidly becoming scarce. . . . In many parts of Tanzania there are still some open resources as new land can be converted into fertile plots at low costs. The future shape of Tanzania's rural society is to a large extent determined by this crucial distribution process. The relevant questions are: who will dominate this last frontier? What opportunities will those who now find themselves among the landless enjoy in the coming years? My experience is that, by and large, the controller throws his weight behind the rich farmer and in that way enables him to expand his landholdings to the detriment of his poorer neighbours. . . .

In *Staff, Kulaks and Peasants* (in Cliffe, 1973) I related a political drama which took place in the village of Itumba (administrative centre of Bulumbia division in Rungwe district) in 1966 and 1967. The case study describes how one wealthy farmer called Chomo, with the help of some staff people, maintained his position in the face of mounting opposition from the majority of the population. The fight became particularly bitter when the ownership of a valuable sugar-cane garden was at stake. Chomo received substantial support from the side of the agricultural extension officer (Mwakalinga) and the medical dispenser. From the political drama we extracted the following information on the position of the controllers, and their allies the wealthy farmers.

Power Base of the Controllers

a – The staff directly control a number of "legitimate arenas". Decisions reached in such arenas are recognized by the outside world as authoritative and are backed up by force if necessary. Examples of such arenas are the Primary Court, the investigations of the local police commander; the enquiries set up by the Divisional Executive Officer as "Justice of the Peace". Indirectly, the staff have an important say in a number of other arenas, the most important of which is the Village Development Committee.

b – Furthermore, the staff control access to certain material resources such as, for example, medicine and medical treatment, which can be obtained from the medical dispenser and mid-wife. Other valued goods and services which one can obtain through "staff people" are: employment in a government service as messenger (or other forms of unskilled labour); expertise of government officials: farm implements, sowing-seed; and transport.

c – Another important power basis of the controllers is their alignment with the large farmers. Objective evidence that such a coalition operates – and that both partners derive considerable benefits from it – is not difficult to procure. In return for information and certain goods (viz. gardens, food such as vegetables, finger-millet and sugar-cane) the staff help their large farmer friends in a number of ways. Not only do they assist them in occupying official functions, they also throw their weight behind these large farmers in disputes; this became apparent when the political drama in Itumba unfolded. From the same drama it appears that the following transactional relations existed between staff member Mwakalinga and Chomo, the largest local farmer.

. . . Chomo ceded part of his sugar-cane garden to Mwakalinga and gave a river garden on loan to the medical dispenser;

. . . Chomo escorted Mwakalinga to the hospital and took charge of mourning proceedings when his son died.

. . . Chomo regularly received information from his staff contacts which enabled him to forestall his enemies' moves;

. . . Mwakalinga assisted Chomo with technical advice and a loan of money in order to make it possible for him to appeal to a higher court, after the local Primary Court had ruled that one of Chomo's best fields (a sugar-cane garden) would have to be handed over to his enemies. The magistrate appeared to have come to this judgment only after considerable pressure had been exerted by the mass of the peasants in the village.

The Controllers' Perceptions and Strategies

The staff people know that they occupy a powerful position in rural areas; they feel entitled to the prestige and emoluments of an elite grouping. A basic tenet of these controllers is to equate success and wealth with the innate capacities of the peasants concerned and their (the peasantry's) ideological motivation for furthering the interests of their country. The majority of the staff people believe the poorer peasants to be lazy, ignorant and prone to practise witchcraft, the argument being that as they make no progress while others succeed they would tend to become envious of the more privileged farmers. Such opinions are sometimes sincerely held, and sometimes no more than rationalizations of their own interest in aligning with the richer peasants.

. . . The controllers follow two important strategic guidelines: "betting on the strong" and concentrating their attacks on weak spots. . . . Official instructions ensure that progressive farmers will represent the peasant population on government committees. Apart from these instructions, however, there is no clear-cut policy of the various government services in this respect. Government personnel work in a climate of *laissez-faire* which permits them to select their audience according to their own inclinations and interests. Generally the controllers are likely to choose the wealthy farmers as coalition partners, i.e. to bet on the strong rather than on the weak and the many. In Itumba, as we have seen, many exchange relationships have developed between staff people and wealthy farmers. Though this is the most frequently occuring type of coalition, it should not be viewed as the immutable and permanent alliance.

Another characteristic strategy of the controllers is the tendency to concentrate attacks on "weak spots" and ask only those peasants to comply with unpopular measures who are expected to offer a minimum of resistance.

Many fields in Itumba are cultivated for periods of four to six years continuously, before these fields are left to lie fallow for a period of three years. The widow Namatanga let one of her fields lie fallow in 1965. In November 1967 – at the beginning of the new agricultural season Kalinga, one of the more wealthy peasants, visited the Divisional Executive Officer and asked his permission to take over the widow's plot. The official called Namatanga to his office and urged her to start tilling the field immediately. The Divisional Executive Officer warned her that if she did not comply with his request, he would regrettably be forced to confiscate her plot and hand it over to others. He pointed out that there were too many people in Itumba who did not have enough land. In vain Namatanga pleaded that the plot had not sufficiently recovered its fertility.

In the same year Chomo left several acres of river land, which has no regeneration cyclus, unused. These plots could have satisfied the immediate needs of a number of poorer peasants if they had been taken from Chomo and given to the have-nots.

The Peasants' Perceptions

Peasants are inclined to dramatize the collusion of staff and of staff and kulaks. Although the suspicions of the peasants are sometimes without any factual basis they are nevertheless important, they influence their actions and mould their strategy. In the case study the following accusations and suspicions are mentioned.

The medical dispenser was alleged to have kept a stock of medicines reserved for his colleagues and rich farmer friends in times of scarcity. This, according to the peasants, had resulted in a lower mortality rate among children of this group than among peasant children. Furthermore, the medical dispenser was accused of withholding medicine from the divorced wife of Chomo and thus, indirectly, to have caused her death.

In a law-suit between Chomo and a few poorer peasants concerning the ownership of a valuable sugar-cane garden, the Primary Court Magistrate was believed to have come to an impartial judgment only after pressure had been brought to bear on him. In the eyes of the peasants he had relinquished his impartiality by secretively advising Chomo – via his friend the agricultural extension officer Mwakalinga – to appeal.

Chomo was reputed to have supplied the medical dispenser, the Primary Court Magistrate, Mwakalinga and two teachers with vegetables, onions and sugar-cane. It was well known that staff were often among his guests at his beer parties.

[Peasants thus believe that:]
(a) all legitimate areanas are dominated wholly or to a large extent by staff.
(b) Staff control access to vital resources.
(c) In case of conflict staff will close ranks.
(d) In case of conflict the richer peasants are supported by staff.

The Strategy of the Peasants

a – In case of conflict with a member of staff it is extremely difficult to press a charge against him. A possible course to pursue is to enlist the backing of another member of staff before taking action.

b – In case of a conflict do not enter the "legitimate arenas" but try another battleground in which more effective manoeuvres can be performed.

The medical dispenser at *X* was alleged to have regularly had affairs with married women in the community. This charge would have resulted in a civil case if the seducer were a peasant. But on the basis of the above stratagem peasants reacted differently: for two years no action was taken, then, in the middle of the night, people set fire to his houses. The dispenser escaped just in time from the blazing house.

More often peasants have recourse to threats which can be as effective as arson. In 1967 some villagers of Itumba bore grudges against the magistrate. Then, on a given day, the wife of the magistrate was advised by a "helpful" neighbour to leave because "people" intended to set fire to the thatched roof of her house. Two weeks later they left the village on a transfer. The magistrate who presided over the case of the valuable sugar-cane garden was told by people to pass a judgment favourable to the opponents of Chomo. If he failed to do so, "things would happen to him".

Richard Jeffries, *Political Radicalism in Africa* (1978a)

The Mau Mau rebellion, far from being an uprising supported by all the Kikuyu, was rather led and manned almost entirely by the landless and potentially landless – either squatters threatened with eviction from European-owned farms by the increasing profitability of fully capitalist farming, or the growing number of young men unable to secure viable plots in the increasingly over-populated African reserves. The colonial government's response was to encourage the official registration and consolidation of land holdings and to open up cash-crop opportunities for African farmers. In this way it was hoped to produce a rural yeomanry or middle class with a sufficient vested interest in the system to induce political moderation. To the acute distress of Oginga Odinga, Bildad Kaggia and other radical leaders, the independent KANU Government continued this policy, with similar disregard for the claims of the landless ex-Mau Mau fighters and detainees – either the claim that their particular land rights had been deliberately ignored in the process of land registration during their detention or the wider political claim that their fight (and, as they thought, that of KANU) had been for an end to all landlessness. Although the government's buying up of white farmers' lands for resettlement schemes provided small-holder plots for some, it hardly began to cope with the magnitude of the problem, while at the same time the wealthier farmers and members of the urban-based elite were enabled to invest in new holdings and thus develop into a new class of African capitalist farmers.

The radicals were initially concerned to press the cause of the ex-detainees. In reaction to the government's attempt to suppress critical voices and drive them from positions of influence, however, Odinga, Kaggia and others extended their attack. Their charges came to include the general issues of increasing class differentiation, excessive deference to the interests of expatriate landholders, and complicity in the continuing domination of the Kenyan economy and development strategy by western interests. President Kenyatta responded by further widening (and, in a sense, narrowing) the questions at issue to a quite artificial degree. The radicals were accused of being Communists and therefore un-Kenyan, of wishing to do away with all private property and thus of representing only the interests of the landless. Increasingly it was also suggested that they were representatives of a "Luo" tribalism.

These, then, were the ideological positions projected in the "Little General Election" of 1966 after Odinga, Kaggia, and 27 fellow MPs resigned from the ruling party, formed the Kenya People's Union (KPU), and were required to recontest their seats. Superficially, the results of the Election suggest that President Kenyatta's view of the situation was shared by the majority of voters. The KPU won a total of nine seats, all of them in Luo and neighbouring areas. Here, clearly, the KPU (and more particularly Odinga) were drawing at least as much on ethnic solidarity as on any specific commitment to its radical policies. In the Kikuyu areas, overt support for the KPU was slight, indeed Kaggia, for example, gaining only 10 per cent of the vote in his home constituency. Although the poll results here are open to question on grounds of undoubted violence against KPU supporters and a degree of ballot-rigging, the evidence of observers suggests that only a hard-core of embittered landless people were prepared to vote against KANU. The bulk of Kikuyu smallholders rather acted according to plan – that is to say, the plan implicit in the government's land policy – uniting behind the relatively wealthy in defence of newly-won security and perceived economic opportunities (Lamb, 1974).

It might nevertheless be suggested that such an identification was far from automatic, a crucial factor being President Kenyatta's authoritative definition of the situation. Kaggia's performance in previous elections indicated that sympathy for his brand of redistributive populism had been widespread. The electoral salience of this theme was undermined in 1966 not simply because of any perceived Luo threat in the KPU, nor even out of some vague deference to Kenyatta's charisma. The nature of the authority Kenyatta brought to bear on the Election was of a thoroughly institutionalized kind. The clear implication of his eve-of-poll speech was that voting for the KPU would be equivalent to supporting the Luo traitors and surrendering all entitlement to consideration in the future distribution of government-controlled resources.

The underlying assumption which made this threat so effective was that neither the KPU nor any opposition party could win a party political game played to rules established and suitably redefined by the government itself – an assumption forcefully confirmed by the disqualification on "technical" grounds of all KPU candidates in the General Election of 1968. The in-depth support acquired by the Kwilu rebellion in the Congo (*Fox*, below) occurred in a situation of extreme governmental fragility in which there seemed a real possibility that the rebels might win. In Kenya, by contrast, as in most of the ex-colonial African states, the transfer of administrative power was conducted sufficiently smoothly and effectively as to ensure that rural discontent could for the most part be contained by the threat of retaliatory discrimination. . . .

In virtually all of the postcolonial African states, indeed, the state apparatus has extended its control over rural economic activities so as to intensify the surplus appropriation on which its own existence is based, while increasing peasant dependence on its allocation of the most important rural resources. Where the manipulative exploitation of this dependency has not itself ensured the political passivity or division of the peasantry, the potential organizational sources of concerted resistance have, generally speaking, been systematically destroyed. One of the few exceptions serves merely to confirm the general rule.

This consists in the series of major concessions to peasant interests wrung from the Senegalese government by the leadership of the (Sufi) Mouride religious brotherhood in 1971–5. Post-independence change in the political economy of Senegal has consisted very centrally in the promotion of a new class of African governmental intermediaries between producers of peanuts – Senegal's most valuable export crop – and the French export companies which process and market peanut oil in Europe. Shortly after independence, a monopoly not only of the local marketing of peanuts but also of the provision of credit and agricultural supplies to the peasant producers was entrusted to a state body, ONCAD, whose organizational inadequacies, malversation and legalized exploitation rapidly became apparent. ONCAD peanut seed loans, a mandatory service, were extremely expensive at a 25 per cent interest rate for a four-month period and, together with other credit transactions of dubious facility, gave rise to much peasant indebtedness. Producer prices for peanuts were consistently and artificially held down, between 1968 and 1974, enabling ONCAD to make a substantial profit even during the drought years. As import prices at the same time rose sharply, the peasants' lot worsened dramatically in absolute terms, "while the proliferation of civil service villas in Dakar offered striking enough visual testimony to the state administration's success in providing for its own senior employees" (D. O'Brien, 1977).

Even though, against this background, rural discontent (known in government circles as the "malaise paysan") became increasingly conspicuous, there seemed very little that the Senegalese peasantry could do to redress the situation. The newly installed leader of the Mouride brotherhood – whose members account for at least one-third of Senegal's peanut production – was nevertheless to come up with a highly ingenious and effective answer. The idea of withdrawing from producing peanuts for the market in favour of subsistence agriculture might already have occurred to individual peasants as a drastic solution to their problem. But only the threat of a massive, organized revolt along these lines was likely to spur the government to positive measures to protect its financial base. By taking it upon itself to prepare its members for a form of agrarian strike, the leadership of the Mouride brotherhood adapted its charismatic authority to create what was, in effect, an extremely powerful rural trade union. A series of rhetorical and symbolic confrontations between the government and the Khalifa-General amounted to the agrarian equivalent of round-table negotiations with, from the Senegalese peasantry's point of view, impressive results. In 1971 and 1973 (the two principal drought years), the government was forced to intervene to cancel all outstanding peasant debts. The Mouride leadership could plausibly also claim a great deal of the credit for the decision in 1974–5 to all but double the producer price for peanuts.

The content of some of the Khalifa-General's declarations, with scarcely veiled references to the government as cast in a satanic role, has apparently led some Senegalese to believe that the brotherhood might become a vehicle of political revolt. As O'Brien remarks, however, "the brotherhood's history does show a certain Mouride aptitude for supping with the devil and Mouride leaders certainly know how to measure their spoons for the occasion". One might add that, so long as President Senghor maintains his customary preparedness to sup with the saints, they will most probably be content with economic concessions which not only alleviate peasant misery but help bolster their own, previously waning, political power and prestige.

Part IV

Prophets, Priests and Rebels

Introduction

As has often been the case elsewhere, the subordination of peasants, illustrated above, and the associated forms of consciousness and ideologies, have drawn heavily on religious ideas and institutions (Moore, 1966). Africans have adapted Muslim and Christian notions to indigenous cosmologies and to their own changing circumstances (Horton, 1971, 1975; Peel, 1968; Ranger, 1972). All these sources have been used to encourage submission to hierarchical and exploitative social orders, or to facilitate the adaptation of communities to the opportunities and inequalities of a capitalist economy (Long, 1968; Cross, 1973; Paden, 1973), though in some cases (Mayer, 1961) rural indigenous beliefs and cultural practices have acted as a defence against the encroachment of urban and commercial cultures.

Yet none of these religions is wholly submissive. Christianity and Islam have their own radical traditions (e.g. Hodgkin, 1980), which in Africa have been most expressed in millenarian and Mahdist movements. Innovative, this-worldly and forward-looking, they can, as *Hodgkin* and *Fox, de Craemer and Ribeaucourt* show, create new forms of solidarity transcending ethnic and other divisions in the attempt to resist colonial conquest, economic exploitation and political oppression (see also Paden, 1973; Weiss, 1967; Lubeck in Sandbrook, 1975b). *Van Binsbergen* analyses the way Zambians have tried to reconstruct their material and symbolic orders through religious and political movements, but have been less successful in achieving them. The Lumpa's attempt to create a material base for their own religious communities brought them into conflict with local groups and the prerogatives of the state, which promptly suppressed them. The African Watchtower movement, like other syncretist religions, inspired both peasant and worker resistance in the colonial period, but became more quietist thereafter (*Perrings*, below; Mwase, 1975; Linden, 1971; Sundkler, 1961; Wipper, 1978).

Indigenous religious influences impose similar limitations on rural resistance. *Fox, de Craemer and Ribeaucourt* and *Davidson* show how magical beliefs and practices, though important in mobilizing resistance and capable of being combined with secular ideologies of class oppression and revolt, can ultimately destroy a movement unless overcome by firm and explicit political leadership, as in the case of Guiné (on Zaïre see further Gran, 1979; Verhaegen, 1967–9). Other rural rebellions, especially those resisting settler expropriation of land, have drawn less on religion and more on secular ideologies. Both the Algerian and Kenyan peasant resistances were strongly influenced by urban leaderships and the struggle to regain land appropriated by settlers or indigenous landlords (Wolf, 1972; Kitching, 1980; Ochieng', 1977; Newsinger, 1981). In southern Africa the ubiquity of labour migration has influenced the form of peasant revolt (Beinart in Klein, 1980; Mbeki, 1964), while in areas of predominantly peasant agriculture, like West Africa, it is state intervention which has prompted it through both exploitative taxation and massive regulation of production (Beer, 1975; Beer in Williams, 1976; Amselle, 1978). As in the case of Zaïre, the leadership of such movements is drawn largely from categories frequently associated with rural rebellion: the middle peasantry, traders and rural artisans, wage earners and minor officials.

Religion and Resistance

Thomas Hodgkin, *Mahdism, Messianism and Marxism* (Gutkind, 1977)

Mahdist and Messianic movements have certain common characteristics.

(1) The central role of the Messianic leader, prophet, or Mahdi.
(2) The millenarian expectations, or hopes, of the movement.
(3) The rejection of established authority, both religious and secular, as oppressive and illegitimate.
(4) The appeal to "the masses" and the effort to mobilize them in support of the Mahdist–Messianic idea.
(5) Associated with this, the attempt to use the universality of the Mahdist–Messianic message as a means of overcoming traditional conflicts and antagonisms.
(6) The establishment of some form of continuing organization, based upon adherence to this ideology.
(7) The use of certain external symbols to express the common purposes and beliefs and distinctive character of the movement.
(8) The assertion of Puritan values in matters of personal conduct (abstinence, self-discipline, etc.); the rejection of "the things of this world".
(9) The situation of "crisis" in which such movements tend to emerge.

Essentially both Mahdism and Messianism are ideologies which are particularly appropriate for "the oppressed" in situations in which they have not only become conscious of oppression but are willing to respond to a movement which seems to offer a revolutionary way out: "If the present belongs to the oppressors, the future belongs to us, the revolutionary community – and outside the community there is no salvation and no future."

But, in spite of these basic resemblances, there are also some significant differences between movements that are generally described as "Mahdist" and those described as "Messianic". In particular, Mahdist movements, emerging in societies which have been fairly effectively Islamized over a period of time, have had a well-established body of Mahdist beliefs on which to draw.

First, the concept of crisis, during the period preceding the end of time in which the Mahdi will appear. "Upheavals and dissension will divide the Muslim community and lead to political strife, social disorder, and moral degeneration. . . ." (Al Hajj, 1967).

Second, the idea that the Mahdi, as the divinely guided one, in direct communication with God or his Prophet, can exercise a special revolutionary initiative in his interpretation of the Qur'an and the Sunna, unrestricted by the established *madhhabs*.

Third, the idea that the Mahdi, as ultimate Caliph of the Prophet, has the responsibility for conducting *jihad*, particularly against nominal and backsliding Muslims who reject his mission, and ensuring the universal triumph of Islam.

Fourth, the association of the appearance of the Mahdi with the approaching end of the world and a brief intervening Golden Age, during which he will "fill the earth with equity and justice, even as it has been filled with tyranny and oppression".

The Messianic movements on the other hand which have emerged in non-Muslim Africa have generally drawn their basic ideas either from the Judaeo-Christian tradition, or from "traditional" African belief-systems, or, very often, from some combination of these . . . Often the ideology has been worked out afresh by the movement through the application of certain basic concepts drawn from the Judaeo-Christian tradition – of a Messiah, of an oppressed people, of salvation as an event in historic time – to their own situation. The central idea is that the Kingdom of Heaven must be understood in a this-worldly, not an other-worldly sense – as a perfected social order, to be achieved in the very near future and enjoyed collectively by the faithful.

Messianic movements in non-Muslim contexts are not committed to the same sort of attitude to institutions as Mahdist movements. It is an essential part of the Mahdist threory to regard *jihad*, in the sense of an armed revolutionary struggle, as the method whereby a perfected social order must be brought into being. Messianic movements on the other hand, while they may accept the view that the expected transformation of society depends upon revolutionary action of their part, may also regard it as dependent upon some cataclysmic external event which it is their duty simply to await. In other words Messianism seems compatible, in some degree, with quietism as well as with activism. Similarly, at the level of objectives, Mahdist movements are committed to the idea of a Mahdist state, i.e. a perfected Islamic state, which they must seek to realize. Messianic movements are not necessarily concerned with state-building, though in practice this may become their objective. . . . What was the nature of the crisis that stimulated the transformation of latent Mahdism into active Mahdism during the period from 1880 on – above all in the eastern Sudan, the only region in which an effective Mahdist state was able to establish and maintain itself for a substantial period, but also generally, in many parts of *bilad al-sudan*.

In a general way one can explain the activisation of latent Mahdist beliefs during this period by the increasing pressure of European imperialism upon the Muslim world and the economic, social, and political disintegration arising out of these pressures and, later, out of actual European invasion and occupation and the defeat or capitulation of Muslim governments. This, understandably, appeared to indicate the existence of the kind of crisis associated historically with the appearance of the Mahdi. . . .

Against this background one can understand how the idea of *hijra* became associated with and reinforced by Mahdist beliefs in the popular opposition to European–Christian rule which expressed itself in the final crisis of the Sokoto Caliphate. The choice of *hijra*, as opposed to collaboration with the Unbelievers, had already been made by Ahmadu Shehu, son of al-Hajj 'Umar and ruler of Segu, who, after Bandiagara had fallen to the French, had moved East with a considerable following to Sokoto, where he died in 1898. His son, Bashir, together with a section of the ruling and scholarly classes from Sokoto and its dependent Amirates accompanied the legitimate (now officially deposed) Caliph, Attahiru Ahmad, when he opted for *hijra* after the fall of Sokoto [in contemporary Nigeria] in March 1903. But what makes Attahiru's *hijra* particularly interesting historically is the scale of mass participation and support which it enjoyed. Hence the strengthened appeal, in a situation in which the country was now in actual occupation by the Europeans, of Mahdist ideas – reflected in the choice of the Mahdist town of Burmi [in today's Bauchi State, Nigeria] as the place of refuge for Attahiru and his supporters and the base for their final stand against imperialism. And within the British-occupied territories of the Caliphate a succession of Mahdist, or post-Mahdist, movements emerged – "the most celebrated . . . (being) that which culminated in the Satiru rebellion of 1906" (Adeleye, 1971).

If we turn from the Muslim to the non-Muslim world we can find a clear example of the use of messianic and millenary ideas to provide ideological support for a movement of "primary resistance" to European imperialism in Ranger's admirable study of the Shona rebellion. Like the later Maji-Maji rising in Tanganyika (Iliffe, 1979), he argues, the rebellion involved –

> defiance of a power which enjoyed great technological superiority and began with a superiority of morale based upon it and upon confidence in its ability to shape the world. The [African] religious leaders were able to oppose to this a morale which for the moment was as confident, if not more

so, based upon *their* supposed ability to shape the world; and they were able to oppose to modern weapons the one great advantage that the Africans possessed, that of numbers. (Ranger, 1967: 352.)

He goes on to stress the "ambiguity" of the attitude of these resistance movements to European ideas and technology. There is repudiation but also desire; a rejection of white mastery but a longing for African control of modern sources of wealth and power in an African environment. . . . Mkwati and Kagthi [religious leaders of the Shona rebellion] . . . were not reactionary in the simple sense of looking to the restoration of the *status quo* of 1890; their programme was in some ways revolutionary in its vision of a new society. In Mkwati's millenarian promises "there was a strange mixture of return to the past and control of the new".

Lobengula was to return from the dead – and to reign from Government House, Bulawayo. When Mkwati was trying to rally the north-eastern rebels in August 1896 it was reported that he promised them that they only "had to wait until all the whites are dead or fled and then they will enjoy the good things of the town and live in palaces of corrugated iron" (Ranger, 1967: 354.)

. . . These Messianic–Mahdist movements were important, both in themselves and as regards their influence on subsequent African history, in at least three ways. First, through the universalism of their ideologies, and the forms of organization which they attempted to construct, these movements tried, with varying degrees of success, to provide a new basis of solidarity, transcending the more restricted ties of kinship, locality, ethnic or linguistic group, or precolonial state. . . .

True, this new revolutionary form was by its nature unstable and difficult to maintain over a long period. There was an understandable tendency, once the leadership had to confront the problem of constructing some kind of continuing system and preserving it against increasing internal and external pressures, to revert to reliance on those same traditional ties, loyalties, institutions, that the revolution had sought to abolish or transcend.

Thus Holt (1958: 246) describes the Khalifa Abdallahi, during the later phases of the Mahdist state [in Sudan] attempting to "restore the administrative system . . . by bringing back the men and methods of the old régime and thereby much of the corruption, dilatoriness, and oppression which the Mahdi had hoped to sweep away". (Modern analogies will readily suggest themselves.)

Second, Messianic–Mahdist movements were in a basic sense forward-looking: they were "movements of innovation looking to the future and the regeneration of the world". These particular movements present a view of a future social order which is essentially different from any kind of society that has existed in the known or remembered past. They may refer back to the early Caliphate or to the state of man before the Fall; the Mahdi–Messiah may see himself as re-enacting the life and experience of the Prophet or Christ; or they may make use of concepts and symbols derived from traditional religion. But they were essentially different from those forms of resistance or rebellion whose primary object was to retain or restore the precolonial political and social order. The revolution, as they conceived it, must involve the total transformation of society, and of man as a social being; the assertion of a new ethnic and a new basis for human relationships; the ending of all forms of oppression, not merely those specific forms of oppression associated with external domination of the colonial state.

Third, Messianic and Mahdist movements have provided a structure of ideas and institutions through which "the masses" have begun to plan an active, formative, and conscious part in modern history. In broad terms these movements would generally seem to have involved some form of alliance between large sections of the peasantry (including semi-proletarianized elements) and, in the case of the Sudan, the nomad population, with a revolutionary leadership drawn largely from what one might call the underprivileged intelligentsia – Sufi shaykhs, small ulama, catechists, monitors, interpreters, clerks, and NCOs who had worked in the administrative, commercial or military sectors of the colonial apparatus.

The points of resemblance between the theories of Messianic and Mahdist movements and certain aspects of Marxism are evident enough. These include the idea of history as involving a continuing conflict between oppressors and oppressed, and leading, by a process conceived as historically necessary, to the ultimate victory of the oppressed; the "apocalyptic" idea of the just, or classless, society, based on the principle of "to each according to his needs", as in some sense the goal of history; the idea of the total corruption and degeneracy of the existing social order, and the consequent necessity for the total reconstruction of all institutions, all aspects of human life and relationships; the idea of social change in a progressive direction as depending not simply upon providential guidance, or some cataclysmic external event, but also (in part, at least) upon revolutionary activism and the intelligent and continuing participation of the masses in the effort to transform the actual world.

In part the points of difference between the two types of theory arise from the fact that Marxism involves a much more carefully constructed, and objectively better grounded, method of historical interpretation and sociological analysis than the methods employed by Mahdist and

Messianic movements. The classless society of Communism is conceived, not as imminent, but as realizable after a complex and protracted period of effort, conflict, and transition, involving many retrogressive as well as progressive phases – even though there have been moments in the history of the past hundred years when Marxists have in practice taken a somewhat millenarian view of the prospects of world revolution. Moreover bourgeois society, and even the colonial systems which Western bourgeois states have imposed upon the peoples of the non-Western world, are conceived as containing within themselves possibilities for the kind of total transformation of society in a Socialist (and ultimately a Communist) direction which Marxists believe to be necessary and desirable. "Millenarian movements", Hobsbawm (1959: 58) argues, "share a fundamental vagueness about the actual way in which the new society will be brought about." But, I think he exaggerates the extent to which "pure" millenarian movements have tended to adopt a passive or "waiting", attitude to revolutionary change. This is certainly not true of Mahdist movements, nor, I think, of most of the non-Muslim Messianic movements referred to here. They are closer to the classic Marxist position that revolution is at the same time historically necessary and dependent upon the beliefs and actions of revolutionaries. Their difficulty was rather that of all Utopian movements: the lack of a clearly defined strategy of revolution, reliance upon a variety of methods – *jihad* or armed rebellion, magical-religious techniques, *hijra* or withdrawal from the European-dominated political order, expectation of external support – inadequate to achieve their revolutionary objectives.

Yet, when all this is said, it remains surely true that Utopianism is, as Hobsbawm suggests, in some degree a characteristic of all revolutionary movements, however "primitive" or "sophisticated" they may be in respect of their social theories or political strategies. It is essential for revolutionaries to believe that "the ultimate in human prosperity and liberty will appear after their victories" (Hobsbawm, 1959: 60–1). It seems doubtful even whether the fact that, for participants in Mahdist and Messianic movements, "the future" normally includes the prospect of the enjoyment of bliss in some form of other-worldly existence, while for Marxists it is *limited* to future phases of human history, makes all that practical difference. In both cases suffering, death, martyrdom are endured for the sake of a future which is believed to be their entire and sufficient justification. Hence the efforts of "venal Mallams" among sociologists and political scientists to discredit revolutionary movements under Marxist (or partly Marxist) leadership on the ground that these are simply modern expressions of "archaic" and "primitive" millenarian ideas are otiose.

Wim van Binsbergen, *Lumpa: Religious Innovation and Peasant Revolt*
(1980)

. . . In every society the members have explicit and mutually shared
ideas concerning the universe, society, and themselves. These ideas are
supported by implicit, often unconscious cognitive structures. . . . The
total arrangement of these elements can be called the symbolic order, or
the superstructure. The superstructure defines a society's central
concerns, major institutions, and basic norms and values. Against these,
actual behaviour can be evaluated in terms of good and evil, status and
success. The superstructure is the central repository of meaning for the
members of society. It offers them an explanatory framework. While
thus satisfying the participants' intellectual needs, the superstructure
also, on the level of action, patterns behaviour in recognized, predictable
units which the participants learn in the course of their socialization.
Thus the superstructure provides the participants with a sense of
meaningfulness and competence in their dealings with each other and
with the non-human world. Ritual and ceremonies, as well as
internalization in the personality structure of individual members of
society, reinforce the superstructure and let it persist over time. On the
other hand, every society has what we can call an infrastructure: the
organization of the production upon which the participants' lives
depend, and particularly such differential distribution of power and
resources as dominate the relations of production.

. . . In a relatively stable situation infrastructure and superstructure
are likely to be attuned to each other, the latter deriving the
meaningfulness and competence it conveys, from the infrastructure it
expresses, reinforces, and legitimates. But in situations of rapid change
the superstructure has no longer grip on, is no longer fundamentally
relevant to, the practical experience of participants in economic life. The
superstructure therefore ceases to convey meaningfulness and
competence. This creates in the participants existential problems: the
subjective experience of alienation. For these problems two solutions
exist. Upon the debris of an obsolete superstructure the participants may
try to construct a new superstructure that is more in line with the altered
relations of production; I shall call this *superstructural reconstruction.*
Alternatively, participants may attack the alienation problem on the
infrastructural level: reversing or redefining, . . . the altered
distribution of power and resources, and the production process as a
whole, so as to bring it in line, again, with their superstructure that has
remained virtually unaltered. . . .

In order to work at all if even during a short time, attempts at superstructural reconstruction apparently have to do three things. First, they have to propound a new arrangement of symbols. Thus they can restore the sense of meaningfulness, subjectively and temporarily, even if the infrastructure from which such meaningfulness ultimately derives is left unaffected. Such a new arrangement of symbols must then focus on symbols that are eminently effective and unassailable in the eyes of the participants. The new superstructural reconstruction may be predominantly religious (e.g. Lumpa), political (e.g. Zambian nationalism), or presumably take some other course; it is essential that the central symbols appear *absolute* to the participants. Secondly, superstructural reconstruction must restore the sense of competence by stipulating new forms of action. This action may vary from collective ritual to campaigns to check party cards. It is important that participants are brought to look upon such action as bringing about the new, desired social order where their alienation problems will no longer exist. At the same time these actions translate the movement's central symbols into the context of tangible, lived-through reality, thus reinforcing them. Finally, attempts at superstructural reconstruction, in order to be at least initially successful, cannot stop at the level of merely individual interpretations and actions, but must create new group structures (e.g. restructured rural communities, churches, political parties) within which the participants can lead their new lives once their alienation problems will have been solved subjectively. Recruitment into these new groups must be presented as the solution to the problems of individual people. Expansion of the new group is often considered the main method to create a new society in which the alienation problem would no longer exist.

On the infrastructural level, two major changes occurred throughout Central Africa since the 18th century. The first consisted in the increasing involvement of local farming, fishing and hunting communities in a new mode of production that was dominated by long-distance trade and by the payment of tribute to the states that emerged in Central Africa partly as a result of such trade. The second major infrastructural change was the penetration of capitalism. Directly, capitalism induced the rural population to leave their villages and work as migrant labourers in the mines, farms and towns of Central and southern Africa; to adapt their rural economy, and increasingly their total life, to the consumption of manufactured commodities; and, in selected areas, to embark on small-scale capitalist agricultural production. Indirectly, the infrastructural accommodation to capitalism was promoted by the colonial state, e.g. by the imposition of hut tax; the destruction of pre-existing networks of trade and tribute; the transformation of indigenous rulers into petty administrators for the colonial state; the regulation of migration between the rural areas and the places of work; the provision of schools to serve the need for skilled workers and clerks; urban housing; medical services; the occasional promotion of African commercial farming, etc. . . .

In the old superstructure, the link with the local dead was the main legitimation for residence, political office, and for such a variety of specialist roles as divining, healing, hunting, ironworking, musical crafts. Through residence, veneration of the local dead, and ritual focusing on land spirits, a special ritual link with the land was established. Without such a link no success could be expected in economically vital undertakings such as agriculture, fishing, hunting and collecting. The participants' view of the society and of an individual's career arranged village life, the economic process, politics and ritual in one comprehensive framework, where each part has meaning by reference to all others. This view was, therefore, religious as much as it was political or economic.

When the trade-tribute mode of production expanded, the emergent major chiefs initially had to legitimize their political and economic power in terms of this same view of society. Chiefly cults came up which enabled the chiefs to claim ritual power over the land's fertility, either through ritual links with deceased predecessors, or through non-royal priests or councillors representing the original owners of the land. Thus, as a result of infrastructural change, symbolic themes already present in the superstructure were redefined; a new power distribution was acknowledged in the superstructure; and a pattern that in the old superstructure referred to merely local conditions was now applied to extensive regional political structures which often comprised more than one ethnic group. However, in this altered superstructure the merging between religious and political aspects was still largely retained.

Along with these chiefly cults, two other types of religious innovation can be traced back to the late precolonial period and to the infrastructural changes then occurring: the appearance of prophets, and the emergences of cults of affliction. Cults of affliction concentrate on the individual, whose physical and/or mental suffering they interpret in terms of possession by a spirit, whilst treatment mainly consists of initiation as a member of the cult. Central-African prophets and the movements they trigger fall into three sub-types; the ecological prophet whose main concern is with fertility and the land; the eschatological prophet who predicts the imminent end of the world such as it is known to his audience; and the affliction prophet who establishes a new, regionally-organized cult of affliction, which in many respects resembles an independent church. The colonial era saw new types of religious innovation. Preachers and dippers (advocating baptism through immersion) appeared. They were connected, some more closely than others, with the African Watchtower movement, which in itself derived indirectly from the North-American Jehovah's Witnesses. There were other independent churches which pursued more or less clearly a Christian idiom. Finally, mission Christianity had in fact penetrated before the imposition of colonial rule (1900), but started to gain momentum much later. . . .

Despite their differences in idiom, ritual and organizational structure, the same few trends in symbolic development dominate all these cases of religious innovation. All struggle with the conception of time. The cyclical present implicit in the old superstructure (highlighting agriculture, hunting, and gathering at the scale of the small-village community) becomes obsolete. In the course of these religious innovations, it gives way to a linear time perspective that emphasizes personal careers and historical development, even to the extent of interpreting history as a process of salvation in the Christian sense. In some of these religious innovations, the linear perspective is again supplanted by the eschatological; the acute sense of time drawing to an end. Almost all these innovations try to move away from the ecological concern for the land and fertility that dominated the old superstructure. The village dead as major supernatural entities venerated in ritual give way to other, less particularistic entities, especially the High God. In line with this, all these innovations tend to move away from taking the old village community, in its form, as their basic concept of society. In the cults of affliction this process manifests itself in their extreme emphasis on the suffering individual and their underplaying of morality and social obligations. In some of the other religious innovations the same process reaches further: they explicitly strive towards the creation of a new and fundamentally different community, a new society to be brought about by the new religious inspiration and new ritual. Finally, in so far as in the old superstructure sorcery was considered the main threat to human society, these religious innovations each try to formulate alternatives to sorcery. The cults of affliction and the mission churches attribute misfortune and suffering to causes altogether different from sorcery. Most of the other innovations continue to accept the reality of sorcery, but try to eradicate it once for all so as to make the new, transformed community possible.

One stream of superstructural reconstruction is of exclusively rural origin; the religious innovators and their followers are peasants. This applies to cults of affliction, and to the cults created by ecological, eschatological and affliction prophets. The other stream springs from what we can provisionally call the "intensive contact situation". This comprises the places of work which attracted labour migrants from throughout Central Africa (mines, farms, towns), and moreover the rural extensions of these centres: district administrative centres (*bomas*); rural Christian missions; and military campaigns involving thousands of African carriers, and fewer soldiers, near the Zambian–Tanzanian border in the First World War. Watchtower dippers and preachers, other independent churches, and mission Christianity are the religious innovations belonging to this second stream. The first stream comprised people still largely involved in a precapitalist mode of production: shifting cultivation, hunting and gathering. However, state expansion and the impact of capitalism, have infringed on their local autonomy, draining their products and labour force (through slave-raiding, tribute, forced labour, migrant labour and urbanization), and encroaching on their rights on local land, hunting and fishing (e.g. by the creation of chiefs' hunting reserves, and later by the founding of commercial farms, towns, mines, native reserves, and forest reserves). From free, autonomous farmers whose system of production was effectively contained within their social horizon and subject to their own control, they became a peasant class in a world-wide society. But while the facts of this process of incorporation and expropriation are unmistakable and have come to affect every aspect of village life, the agents of control in their new situation have largely remained invisible at the village level. The physical outlets of the state and of the capitalist economy were confined to the district centres and the towns along the line of rail, outside the everyday experience of the peasants. Particularly after the creation of indirect rule (around 1930), administrators and peasants alike could foster the illusion of an essentially intact traditional society whose time-honoured social institutions, though heavily assailed were still functioning. Under these circumstances, the rural population's reaction against being forced into peasant class position could hardly be expected to confront, immediately, the outside forces responsible for their expropriation. One does not expect anticolonial responses in this context. A precondition for such responses would have been that the peasants had acquired some explicit assessment of the power situation in the wider society in so far as this affected their situation – and were prepared to challenge these structures. But as Gluckman (1971: 15) has pointed out: "there were plenty of hostilities [between Black and White]; but they did not continually affect the daily life of Africans; and the picture of Africans in constant and unceasing antagonism to whites is false for the rural areas".

Instead, the peasants sought a solution for their predicament of alienation entirely at the local level; and not primarily through the creation of new relations of production, but mainly through the formulation of a new superstructure.

The various rural-based religious, innovations were attempts to render, on a local scale, village life once again meaningful but new symbols, restoring the sense of competence by new ritual. Whereas the cults of affliction attempted to do this on the exclusively individual level, the various prophetic cults went further. The latter aimed at ushering the local population into a radically new community. However, usually this community was entirely conceived in ritual terms. Most prophetic cults did not attempt to work out the infrastructural requirements, in terms of relations of production, by which such a new community might really have formed a lasting answer to the predicament of peasantization; Lumpa was an important exception to this.

The second stream of superstructural reconstruction sprang from a quite different social situation. In the places of migrant work, the *bomas*, the missions, and while involved in a military campaign, the Africans had not just experienced the distant effects of the expansion of state systems and capitalism. In general, they were born and raised within the peasant context retaining more or less close links with their village kin. Yet they had entered into a different class position, or were on their way of doing so. They lived outside their villages, in a social setting dominated not by the inclusive, reciprocal social relationships typical of the village, but by formal organizations, patterned after those of modern North-Atlantic society. Their daily working experience was determined by forms of control characteristic of capitalist relations of production. In this situation, their livelihood was entirely dependent upon their taking part in the production process as wage-labourers. Therefore their class position was largely that of proletarians, even though the majority attempted to keep open the lines back into the village, and still had rights to rural land should they return home. The forces of the state and capitalism that in the villages remained distant, anonymous, and often below the threshold of explicit awareness, were in this proletarian situation blatantly manifest. These forces pervaded every aspect of the worker's social experience, and were personified in concrete people: white employers, foremen, administrative officers and missionaries. Exploitation, economic insecurity, humiliation and racial intimidation were the specific forms in which these more immediate causes of the African predicament were driven home in this situation. Essentially all this applies equally to the rural Christian missions. I am not denying that the flavour of human relations in the missions may have been somewhat more humanitarian than in the migrants' places of work. But infrastructurally the missions represented a social setting very similar to the latter, in such terms as: formal, bureaucratic forms of organization and control; race relations; predominance of capitalism, as manifested in exclusive land rights, wage labour, and distribution of manufactured commodities.

For many thousands of people in the intensive-contact situation mission-propagated Christianity seemed to provide the solution they were looking for. This religious innovation promised a new life and a new society. Its organizational structure as well as its moral and ethical codes were, not surprisingly, well attuned to colonial society and capitalism. However, for this very reason conversion did not solve the predicament of alienation; it added but a new dimension to it.

In the intensive contact situation a general and explicit reaction was generated against white domination in both the political and the religious field. African Watchtower and other independent churches (including the African Methodist Episcopal Church), are the more predominantly religious manifestations of the second, non-rural stream of superstructural reconstruction. The political manifestations led through Welfare Societies and labour agitation at the Copperbelt, to the nationalist movement which took a concrete form after the Second World War.

Given the fact of circulatory labour migration, in which a large proportion of the Central-African male population was involved, the two streams of superstructural reconstruction could not remain entirely screened off from each other. Significant exchanges took place between the superstructural responses of peasantization and those of proletarization. The introduction of peasant cults of affliction into the intensive contact situation is a common phenomenon in Central Africa.

In the late 1920s and the 1930s Watch Tower was propagated in the rural areas of Central Africa at a very large scale. The proletarian preachers and dippers expressed anticolonial attitudes, and attracted state persecution on this basis. However, the massive peasant audiences they inspired and brought to baptism, seemed to respond less to their anticolonialism and their analysis of the wider society. Instead, the peasants were looking for reconstruction of just the local, rural society, by ritual means, and therefore chose to emphasize selectively the eschatological and witch-cleansing elements in the preachers' messages. And the latter were not hesitant to oblige. . . . The various peasant responses reveal the attempt to reconstruct a whole, self-supporting, autonomous rural community. Most of these attempts were unrealistic and failed entirely. Yet in essence they are extremely radical in that they attempt to reverse the process of peasantization, by denying the rural community's encapsulation in a wider colonial and capitalist system. By contrast, the "urban" responses were decidedly less radical. For they took for granted the fundamental structure of capitalism, and aimed not at an overthrow of capitalist relations of production, but at material and psychological improvement of the proletarian experience within this overall structure. . . . After UNIP (United National Independence Party) realized territorial independence, this nationalist party and its leaders have greatly enhanced state control as a means to consolidate the capitalist structure of Zambian society. The infrastructure was left intact, and after the replacement of this structure's white executive personnel by Africans, its further expansion was stimulated. The growth of UNIP in the rural areas, where the party increasingly implements and controls state-promoted projects of "rural development", represents a further phase in the domination of rural communities by the state and capitalism.

*   *   *   *   *

. . . Lenshina was born around 1920, as the daughter of a Bemba villager who had fought against the Germans near the Tanzanian border, and who had later been a *boma* messenger. Though growing up near Lubwa mission, Lenshina was not a baptized Christian when she received her first visions in 1953. Her husband had been a carpenter with Lubwa mission, but by that time was no longer employed there. Lenshina referred to the mission with an account of her spiritual experiences. The white missionary-in-charge took her seriously, saw her through Bible lessons and baptism (when she received the name of Alice), and encouraged her to give testimony of her experiences at church gatherings. However, when this missionary went on leave abroad, and Alice began to develop ritual initiatives on her own, even receiving money for them, the African minister-in-chårge felt that she could no longer be contained within the mission church. From 1955 onwards Lenshina propagated her message on her own behalf, thus founding an independent church. She collected a phenomenal following around her, which by 1958 was estimated at about 65,000. Many of these were former converts of Lubwa mission and of the neighbouring Roman Catholic missions. In Chinsali district and adjacent areas, the great majority of the population turned to Lenshina's church, which was soon known as Lumpa ("excelling all others"). An organizational framework was set up in which Lenshina's husband Petros Chitankwa, and other male senior deacons, held the topmost positions. Many thousands of pilgrims flocked to Lenshina's village Kasomo, which was renamed Sioni (Zion); many settled there permanently. In 1958 the Lumpa cathedral was completed to be one of the greatest church buildings of Central Africa. Scores of Lumpa branches were created throughout Zambia's Northern Province. In addition, some appeared along the line of rail, and even in Zimbabwe. However, the rural membership of the church began to drop in the late 1950s, from about 70 per cent to about 10 per cent of the local population. After various clashes with the chiefs, local missions, the colonial state, and the anticolonial nationalist movement, armed resistance against the state precipitated the 1964 final conflict which meant the end of the overt existence of Lumpa in Zambia.

Lumpa laid strong emphasis on the eradication of sorcery, mainly through baptism and the surrender of sorcery apparatus. It displayed the linear time perspective implicit in the notion of salvation, while eschatological overtones only became very dominant in the few months preceding the final conflict. Lenshina assumed ritual ecological functions such as distributing blessed seeds and calling rain, but on the other hand imposed taboos on common foods such as beer. The church's idiom highlighted God and Jesus, while denouncing ancestors, deceased chiefs and affliction-causing spirits as objects of veneration. Finally, the church aimed at the creation of a new, predominantly rural society – but this time not only by the ritual means of witchcleansing but also by experiments with new patterns of social relations and even with new relations of production and control which at least went some way towards infrastructural change. In this last respect lies the uniqueness of Lumpa – as well as its undoing. . . .

From the very beginning the symbolic idiom in which Lenshina expressed her message belonged not to the stream of proletarianization, but to that of peasantization. This is clear from Lenshina's emphasis on ecological ritual, sorcery-eradication, and the construction of a new, exclusively local, rural society. As the movement spread over north-eastern Zambia, these peasant elements became more and more dominant. . . . In its emphasis on the creation of a new, local society, the incorporation of that society in the wider structures of capitalism and the colonial state (the frame of reference of the proletarization response, including nationalism), became increasingly irrelevant. . . . By becoming more and more specifically a peasant movement, Lumpa could no longer accommodate those of its members whose experiences at rural missions, bomas, and in town were more deeply rooted in the proletarianization process. This partly explains the decline of Lumpa in north-eastern Zambia since the late 1950s. By that time many of the Lumpa adherents returned to their mission churches. Others heeded the call of the rapidly expanding rural branches of UNIP. Entrenched in its exclusively rural and local outlook, Lumpa was working out a form of peasant class struggle quite incompatible with the nationalist emphasis on wider incorporation and on the state. By the same token, the urban branches of Lumpa became increasingly divorced from the rural developments in the church. . . .

On the level of social relations, the belief in the eradication of sorcery created a new social climate where the very strict moral rulings of the Lumpa church were observed to an amazing extent. This was for instance noticeable in the field of sexual and marital relations. . . . In many respects, moreover, Lumpa tried to revive the old superstructure, in which concern for the land and fertility, protection against sorcery, general morality, and political and economic power had all combined so as to form one holistic conception of the rural society. However, the new society was to be a theocratic one, in which all authority had to derive from God and his prophetess, Lenshina. The *boma*, chiefs, Local Courts, as they had no access to this authority, were denounced and ignored. In the judicial sphere, cases would be taken to Lenshina and her senior church leaders, who tried them to the satisfaction of the Lumpa adherents involved. . . . Very frequent communication was maintained between the various branches and headquarters, e.g. by means of pilgrimage and the continuous circulation of church choirs through the countryside. Under these conditions the creation of an alternative, church-administered authority structure was no illusion, but a workable reality. . . . The very substantial donations from Lumpa church branches, individual members, and pilgrims, accumulated at Sioni. They were used not only for Lenshina's household and retinue, but also towards the creation of rural stores. Trucks were purchased, both to stock the stores and to transport church choirs between the branches and headquarters. The huge Lumpa cathedral was built in 1956–8 by the various church branches in a form of tribute labour, with no outside assistance. The continuous circulation of pilgrims and choir-members through the countryside of north-eastern Zambia represented another interesting economic feature. These Lumpa adherents had to be fed gratis by the local villagers, to whom they were often strangers. They were not always welcome and were likened to locusts. Yet this institution suggests the potential of the economic network created by Lumpa.

The most significant move towards a new infrastructure revolved on land and land rights – as befits a peasant movement. Lumpa's attempt to create a new rural society and (to some extent) new relations of production, inevitably called for a territorial basis on which a contiguous, exclusively Lumpa population could pursue their new social, economic and religious life. Lumpa adherents began to resettle, primarily around Sioni, where apparently hundreds of them concentrated. Accepting only theocratic authority, they did not ask permission from the chiefs. In this way they challenged the fundamental property rights on which their rural production system had been based for two centuries or more. This conflict over "unauthorized" settlement led to the first violent clashes between Lumpa and the police, in 1959

(Roberts, 1970: 544). Soon, Lenshina tried to purchase land, which was greatly opposed, and resented, by the chiefs and by the increasingly non-Lumpa population. As UNIP/Lumpa tensions mounted, Lumpa adherents withdrew into a number of exclusively Lumpa villages, which were again "unauthorized" from the point of view of the chiefs and the state. In July 1964 Kaunda's ultimatum to abandon these villages expired. Two police officers on patrol visited one such village; the inhabitants allegedly understood that they came to demolish the village, and killed them. This started the final conflict, whose outcome was, *inter alia*, the demolition of all Lumpa villages and of the Lumpa cathedral. [Some 1500 people died; Lumpa was banned; many Lumpa adherents exiled themselves in Zaïre; Lenshina was detained until 1975.]

Rebellion and Revolution

Renée C. Fox, W. de Craemere and J.-M. Ribeaucourt, *The Second Independence: the Kwilu Rebellion in the Congo* (1965)

The team of the Kwilu government (established in 1962, after the death of Lumumba, and the imprisonment of Gizenga, his Vice-Prime-Minister from Kwilu) quickly became known through the Congo as a young, educated, dynamic, socially progressive group, and the Kwilu gained the reputation of being a ''pilot'' and a ''model'' province. . . .

The provincial government instituted tight and far-reaching influence and control over the life of the population in many different areas. A program for the planned development of villages throughout the province was devised. The provincial government also organized activities in the realm of public health, the building of roads, and the modification of methods of agriculture. It made the collection of taxes more efficient and stringent, and further developed the police force. . . .

Despite the formal national reputation of the Kwilu as a model province the planning, organizing and integrating done by the government was not unequivocally appreciated by the population of the Kwilu. The people of the villages apparently resented the degree and kind of control exercized over them by government officials whom they regarded as not having a traditional village mentality, or a sense of identification with the plight of the population living and working in rural areas. They saw these officials not only as men who did not really represent them, but also as individuals who lived in much greater luxury than the masses, and who exploited the people through the frequent collection of taxes and fines, through the drafting of workers into enforced labor projects for which were not paid, and through the arbitrary use of the police, the gendarmerie and the army, and of false witnesses in trials. The villagers also felt that the provincial government was favouring the development of centres like Kikwit and Idiofa over that of smaller communities. . . .

From the start [of the Kwilu rebellion, led by Pierre Mulele] government, religious, industrial and educational agencies and personnel were the deliberate targets of the rebels. . . .

The general doctrine of Mulelism offers a definition of what is wrong in the Congo four years after Independence; a diagnosis of the causes of these difficulties, imperfections and injustices; and suggestions and enjoinders about what can and ought to be done about them so that an idyllic, truly independent society is brought into being. The main tenets of the doctrine seem to be the following:

> Ideally, a country is a territory in which people live together and obey the laws their government has proclaimed. Men of the government are chosen by the people of the country; the laws are proclaimed in the name of all men to protect the well-being of all.
> This country, the Congo, has a bad government. All the wealth of the country is in the hands of the governors. They protect only their own well-being, and that of their families. They eat well, drink well, dress well. And as for us, we have become their "slaves".
> In a country of this kind, the people are divided into two classes: (1) the rich, the capitalists, who profit from the work of others "like the mosquito sucks the blood of men". (2) Workers and peasants: the poor, or the "popular masses".
> During the electoral campaign, the Party (PSA Parti Solidaire Africaine – see Weiss, 1967) promised us: (1) Free medical care for men of the village without work. But up to now, have they given it to us free? (2) Free education: When our children attended classes, they said, we would not have to pay. But now, in order for our children to go to school, a large fee is demanded of us. Many of us are unemployed, and have no money with which to pay the fee. How, then, can our children pursue their studies like the children of the governors? And without an education, can one of our children become a deputy or a minister later in life, like one of their children can become? The governors have increased the cost of education in order to chase our children away, and in order to keep their money and material possessions for themselves and for their children. (3) The Party also promised us machines to plough our fields. Have they given them to us? No. And so we continue to suffer as we work the earth.
> All the wealth of the country is in the hands of "foreigners": (1) Foreigners or imperialists who steal the wealth of the country. (2) Persons of the bad government who help them steal the wealth of the country. "Thanks to the aid of foreigners, they live without caring that the majority of their brothers are dying of misery." This class has at its disposal and uses the violence of policemen and soldiers. The persons of this group include not only government authorities, but certain functionaries, merchants and businessmen, teachers and missionaries who think, live and act like the politicians "with the heavy purses". All the rest of the people who live in misery: the poor, the peasants, the workers. "They are like dogs who hunt and catch wild game for their masters, but are only permitted to eat the bones. . . . The hunter who has not suffered or worked as hard as the dog, will always have the best portion. . . ."
> These classes are always "in struggle". There are two kinds of struggle: (1) Struggle to diminish suffering, or a reformist struggle. These reformist struggles have been led by intellectuals and workers, not by village people. The means these reformists have used are: placing good deputies in

parliament; organizing and working through labor unions; writing criticisms in the newspapers; and staging mass protests. ''But four years have passed . . . and have we acquired any benefits? Not in the least; we are in even greater misery. What must we do, then, to remove these miseries?'' (2) Struggle to plough up again and reorganize this country: engage in a revolutionary struggle. This must be a battle of all the people of the country – the popular masses – who must raise themselves out of their suffering.

All men, no matter what their status and work, were once village people. ''Village people are like the water, and all the others are like fish in the water.''

– The people of the villages must fight against the governors and vanquish them. We must refuse to obey bad chiefs, soldiers and police, and refuse to pay taxes. If the soldiers and police come armed, we, the rural population, must enter into combat with them and repel them. And we must destroy roads and bridges. When the government is overthrown, we will establish a new regime in which all must and will work in order to eat; in which foreigners cannot come to take the wealth of the country; and in which we cannot steal the wealth of other persons either. A beautiful house, complete with furniture, will be built for each person by the new government.

– This way of living is called communism. This is what we wish, for we wish all men to be happy. The man who leaves the Party of the people will die in the same way as a fish who leaves the water.

– We have to help the people enter into combat. Combat is war against our enemies. For that we need cadres, soldiers and police, and money and material to form them. We must all help those who are fighting against the bad government. We will help them in giving them manioc, wine, and the like, so that they will have the strength to continue the battle. Thus, we must all unite in order to free our country. . . .

For the rebels of the Kwilu, Mulele is a leader-savior with awesome magical qualities and powers that will protect his followers, as well as himself, as they go forth into battle against the defined enemies of the revolution and of the new society of happiness and justice that will be brought into being by the revolution. Mulele is regarded as being invulnerable to bullets. Mulele is also believed to be omnipresent; capable of making himself into an animal or a snake, and of travelling long distances like a spirit or a bird. His followers are convinced that they share his invulnerability. The death, none the less, of many rebels in combat is either not commented upon at all, or explained as an indication that those persons have lost the powers of invulnerability conferred on them by being associated with Mulele, because they had transgressed certain norms and practices of the movement, or because they did not believe sufficiently in victory. . . .

One is struck by how similar the beliefs clustering around the person of Mulele are to those that were associated with the leaders of the various messianic religious movements that appeared in the Kwilu in the years just before and just after Independence. The leaders of these movements were also reputed to have special magico-religious powers of invulnerability, invincibility and metamorphosis, with which they could protect their followers as well as themselves. Like Mulele, they were considered to be prophets and liberators – saviors who had come to announce the end of an era of oppression and suffering under an unjust regime, and to lead the people into victorious battle against the oppressors. . . .

The norms and the taboos that the rebels in the Kwilu were ideally supposed to exemplify and obey are as follows:

Partisans must live a communal life.
They must obey the orders of their chief.
They must not fight among themselves.
They must be brave, have discipline, and exhibit endurance and perseverance.
They must do whatever manual work is required, voluntarily, and look upon such work as honorable and dignifying.
They must not speak French. (Lingala is the accepted language.)
They must not pray.
They must not eat certain meats.
They must abstain from all things European.
They must not wash or cut their hair before going into battle.
Partisans must help villagers; they must teach them and give them counsel and advice.
They must respect all men and all women.
They must not arbitrarily hit or hurt others.
They must not confiscate anything that belongs to villagers – "not even a needle or a thread". Anything that they destroy they must pay for with good will.
All property confiscated from the enemies of Mulelism must be handed over to the chiefs of the partisans.

Implicit in these injunctions to the partisans is the idea that disobeying any of these norms or failing to live up to them will reduce the invulnerability of a rebel in battle and make him more susceptible to bullets. . . .

The tribes in the Kwilu which have tended to give their support to Mulelism include the BaMbunda and the BaPende, the tribes of Mulele and Gizenga respectively. They are also the tribes that most vividly remember the revolt of the BaPende in 1931 (which took place partly in reaction against the exploitation of the cutters by palm oil refineries).

. . . Women as well as men have gone along with the Mulelists in the Kwilu; people of age who are married, as well as young people who are still single. Some of the young people in the movement are neither in school nor employed; but the movement has also attracted a certain number of secondary school students, and even seminarians. Though school teachers are defined by the movement as *"penepene"* ["very close to" colonialists], Mulelism has none the less succeeded in recruiting a significant number of teachers. Many of these teachers have entered the movement partly through the intermediary of the PSA of which they were members; and most of them tend to be relatively young persons, twenty to twenty-five years of age. Once in the movement, they are frequently given the position either of "chief" of a band or of propagandist for the movement. Among the motives that seem to have interested these teachers in the movement is the promise made to them that in the new society of the second independence, teachers will be appointed officials and ministers of the government. Some of the teachers who have become Mulelists were disgruntled with the long periods that they had to go without pay for their services, due to what they considered the inefficiency and corruption of the local and central governments. Certain teachers felt especially indignant about the brutality and destruction they had seen perpetrated in the Kwilu by soldiers of the National Congolese Army.

Other Mulelists include workers employed by private companies in the Kwilu (primarily palm oil industries) and by Catholic and Protestant missions. The chiefs of the rebel bands tend to be recruited from among men who have had positions as clerks, as well as from the ranks of teachers. A certain number of merchants and owners of stores are in the movement although they, like the schoolteachers, belong to a class that in general is defined as an enemy of Mulelism. As we have seen, some of the traditional tribal chiefs of the Kwilu have taken a stand against the rebels, but many more have supported them. Finally, even some policemen and subaltern agents of the administration have joined the Mulelists, among them ex-policemen formerly stationed in Leopoldville, who were discharged and sent to the inland after they had staged an insurrection in the summer of 1963 in an attempt to gain more pay.

In sum – the social distribution and the motivation of the followers and the adherents of Mulelism in the Kwilu suggest far more than a banding together of "oppressed classes" versus "exploitative classes of privilege". Tribal, political, economic, religious and magical influences of various kinds have attracted persons of many different social groups in the Kwilu to the movement (and detracted still others). In later stages of the Kwilu rebellion, when the partisans began to make wholesale use of methods of terror and violence, many other people supported the rebels primarily because they were afraid.

Basil Davidson, *Political Leadership in Liberation Struggles* (1978)

At the end of 1963, after nearly a year's guerrilla effort the PAIGC was heading for its ruin; abuse and crime against village people in the guerrilla-held areas had led to something like a reign of terror. Luiz Cabral (subsequently President of Guiné-Bissau) recalls:

> The people were in fear, and our struggle risked destruction at the very moment when our fighters had taken to arms. We found that abominable crimes were being committed in our name, and that people had begun to flee from some of our liberated zones.

What had happened? According to Francisco Mendes (now Prime Minister of Guiné-Bissau:

> These problems became acute after our militants began to receive arms from the exterior and to reinforce guerrilla bases during the second half of 1963. Such problems were worsened by long distances between bases, and poor communications. With fighting groups more or less autonomous, an overall control was hard to exercise. And most of our militants were young and inexperienced.
> At that point, many fighters began to exploit their new authority for personal reasons. They began to reject the overall authority and unity of our party, and to abuse the people, especially the women, in zones they controlled. Above all, they began to group themselves on a tribal basis, to build an autonomy on tribal affiliation and religious belief, to give priority in recruitment and the handing-out of arms to members of their own tribes or families, or through their tribal chiefs if they had any.

Other aspects of the situation that had overwhelmed Mulele and Soumialot [see *Fox*, above] one by one appeared. Mendes: "These men also began to seek advice in old customs and beliefs about witchcraft, invoking the spirits of their ancestors or the spirits of the forest with the help of charms and ceremonies, asking their diviners to find out if their actions could be successful. They became the victims of these beliefs. They made others the victims of them, too." Just as in the Congo, the belief in bullet-immunizing charms became common, and, again as in the Congo, "the belief that death or wounding in battle was brought to this or that militant by witchcraft. There began a hunt for 'witches', and some of those accused of withcraft were shot and others were even burned alive."

Bernardo Vieira, with Umaro Diallo as his second in command, was then in charge of crucial southern areas. They met this calamity at its most severe, no doubt because the peoples of the south, chiefly Balante and Nalu, had retained a strong hold on their ancestral cultures.

What they had most to fight against at first, Vieira and Diallo recalled, was "tribalism – at that stage a worse enemy than the Portuguese. We had to mobilize our people and explain realities to them, the realities in which they lived: not big things like imperialism and colonialism, of which they'd never heard, but colonial taxes, forced labour, local oppression. That was now we could build unity in our struggle. We had steady success, but tribal conflicts and beliefs became the major obstacle." . . . "Each tribe had its own customs, modes of making sacrifice, beliefs. We were not as we are not against religion, as such; and so we didn't want to interfere. The people really believed in their religion; besides, unnecessary clashes with witch-doctors . . . had to be avoided because these persons had great local prestige." But matters now reached a point where they had to interfere, both because of the principles of their politics and because they would otherwise lose control of the movement they had launched. . . .

Loss of control to magical belief was very widespread according to Vieria:

It happened in many places. In our zone there was a witch-doctor at a crucial creek-crossing who had a lot of persons seized and beaten. Umaro and I went there and set them free. The local people were angry with us: they said that we wouldn't even allow them to "wash" their village. Sometimes the witch-doctors accused persons of giving information to the enemy so that the enemy came and bombed them. They said that the witches brought the aircraft there. And the villagers killed these "witches" and sometimes burned them alive. Or they seized all the goods and belongings of an accused person.

In this situation,

it came to a test. I decided to arrest a widely known witch-doctor, a woman called Kubai. She was going about everywhere in our zone, raising accusations, sowing fear; I arrested her and accused her of crimes, making her frightened. After a while she said she would tell the truth: that all her accusations were lies, lies she had learned to tell from her father. I even got her to say how many people she had caused to be killed. Then I called the villagers where we were, and she said all this in public, openly, before them all. And I called more people from other villages, and she told the truth to them as well. And people began to understand.

The evidence shows that it required great courage and determination to withstand the pressures of these beliefs and practices, but also, crucially, that it called for a fixed loyalty to the revolutionary teachings of Cabral as well as an unusual clarity of mind about the purposes of those teachings.

Some of our commanders let themselves be dominated by such beliefs, even if they didn't much believe in them. Some even killed "witches" themselves. Umaro and I had to stand against all that, we had to cut through all that. Yet it was difficult to convince some of our comrades. Then it got to the point even where witch-doctors were learning commanders' military plans and deciding which actions should be made and which should not. Commanders began to refuse our orders. . . . Characteristically deciding that the issue must be brought to a head, no matter what might follow, Amílcar Cabral decided to call a congress of all leading commanders and militants, in February 1964. . . .

Commanders and leading militants were assembled by many days of hard marching. The congress took place in a forest clearing in a zone less subject to the witch-hunt "reign of terror" than others in the south, and at a moment when tough fighting was in progress against a Portuguese offensive aimed at re-taking the nearby "island" of Como. Only three commanders refused to attend. But most of the others, save for those remaining loyal to PAIGC policy, came as though they were independent potentates: "just like tribal chiefs, each with his personal servants, followers, and guards" (Mendes). Each sat down separately around the clearing, each entourage obeying its own commander and nobody else.

Three factors proved decisive. These were the nature and unity of the leadership and the character and quality of Amílcar Cabral himself. Begun in an atmosphere of suspicion and hostility, the congress gradually thawed a little. All who had come, however recalcitrant some of them might be, still believed that they were followers of Cabral; and all of them still faced the same enemy. . . . Cabral steered the congress according to his plan, leading it to a crucial session which lasted from eight in the evening until near dawn the next day. In this session he turned to "questioning all the civilian militants [who had also been invited to attend] from various zones. These spoke one by one of the barbarities which were being committed against the civilian population." (Luiz Cabral.)

As the night wore on, angry or bitter revelations built an atmosphere of shame and revulsion. Cabral waited until all had said their say, and then spoke at length. Mendes:

> He said that he had not created the party to give any tribe or group an advantage over others, but for the liberation of our whole people. He said that the party had to be the instrument of a *national* unity. He said that this unity must be forged in our struggle against the colonialists. He spoke of the old resistances that had all failed – and why? Because then each people had fought for itself, and so the Portuguese could always win. Now was the time to resist with all our people fighting together against the same enemy.

About witchcraft, he said that this was indeed a reality in African belief, but that we must go beyond it.

Then he dwelt on the crimes and abuses, "and condemned all who were guilty of them". Towards dawn, as he wrestled with the conscience of the dissidents, there came a dramatic moment. One of the guilty affirmed: "Very well, if you think I am to blame for these things, then disarm me and investigate." Cabral replied: "Yes, I agree. I order you to be disarmed." All sources affirm that this was an agonizing moment of decision. But the man put down his weapon on the ground in front of him. Cabral said: "Now I order the others to be disarmed." And that worked, too: first the rank-and-file fighters in the entourages put down their arms, and at last their commanders. With the loyalists remaining under arms, the courage and clarity of this leadership had won.

. . . No attacks were made on religion provided that it made no further threat to unity. Bernardo Vieira: "Even to the end of the war (in 1974) our fighters wore *gri-gris* (amulets) if they wanted. They would even ask for leave to go to their villages and undergo the cure of the country: that is, receive the blessing of the ancestors. And we allowed this": with good reason, for once the diviners had understood the process now in play, the advice of the ancestors fell duly into line with it. "They came back to us strengthened in their self-confidence. They fought better. They had more courage."

I have dwelt on these details because they define a moment in the development of ideas, absolutely decisive for any further progress, when the primacy of ancestral belief was made to give way to a fully secular interpretation of reality.

Part V

The Urban Poor

Introduction

This part focuses on the sociology, actions and consciousness of sections of the urban poor (as does Sandbrook, 1982). It ignores other questions of urban sociology, town life and the sociology of work. For the first of these see Gugler, 1978, and Aronson, 1978; and for case studies of factory and railway labour Peil, 1972, Kapferer, 1972, and Grillo, 1973 – though the great bulk of material on the sociology of work is conceived solely from the standpoint of management. City life, its flavour and variety, rarely discussed (and rarely experienced) by academics, is probably best appreciated by novelists, notably the Senegalese Sembene Ousmane (e.g. 1970, 1972) and South Africans such as Themba (1972) and Matshoba (1979).

The process of proletarianization described in *Cohen*'s article led initially to the creation of communities of miners, agricultural workers and railway construction labourers. Despite their relative isolation and high turnover, these communities responded to the harsh conditions of recruitment, work and discipline (Gutkind, 1974; Clayton, 1974; F. Wilson, 1972) with a remarkable range of organization and protest. *Cohen* describes the "hidden forms" taken by such protest, and relates them to the development of worker consciousness, while *van Onselen*, *Perrings* and *Gordon* consider the particular case of mine labour, which developed a combination of a special work culture, defensive organizations (often religious in character) and techniques of labour withdrawal and contestation ranging from sabotage to the fully fledged strike (see also Bonner in Bozzoli, 1979; Johnstone, 1976; O'Meara, 1975). All these are shown by railway labour, though to a lesser degree (Mason in Gutkind, 1978; Jeffries, 1978b), and even by farm tenants and agricultural labourers, among whom messianic movements were common (see Part IV, and Marcum, 1969).

In parts of southern Africa the pre-war systems of labour recruitment and discipline have continued with modifications (see, e.g., Gordon, 1977; Murray, 1981), but elsewhere unskilled and migrant labour has been replaced increasingly by a more skilled and urbanized labour force, arising from both the needs of state and multinational capital and from pressures from organized labour (see, e.g., Stichter in Sandbrook, 1975b). Still principally drawn from the countryside, it continues to have strong rural ties (Gibbal, 1974; Grillo, 1973), which has led to the denial that it constitutes a proletariat. Instead, the labour force is seen as divided into a "semiproletarianized peasantry", mostly rural-born, poorly organized and showing elements of peasant consciousness (Arrighi, 1973, ch. 3), though capable as are peasants of moments of militancy and violent protest; and a small highly organized and conservative "labour aristocracy" intent on preserving its relative privilege through the trade union movement and political links to the bourgeoisie.

While conservative attitudes (Waterman in Williams, 1976) and the pursuit of sectional interest by African workers undoubtedly exist (see, e.g., Sandbrook, 1975a) the "labour aristocracy" concept seems empirically false and analytically valueless (Gerold-Scheepers, 1978; but see Saul in Sandbrook, 1975b). The corresponding notion of a "semiproletarianized peasantry", seems to identify class status with class origin and again ignores empirical evidence (Waterman, 1979). Recent research indicates rather that African worker consciousness is (and has been) ambivalent. This arises not from the movement of labour from country to town (from "traditional" to "modern"?), but from the nature of the urban political economy, in particular the presence of a large "informal sector" of traders and artisans and the opportunities that provides for a movement out of wage labour.

Organized African labour has a long tradition of militancy and political radicalism, as *Crisp* argues (see also Allen, forthcoming; Sandbrook, 1975b; Gutkind, 1978; Joseph, 1977; Sandbrook, 1977b). At the same time union action can frequently be seen as merely economistic, with militancy arising more from a desire to maintain differentials or secure a place in the union hierarchy than to challenge the state or employer (e.g. Sandbrook, 1975a). Similarly union officials have been co-opted with such ease by parties, governments and international labour organisations that they are now frequently distrusted by their members (Mihyo, 1975; Burawoy, 1972; Peace, 1979a; Sandbrook, 1975a).

Corresponding to the use of the union by its officers to achieve upward mobility is the use of wage labour to achieve a shift into trade or artisan production by individual workers. The belief that this shift is desirable, and that it can be made by savings and the help of urban patrons (e.g. Peace, 1979b) produces a decidedly individualistic strand of consciousness (Lloyd, 1975). Yet the reality is increasingly that mobility is slight, and that an "urban brother" (Peace, 1979a) is more use than a "big man". The predominant strands in worker consciousness are thus, as *Sandbrook and Arn* argue, a form of class consciousness in communities made up largely of workers, and a form of populism in those much commoner communities in which workers mix with other sections of the urban poor (see also Peace, 1979a; Jeffries, 1978b; Sandbrook, 1975b).

The rest of the urban poor share both the workers' hopes for and lack of mobility; but unlike workers, the majority of casual labourers, petty traders, petty commodity producers and criminals have a precarious and impoverished future, as *Gerry* vividly shows (see also Le Brun, 1975; Hugon, 1977; Hart, 1973). Hopes have been expressed both for their economic vitality (see Leys, 1975, ch. 8) and for their political potential in the form of a "revolutionary lumpenproletariat" (see R. Cohen, 1973). In practice they appear both economically dependent on and threatened by capitalist production, and at best ambivalent in their political stance (Gutkind, 1975).

Blacks in South African cities, as in the countryside, have a long history of struggles over a variety of recurrent issues involving other sections of the community, the recent Soweto revolt being one high point (Roux, 1942; Wickens, 1978; Du Toit, 1981; Webster, 1978; Bozzoli, 1979; Hirson, 1979; Moorsom, 1978). These studies show, as does Perrings (1979) for Katanga, the significance of rural conditions for urban struggles and of events in urban areas for rural conflicts. They show how different urban struggles relate to one another, reveal class and other divisions (e.g. migrants *v.* residents), and show the tensions arising from diverging interests and objectives. The interaction between workers and students, and between community and national issues, is clearly central to strategies of political struggle in South Africa.

Hidden Forms of Labour Protest

Robin Cohen, *Resistance and Hidden Forms of Consciousness* (1981)

The previous literature on African labour-protest has for the most part been confined to those indices of worker dissent that are easily observed, or accessible to measurement. The number, scope and duration of strikes, the number of man-days lost, the rate of labour turnover, the extent of worker participation in union organizations, radical social movements and street demonstrations – all these are, quite rightly, considered as evidence of labour-protest. . . . The groundwork for a richer approach for the study of African labour-protest can, however, be found in van Onselen's work (1976) on Rhodesian mines in which he writes:

> In a labour-coercive economy . . . worker ideologies and organisations should be viewed essentially as the high-water marks of protest: they should not be allowed to dominate our understanding of the way in which the economic system worked, or of the African miners' responses to it. At least as important, if not more so, were the less dramatic, silent and often unorganised responses, and it is this latter set of responses, which occurred on a day-to-day basis that reveal most about the functioning of the system and formed the weft and warp of worker consciousness. Likewise it was the unarticulated, unorganised protest and resistance which the employers and the state found most difficult to detect or suppress.

In specifying a new problematic it is first necessary to isolate some generic features of a capitalist labour-process before identifying characteristic worker responses, and their particular African manifestations. It is postulated here that the labour-process under capitalism involves both the creation of a working class and its habituation to industrial production in five major ways:

(a) The potential worker is forced to abandon his own forms of subsistence or income and to rely, increasingly fully, on wages. . . . There is more typically a high element of compulsion in this creation and control of a stock of labour-power (for short, Enforced Proletarianization).

(b) Once at work, the worker has to accept the unequal authority structure of the workplace (Managerial Control).

(c) The worker has to adapt to the physical and psychological conditions of his employment (Psychological Adjustment).

(d) He has to accept an unequal distribution of reward for the labour-power expended (Differential Reward).

(e) He is forced to recognize the overall political and juridical structure that permits, or encourages, the growth and establishment of capitalist social relations (Political Control).

Even within the most advanced capitalist modes of production not all elements of the labour-process are fully commandeered by Capital. In Africa one would anticipate that the element of control would be much reduced in view of the incomplete character of capitalist penetration, and the remaining (though drastically reducing) possibilities Africans have for producing a wage-supplement. . . . The opposite side of the coin to the face which shows incomplete capitalist penetration is that which would suggest that workers are not always able to mount an effective challenge to all elements of the labour-process. None the less African workers did (and do) resist incorporation into capitalist production in many ways. . . .

Workers' Responses in Africa

Desertion   This was a common means of escaping habituation into the capitalist mode all over Africa. One report from Nyanza, in 1907, said that railway workers were "extremely apt to throw down their tools and run away on the slightest pretext". Another from the Kikuyu area complained "no man can run a farm with monthly relays of raw natives: labour of this kind is always capricious and liable to desert". In 1909, 31 out of the 48 complaints received by the Nairobi Labour Office all concerned cases of desertion. . . . Similar data for Northern Nigeria are reported by Mason (in Gutkind, 1978), while desertion of soldiers from colonial armies, often used as "labour brigades", was also common, as were cases of self-mutilation to escape conscription (e.g. Echenberg, 1975). In the case of southern Africa, a similar structure exists. Van Onselen (1976: 230) quotes the lament of Mashonaland mine owners: "The police use every possible effort, but the fact remains that whole gangs can, and do, abscond and are never traced or heard of again." He goes on to show that where total contraction out of the wage–labour system was not possible, workers deserted in one mine after another to try to secure better wages and working conditions.

Colonial governments and mine owners alike responded to the high rates of desertion by attempts to control and supervise both the recruitment and mobility of workers. In the French colonies highly supervised forced labour was used until the 1930s. In the British colonies, Masters and Servants' Ordinances and other legislation (registration bureaux, work certificates like *kipande*, etc.) were all designed to criminalize worker mobility, and reduce the rate of desertion. . . .

The rate of desertion depends on the degree of control exercised, but also, more saliently, on the degree of viability that remains to the precapitalist mode of production. Herein lay a contradiction for the underdeveloped form of capitalism prevalent in Africa. "The ideal solution . . . was one in which agricultural production remained sufficiently virile to produce an exportable primary product and absorb return migrants, but not so viable that it threatened the supply of cheap unskilled labour. Such a delicate balance was impossible to achieve and may indeed be considered one of the central contradictions of the colonial political economy." (R. Cohen in Gutkind, 1976.)

Community Withdrawal or Revolt   Most of the colonial historical sources have rich and bloodthirsty descriptions of the early wars of "pacification". The reasons for such adventures may not be totally reducible to the need for the fledgling colonial states to create a reservoir of cheap and available labour but this was clearly a motivating factor and was certainly the major effect of colonial wars. The necessity for the colonial authorities – especially in the areas of white settlement – to create and control a substantial quantum of labour-power, is further demonstrated by the constant repetition in colonial sources that such and such a chief or headman needed to be deposed or killed for failing to honour his treaty commitments to provide labour. The local communities had two alternatives: withdrawal into regions so inhospitable that the labour recruiter or raiding party couldn't reach them or a communal revolt against the authority of the colonial state, its agents or its local collaborators. Examples of these forms of protest are legion, but the degree to which a protest against forced labour was the core of a communal protest has not always been emphasized. . . .

As to evidence of communal revolt, a recent history of the Igbo of Eastern Nigeria documents a not untypical story. The people of Udi, who had given only a token resistance when the British first came, took advantage of the outbreak of the First World War to rise in rebellion. "It was a protest against forced labour on the roads . . . where the unpaid workers, who were expected to feed themselves, often went hungry – 'sometimes they used to eat leaves'. The survey of the railway line seemed to threaten their ownership of land, and herald more forced labour." When the revolt was brutally crushed, the peace terms included the supplying of two thousand unpaid workers for the railway.

After 1915 they were forced to work in the mines as well (Isichei, 1976). In Kenya, millenarian cults, like the Mumbo cult, whose believers refused to pay tax or labour for the administration, grew up precisely amongst those groups, like the Gusii, which had their first exposure to labour demands on a large scale. European depredations of African land were associated with European demands for African labour and it was for control of their own land and labour-power that such well-known revolts as Maji-Maji (1905–7) and Mau Mau occurred. In short, there was a high element of labour-protest in events that have been interpreted by colonial historians as wars of pacification and by the post-1950s Africanist historians as ''proto-nationalism''. . . .

Thus to implant capitalist social relations in an area previously characterized by precapitalist modes, it is necessary to create and control a stock of labour-power. In Africa, this was achieved particularly violently, through wars of pacification, the imposition of hut and poll taxes, the use of forced labour, and the application of a legal code equating worker mobility with criminality. Africans responded by desertion, by withdrawal or by revolt. But acquiescence of the loss of control over labour-power and its product was inevitable, even where symbolic escape was possible. Equally, one might have to accept the fact of wage–labour without accepting the conditions under which labour-power is utilized. It is to these forms of resistance that attention is now directed.

Task, Efficiency and Time Bargaining   In task bargaining a worker deliberately seeks either to restore his traditional skill or craft in the face of management attempts to detail, deskill and massify the productive process, or (more commonly) he seeks to reduce his exploitation by adhering overstrictly to job-specifications and rules detailing his work. A ''work-to-rule'' and job-demarcation dispute are typical examples of this form of protest. . . . Time/Efficiency bargaining is a closely related form of resistance and may be seen in the workers' characteristic and frequently successful attempts to bamboozle the time-and-motion men, the planner and the job-setter. The collective solidarity (''brotherhood'') in such bargaining on a Namibian mine is well described by Gordon (1977):

> White supervisors attribute quota restrictions by the workers to ''laziness'' and point out that in terms of cash earning it is illogical behaviour since it cuts into the underground workers' bonus. Thus, it is felt that laziness must be inherent. But quota restriction, from the workers' perspective, has a logic of its own. It enables them to avoid fatigue by allowing them to work at a comfortable pace. They are thus able to establish a degree of control over their own work targets. . . . Quota restriction prevents

competition at the work-place which would disturb established interpersonal relationships and protects slower brothers . . . walk offs were quite frequent and entailed considerable brotherhood solidarity.

Sabotage Sabotage is rationally based in the determination of workers to slow down the production process and to prevent redundancies with the introduction of labour-saving machinery. Sabotage can also be seen as a means of levelling-down profits to reduce inequality rather than, as in a wage demand, attempting to reduce inequality by levelling-up. A series of incidents witnessed in a Lagos plastics factory by the author (December 1968) demonstrated this clearly. After a wage demand had been refused, the workers systematically jinxed the machinery, the vats, the moulds and the firm's transport. Subsequently, when the workers' consciousness escalated and they decided to occupy the factory and sell the goods themselves, they regretted their earlier enthusiasm, but there is no doubt that the initial outburst was directed against what workers perceived of as excessive managerial profits. Sabotage therefore is linked with the other forms of resistance to the differential reward inherent in a capitalist labour-process.

Creation of a "Work-Culture" The structure of workplace authority is also frequently undermined by the deliberate creation or amplification of social distance between the worker and manager. In-jokes, private linguistic codes, wall slogans and the like are most common; but the creation of a work-culture takes many forms. . . . Work-songs to break the monotony of the labour and to mock the gang-boss, dances, drinking patterns all take on the character of a distinct moral universe, a private culture where, as *Gordon* notes below, blacks can "be themselves" and be masters of their "own" actions. The dialectic between "resistance" and "adaptation" is seen most clearly in the case of a work-culture, which can act either as an insulative force or a set of symbols to mobilise the hunger of workers. . . .

Accidents and Sickness The next set of responses are those which are normally conceived as having little relation to the labour-process itself and are often thought of as extraneous to the relation of production. While there may be an element of unconscious reaction involved, these forms of behaviour do indeed constitute forms of worker resistance and adaptation. Take first the question of sickness and accidents. The incidence, seriousness and distribution of illness and "accidents" are neither fortuitous nor random. The type of industry, the track speed-ups by management, the particular time of the day and time of the week; if all these factors are taken into account, accidents are far from being accidental. . . . With regard to reported sickness, what for managers constitutes "malingering" may for workers constitute an attempt to deny their labour-power to the employer while coping with debilitating conditions the employer has provided. Equally, accidents are deliberately (or even unconsciously) used to evade work or slow it down.

Drug Use   Almost invariably this represents a form of psychological resistance but social quiescence by workers. Often alcohol and cannabis are used as a form of compensation for an unrewarding work experience. This should however be distinguished from managerial and public provision of drug centres as in the large beer-drinking facilities in mining compounds and townships of southern Africa, designed to prevent the recreation hours of workers being used for anytihing more harmful. . . . It can also provide a form of companionship and solidarity: Gordon (1977) observes that drinking together is one of the most important rituals of friendship in a Namibian mine.

Belief in Other-Worldly Solutions   A common form of psychological resistance to work is the adoption of religion or other-worldly beliefs, particularly those that stress relief from suffering in the next world. Yet, while undoubtedly an opiate for most workers, religious belief and practice might also provide some elements in the construction of a workers' ideology (asceticism, solidarity, retribution) and some practical experience of organization. This was undoubtedly the reason why at first all the independent churches were outlawed in the Rhodesian mine compounds (van Onselen, 1976; *Perrings*, below). . . .

Theft   Can be usefully considered as a wage-supplement, which varies in volume with the rise or fall in real wages, as both *Gordon* (below) and van Onselen (1976) remark:

> Daily, hundreds of petty crimes were committed on the mining properties with the specific objective of rectifying the balance between employees and their employers. African workers constantly pilfered small items of mine stores – such as candles – or helped themselves to substantial quantities of detonators and dynamite which they used for fishing. Wage rates were altered on documents and hundreds of work and "skoff" tickets were forged by miners who sought to gain compensation for what they had been denied through the system.

Hidden and Overt Forms of Class Consciousness

. . . It is now necessary to relate the hidden to the overt forms of consciousness. Three theoretical positions can be suggested:

(i) The hidden forms are both more pervasive and more important, they are a "bedrock", "grass-roots", "genuine" sort of consciousness. van Onselen seems to be inclined to this view, though by limiting his theoretical elaboration to a "labour-coercive economy", that of a mining compound, it is easy to reply that in that context only the hidden forms were possible. It is a view, however, that would tend to the romanticization of events that by their very nature cannot but be often disconnected, spontaneous, individualistic and with short-term effect. There is no sense here in which workers can combine for a sustained long-term programme, seize the instruments of production or govern themselves. (ii) The hidden forms are at a lower level of consciousness but can be seen as part of an incremental chain leading towards a "higher", more politicized, form. Yet in the absence of leadership, organization and a galvanizing issue (and in the presence of a repressive state or employer) there is little reason to assume that such a process cannot be sidetracked or aborted. If protest can be kept on a sporadic and informal basis, it can ultimately be seen as a form of adaptation to the conditions of capitalist production. . . . (iii) Overt forms can represent an extant, readily observed consciousness, whereas the forms of resistance described above can represent a latent and subterannean reservoir of consciousness. Workers can transcend the prosaic limits of everyday actions and reactions in given circumstances and with a leadership that is able to amplify and galvanize forms of dissent that have not previously gained a conventional expression. None the less, the variety of response and tenacity of purpose shown by African workers in their attempt to resist the capitalist labour-process have thus far exceeded by far the capacity of African trade unions and revolutionary parties to channel such dissent for progressive or revolutionary ends.

Mines, Migrants and Protest

Charles van Onselen, *Chibaro: Compounds and Social Control* (1976)

What is peculiar in the experience of the Rhodesian mines is not the need to procure, hold and discipline labour that is restricted to the development of capital-intensive enterprises in southern Africa in general, or Rhodesia in particular: on the contrary, these features appear to be shared, in different degrees and at different points of historical development by many industrializing systems. Nor is it the enormity of the price that labour is called upon to pay in the process of capital accumulation and industrialization that in itself makes for a distinctive or unique experience. What is peculiar is the compound system. In terms of its point of historical introduction in southern Africa, of the particular colonial structure at the time and the longevity of the institution, it is unique in capitalist development.

The compounds existed as an embryonic form of labour control in South Africa and in Rhodesia from the earliest days of the respective labour-intensive mining industries. The state and employers, however, precipitated the crystallization of this form of coercion at a particular stage of capitalist development – that point at which the system was confronted either with a labour or production crisis, or both. Everywhere in southern Africa, the compounds served to isolate, regiment and exploit the most vulnerable section of the working class – the black working class as represented by African miners. . . .

Physical Features of the Rhodesian Compound System

The system that came into existence on many of the larger mines in Rhodesia differed in important respects from those that developed in Kimberley and the Witwatersrand. Basically, these differences, and especially those between the Rand and Rhodesia, can be traced to the relative attractiveness of the industry as a labour market within a national and regional economic system. . . . The Rand mines with their poor health record and low wages proved an unattractive labour market in the South African national economy, and had to compete with the manufacturing and other sectors for its labour supplies. They thus required a high degree of compound control to prevent desertions, and in comparison with most of the Rhodesian mines ran virtually "closed compounds".

Despite an appalling health record and low cash wages, the Rhodesian mines still formed the best labour market for workers in the national economy, and for the thousands of workers drawn from further north in central Africa. Unlike its South African counterpart, the Rhodesian industry never had a significant local manufacturing industry competing with it for its labour supplies. In addition, and again unlike South Africa, the Rhodesian miners were widely spread throughout the country and often located in relatively remote rural areas. This meant that large concentrations of black labour did not pose the same real or imagined threat to white communities as they did on the Witwatersrand. There was thus a combination of forces at work which made for a more relaxed or "open compound" system in Rhodesia.

Large mines developed a three-tiered compound system. The inner or square compounds were used to house either short-term workers or recruited labourers – that is, the least proletarianised, unskilled and lowest paid workers – who would have been most prone to desertion. The huts of single workers surrounding the inner compound housed longer-term miners – that is, more proletarianised workers with greater skills and average wages – who were less likely to desert. Finally, separated from both of these tiers were the huts of the married workers and their families – fully proletarianised workers, semi-skilled, with above-average wages – the group least likely of all to desert.

The "three-tier" compound system allowed for differing degrees of control over the black labour force – a degree of subtlety not needed on the Rand mines which made exclusive use of the single male migrant worker. In Rhodesia, as workers became more skilled, relatively better paid and more proletarianised, so managers could relax their control by allowing the worker to change his accommodation from the hated inner compound to the relatively private and relaxed outer areas. . . .

. . . . It was the compound as an institution which provided the framework for the total exploitation of the black workers. It was the compounds together with the Pass Laws which denied Africans the right to respond to "market forces" and sell their labour in the best market. It was the compound, with its state-sanctioned system of industrial violence, which converted reluctant and forced labour into forced production. It was the compound, acting as the college of colonialism, that did much to rob Africans of their dignity and help mould servile black personalities. It was the political control in the compounds, exercised by the state–employer alliance, that did much to prevent the emergence of black working-class movements which could have improved the lot of African miners. And it is the unique and powerful social, political and economic cutting-edge that the compound system represents both for state and employers, that accounts for its continued prominence in central African industry seventy-five years after it was first introduced.

Worker Responses in a Labour Coercive Economy

Weak as their bargaining position was in relation to white power, and relentless as were the methods used to subject them, African workers did find ways of fighting back. These ways were indirect, even subterranean, but they were effective. From the earliest years, they developed strategies which aimed at reaching the best labour markets. In order to render this objective possible with the minimum amount of exploitation *en route* Africans developed stratagems which increased their bargaining power and a system of market intelligence which enabled them to avoid the most obvious pitfalls. The patterns of labour flow within the regional economic system themselves should thus be seen as a creative and sophisticated African response to the emerging capitalist system in southern Africa. The speed and manner in which Africans chose to ''vote with their feet'' was the most basic response of all in a labour coercive economy.

While Africans found means of overcoming the barriers to mobility within the economic system as a whole – thus showing their resistance to the most exploitative wages – they also found means of resisting or opposing exploitation within the compounds themselves. Since the compound system did not make allowance for the ready expression of articulated and literate protest, they found more subtle methods of expressing their resentment at exploitation. They refused to work, worked at half-pace or ran away from employers who exploited them; they stole from and defrauded mine owners; destroyed mining property and equipment, feigned illness and ''loafed''. All of these tactics bear the hall-marks of a highly coercive labour system and many of them are identical to those developed by slaves in the plantations and industries of the American Deep South during the nineteenth century. If many black miners perceived themselves as *chibaro* (slaves) they also chose to resist their exploiters in the metaphor of slavery.

Given the resources and possibilities open to them, the responses of Africans to the emerging industrial system are striking. Their responses were not only rapid but often extremely efficient and inventive. In a new world where literacy, documentation and bureaucracy was used in an attempt to hamstring their physical movement, the response came through newly acquired skills. Those with the ability to write developed a talent for forgery – a service which many extended to their illiterate brothers. Older peasant beliefs and practices too were made to slot into the new industrial setting. The belief in witchcraft for instance – something pre-eminently associated with persons rather than places and country rather than compound – served to protect workers from the hazards of the Bonsor mine. Rural techniques of protest, like cattle-maiming or killing, came to be directed at the new industrial overlords of the country. Everywhere, peasant and mission-school product alike pooled their knowledge in a system of a market intelligence.

These largely silent and unorganized responses of black workers offer eloquent testimony to the existence of a consciousness of who the exploiters were. Black workers did not require meetings, pickets, leaders and ideologies to make them understand who was oppressing them. Well-developed ideologies and organizations are adjuncts to the development of a refined world view, they are not necessarily precursors of industrial resistance. For Africans to resist spontaneously and directly, they simply needed to perceive the single dimension involved in the relationship of exploiter and exploited: this relationship they saw all too clearly.

Charles Perrings, *Workers' Associations: Cushions Against the Compounds*
(1979)

Associations designed to assist their members to cope with the problems of compound life had long been a feature of the workforce on the Copperbelt mines, as early as 1910. The Mbeni dance groups which acted as mutual aid societies appear to have developed in the war and post-war years, and were certainly present on the mines by the early 1920s. They tended, however, to be associated with the ''English'' administration, taking their titles and organization from the ''English'' military example (Mitchell, 1956; and see Ranger, 1975). . . . Their place in the Katanga compounds was taken by similar associations bearing titles such as *Les Belges des Baluba* whose organizational models were drawn from the Belgian administration. Many of them made regular collections for funds for self-help schemes, and two or three were reported in the late 1920s to be attempting to collect sufficient funds for the purchase of a piece of land in the general African section of Elisabethville. . . . The associations were essentially defensive in aim, intended to cushion their members in a working environment that in the earlier years was exceptionally hazardous. Their main appeal was therefore to those at highest risk, . . . and it is evident that among the main beneficiaries of the associations were the new and single recruits.

They were, moreover, mainly tribal in complexion, although anxious to model themselves on the example of the colonial administration, and it is unlikely that they offered a great deal to those with a longer-term commitment to industrial employment.

For such men a far more attractive proposition was the Watch Tower sect or *Kitawala*, a derivative from the Jehovah's Witnesses, which was at the peak of its strength in Central Africa during the depression of the 1930s (Cross, 1973). Its membership was almost exclusively comprised of those exhibiting a high degree of commitment to wage labour or peripheral economic activities, and in 1931 when it was first reported in the Belgian Congo, it was noted that "the Elders are generally of the detribalized class and are often occupied as hawkers or traders". Sholto Cross notes that in Northern Rhodesia "a high proportion of skilled and literate migrants joined the movement – surface rather than underground workers, clerks, hawkers and traders, 'natives of the detribalized class' and those with some intellectual aspirations". . . . They were thus workers who had developed a marked commitment to a particular area of the labour market, for whom mobility was an inappropriate response to the pressures deriving from the chronic insecurity of their position in the industry.

Watch Tower did provide a vehicle for the critique of industrial conditions and colonial society generally, and it was for this reason that it was regarded with such acute suspicion by the colonial administrations in both territories. The Russell Commission was particularly alarmed by what they learned of the Watch Tower, and described it in their report as a "dangerously subversive movement". The reported statement of Watch Tower adherents are certainly very revealing. When adherents were arrested at Jadotville in August 1936, for example, they made the clearest possible declaration of what they saw as the injustices of racial wage differentials in the colonial economy.

> It stands out clearly from this book [The Bible] that all men are equal. God did not create the white man to rule over the black. . . . It is not just that the black man who does the work should remain in poverty and misery, and that the wages of the whites should be so much higher than those of the blacks.

But if the problems were seen very clearly, the solutions were not. Watch Tower gained strength during the depression, but it was the strength of desperation. Its appeal was the appeal of millenarianism in the last resort. It offered no constructive plan of action, only a limitless supply of predictions as to the deliverance of believers. The above declaration, for example, was the justification of a prediction that "1936 is the year which will bring the end of the domination of whites over blacks in the country''. It was by definition a vehicle for protest and not change. This is not to suggest that individuals in the Watch Tower leadership were not aware that many of the answers to the problems of the black worker in the mines lay in his own hands. In the aftermath of the 1935 miners' strikes Fred Kabanga, leader of Watch Tower at Mufulira mine, was for example reported as having made the point to a meeting of mine workers as follows:

> You natives on the mines are still receiving very little pay. This is the fault of the white men who are making all the money. The natives are suffering still. What are you going to do about it? . . . If you keep quiet that is your own affair.

But the conglomeration of ideas that constituted Watch Tower "doctrine" offered no solutions, and increasingly those Africans most deeply enmeshed in the web of dependence on wage labour were moved to develop alternative strategies for survival in which there was no room for millenarian expectation.

Robert Gordon, *Contract Workers in Namibian Mines* (1977, 1978)

Nearly half of the black labour force in Namibia consists of male contract workers, who are recruited in the northern Bantustans of South Africa by Labour Bureaux on the basis of "orders" placed by white employers. Once recruited, the worker is transported to his place of work and there housed in a white-controlled compound for the duration of his contract, after which he is repatriated back to the reserve. Movement outside the compound and workplace is severely restricted by a barrage of "pass laws".

Recently, Rex (1974) has cogently argued that the contract labour system is the most rational form of labour exploitation yet devised: "A very high degree of rationality can be achieved under such circumstances. Enormous economies of scale can be made in what would otherwise be the worker's spending pattern, and he can be effectively sealed off from subversive forces which might lead to his trying to form unions to bargain over the price of his labour. . . ." The conditions *per se* do not, however, by themselves determine how workers or managers will react, rather it is their interpretation of the relevant conditions in their situation which decides how they will attempt to achieve their goals within the framework of the labour repressive structure.

White interpretations are well illustrated by the supervisory ideologies found in Namibian mines. A relatively sophisticated ideology is espoused by top Management at Head Office and by some of the senior officials, whose image or set of premises leads to the elaborate rationalizations and justifications of migrant labor and the compound system of which Francis Wilson (1972) has provided some fine examples.

A second, more elementary and vulgar version is that espoused by white supervisors who are in direct contact with blacks at the work-place. The essential tenets of this definition are that blacks at the mine are indolent, irresponsible, primitive, impulsive and dirty, that they lack honesty, drive and ambition. This conclusion is reached on the basis of isolated observations which are then incorporated into and used to develop a generalized "typification". However, since blacks are believed to be natural liars, the behavior in question is not clarified by asking the blacks about it: instead, corroboration and validation is sought from other whites. . . . The pervasiveness of their typification is even firmly embedded in the speech patterns: all blacks are addressed and referred to as "boy" by the whites.

Yet if the whites' theory were accepted *in toto*, it would be impossible for the mine to operate. Variations to the working theory are accounted for by allowing for differences in individual temperament or, more sociologically, through the medium of ethnic labels. Each label carries a specific moral content. This folk typology by the whites is not anchored in any consistent empirical reality because whites are unable to differentiate physically between the various groups. Their differentiation is based instead on what the workers tell them. . . . The relationship between the imputed moral content of the ethnic identity of the blacks and the number of blacks being supervised by a white should be noted. . . . Thus, blacks from the commonest group are labelled as "morally bad", smaller groups as "morally better", and very small groups as "the best". Many white supervisors articulate the moral contents of ethnic identity in their interactions with blacks. They feel that by insulting blacks in ethnic terms, they will stimulate ethnic pride which in turn produces ethnic competition and thus increase productivity.

Ethnic and temperamental differences mean that all blacks cannot be treated the same way. The pretence of white superiority is maintained by the whites' refusing to take note of every deviation by black workers. They obtain strict obedience by making it relatively easy for the workers to obey; that is, since the blacks are so "lazy" the production targets are lower. As most blacks know, most whites maintain two fronts, a "public" front which calls for a large amount of formal deference especially when there are other whites present, and a "private" front in which the whites allow certain informalities and indiscretions and are more amenable to "informal requests".

Ironically, in order to carry out their assignments, both supervisors and workers "buck" the system. An informal echelon system with its attendant informal "house rules", punishments and privileges develops and is the dominant social characteristic of the Mine. Where an organization caters for all the "needs" of its workers, the scope of these "house rules" is tremendous. The supervisors feel entitled to delegate work informally which is often not in the workers' formal job description and to offer a small number of clearly defined rewards like liquor, cigarettes, articles of clothing and even promotions for "co-operation" . . . Having a good and well-trained gang of "boys" is a source of pride and money to the ganger and this dependence of white miners upon their gang is acknowledged by most supervisors.

The system of rewards is also a tool of coercion for the whites. Thus, for example, when a group of blacks asked their shift boss why they were not receiving presents any more he replied, "Ask the boys who complained to the Compound Manager about my swearing." The white attitude towards the informal reward system is, however, ambiguous. There is always the fear that it will backfire and that, despite the informal rewards, the "boys" will work slower or be "spoilt".

The ideology of the supervisors plays a pivotal part in determining the formal and informal organization of the Mine. Blacks are constantly made aware, both explicitly and implicitly, of how whites see them, and from their point of view this is important because it determines how they will be treated on a day-to-day basis and also because it, to a large degree, provides the opportunity structure in which they make their money both in the formal and informal sectors of the Mine. From our perspective, the ideology is important because it encompasses the employee not only as a worker but also as a human being. How the black workers respond to the social implications of the typification is of obvious significance.

. . . Black workers are unanimous in their belief that they are "oppressed" by the whites and that the whites are united in oppressing them. This is possible because whites control the access to money which everyone needs in order to survive and results from the fact that "whites think they will become poorer if they don't oppress blacks". It is based on fear since "whites know that blacks can do their job if given the opportunity". Instead, blacks feel that they are making money for the whites and not getting an equitable reward for their output. As a result of their powerful position whites can and do treat blacks like "dirt": "They won't let us have women here because they think we are animals." "It makes no difference what job you do or how rich you are, in their eyes you are only a Kaffir." Whites express their superiority in the pattern of forced deference and the superior social facilities to which they have access. In sum, the powerful situation of the whites forces the blacks to see the whites as dishonest, ambitious, untrustworthy, fearsome and above all, unpredictable (see Ndadi, 1974). Worker consciousness is thus of a populist, rather than of a class character (see Gordon, 1975).

Two important points emerge from this interpretation. Firstly, the workers do not see their problems as lying narrowly within the domain of industrial relations but relate it to their position within the wider political economy of the Territory. Central to the platform of SWAPO, the largest political party is its opposition to the contract labour system. It was precisely on this issue that it initially attracted adherents and in its formative years it attempted to project itself as a mass trade union. Secondly, survival in this labour repressive situation depends on keeping the whites as ignorant about the black workers as possible. Black workers developed an underground labour resistance movement, . . . while the compound labour system also serves to make the workers systematically "invisible men" by *inter alia* isolating and treating them like batches of numbers. The system enables whites to show a collective unwillingness to know unpleasant facts which would threaten their self-conception. Whites, for example, are officially discouraged from visiting the compounds or reserves or from having more than the minimum necessary contact with blacks. This enables whites to maintain their moral propriety on the basis of such flimsy myths as "the blacks are satisfied with conditions and any manifestations to the contrary can be attributed to 'agitators' ''.

For the black to challenge the white's definition of the situation is to court "trouble". Migrant workers thus learn how to lie, dissemble, avoid unnecessary interaction with whites and dodge the police. The white definition of the situation is built into the pattern of etiquette. Blacks soon realize that it is skills at the social graces and not technical competence which will determine how successful one's sojourn at the work-place will be. . . . At the work-place the trick is to be labelled a "good boy" by one white employer, and on that basis to try and establish ties of patronage with whites. White patrons are important for they make life more bearable by granting small favours, overlooking certain irregularities, some petty theft. They may also support one in any interaction with the dreaded police or the native commissioner. To protest individually without this supportive base would inevitably result in the black being labelled a "dirty Commie" and punished accordingly.

But a black worker who is deemed by his fellow workers to have established too intimate ties with his patron runs the risk of being ostracized and labelled a "stooge" or "sell-out". To avoid this entails considerable manœuvring and social investment in the ethic of "brotherhood" to demonstrate that one still subscribes to it and that one's bona fides are still acceptable. The ethos of brotherhood provides the main organizational framework for the underground or "private" resistance network. With so many workers in an identical situation, being treated alike, having the same problems and facing the same dangers, it is easy for them to identify sympathetically with one another irrespective of differences in origin or background. This is expressed in "brotherhood". Brotherhood serves to delineate a distinct moral universe which specifically excludes all whites. It provides a screen behind which the workers have developed a "private culture" in which they can be "themselves" and a point from which they can exploit the white imposed system. . . . Brotherhood stresses helping one's fellow brother particularly in the face of white oppression and above all never informing on one's brothers.

This is particularly important because one of the most important ways of making money is through theft from whites. Such theft is justified firstly because the workers do not believe that they are receiving a wage commensurate with their effort, and secondly, because they do not accept the legitimacy of white rule. They justify theft by saying that as the whites stole their country, so they are taking it back little by little through theft. . . .

At the work-place, workers have long realized the importance of numbers in bargaining over the price of their labour. While strikes have been far more plentiful than most whites think, workers are well aware of the risks they take if they decide to engage in strike action. A far safer and more common strategy is the "go slow" and deliberate industrial sabotage by acting excessively "stupid". Such strategies, in addition to the well-founded tradition of gold-bricking and quota restriction, require considerable organization. . . . Brotherhood also transcends the narrow realm of the work-place. Desertion particularly from the farms was and is a common method of expressing dissatisfaction with the system. The success of desertion, whether individual or collective, depends on brotherhood. A successful deserter relies on his working brothers to feed, clothe, accommodate, assist financially and hide him from the Police. In the urban areas it also provided a vital information system about what jobs were available, the attitudes of the employer and whether he would ask for a work "pass".

Trade Unions and Class Consciousness

Richard Sandbrook and Jack Arn, *The Labouring Poor and Urban Class Formation: A Study of Greater Accra* (1977a)

The model underpinning this study draws upon a considerable range of research carried out in West Africa and elsewhere. Gutkind has conducted some of the pioneering work on the African "urban poor". In a series of articles (1967; 1968; 1973; 1975), he dealt with the questions of the "social circulation", organization and consciousness of the unemployed, especially in Lagos, Ibadan and Nairobi. The main conclusion regarding the politics of the unemployed in the first two articles, based mainly upon 120 interviews with "unemployed" in Lagos and Nairobi in 1966, may be summarized as follows. Although the unemployed share a common, disadvantaged fate, they have been unable to create for long any common associations to promote collective action. This is due to the continuing strength of divisive ethnic ties, the lack of financial support for an association, the official co-optation or repression of capable leaders, and the lack of a corporate identity as "unemployed" or "the poor". However, these disadvantaged elements will become radicalized in the future, as they begin to perceive the elite as an exploiting class.

Gutkind (1973) suggests that, at least for some among the unemployed, this change in perception had already taken place. He argues that "political consciousness increases, however modestly, with length of exposure to the conditions faced by the unemployed. Furthermore, the unemployed seem to shift their political focus from local conditions to a broader base, that of the nation as a whole". This thesis is supported by his findings that more of the unemployed now regard upward mobility as being blocked, perceive the social structure as highly stratified, and regard the current social distribution of rewards as illegitimate and exploitative. While these are provocative speculations, their validity is difficult to judge. This study was apparently based upon interviews with only 29 unemployed in Ibadan in 1971: of 71 unemployed male Yorubas first interviewed in 1966, 40 could be traced five years later; and of these, 11 were currently employed. Moreover, the author does not reveal the proportion of those interviewed who gave a particular response.

There is also a conceptual problem. Gutkind, at least until 1973, tended loosely to identify the "urban poor" with the "unemployed". But this is misleading, for the unemployed (if strictly defined) constitute only a small proportion of the African urban work force, or even of those generally considered poor. Recent research has revised considerably downwards the earlier estimates that from 15 to 25 per cent of the urban male labour force were unemployed. . . . Gutkind's studies lacked an analysis of the urban poor – who they were, how they made a living, and especially how the various strata interrelated in terms of interests, aspirations and perspectives.

Gutkind's more recent article (1975), based on "about" 200 interviews, contains a partial rectification of this earlier shortcoming. Here the author seeks to distinguish the various strata within the Yoruba urban poor in Ibadan, and to suggest the relations of conflict and co-operation that obtain among these. Unfortunately, however, the depiction of "sub-class" consciousness and conflict remains unclear. At one point he alludes to a "polarization" emerging between a relatively privileged working class and other elements of the urban masses (though later he also talks about a "truly revolutionary proletariat" coming into being). But at another point he phrases the divisions within the urban poor in terms which are apparently not reducible to those employed in his discussion of polarization. This cleavage is between the *mekunnu* (the common people) – petty traders, semi-skilled workers, labourers, craftsmen, etc. – and the *talaka* (the very poor, those who do not have enough to eat) – the unemployed and the poorest casual workers and unskilled labourers in the large-scale sector. Gutkind contends that considerable hostility exists between these two "sub-classes", with the *mekunnu* regarding the *talaka* as lazy and unreliable, while the latter consider the former as arrogant and, in the case of traders and craftsmen, cheats. Yet surprisingly, given this apparently deep-seated mutual antagonism, the author asserts that both elements are united by a "quite highly developed" populist consciousness. This is based upon a common antipathy toward an avaricious and corrupt class of politicians and civil servants.

Other recent West African studies have presented equally complex pictures of the politics of this social category. The notion of a vague populist consciousness unifying the diverse elements of the urban masses is also contained in the related work on Nigeria by Williams and Peace. Williams's careful study (1974) focuses in part upon the economic situation, aspirations and organizational potential of Yoruba craftsmen and traders in Ibadan. He argues that, while these elements evince a common populist ideology, this is not given any organizational form:

the social relations of production and distribution in which Ibadan craftsmen and petty traders are involved, and the forms of social organization to which these relations give rise, do not bring them into solidaristic relations with one another in opposition to their exploiters. Their relations with the merchant traders and the "haves" generally are mediated through relations of patronage and clientage rather than through impersonal market relations, or corporate forms of social organization.

Peace's research (1979a) on the workers in an industrial estate located in a suburb of Lagos poses the important issue of the role the relatively well-off industrial workers play in the politics of the urban poor. He contends that these workers are, far from a "labour aristocracy" divorced from the concerns of the urban poor, best conceived as the "political elite" of these strata *vis-à-vis* the dominant classes. A common identification of interests is fostered by several factors; industrial wages are in fact not all that superior to those earned in informal occupations; the economic dependence of some poorer urban strata (landlords, petty traders, craftsmen) upon the permanently employed ensures that gains made by the workers are widely shared; and the workers and the other poorer strata share the same petty-bourgeois aspirations. Industrial workers also possess both the higher educational levels and the organizational potential to make possible a leading political role for them in the context of widespread urban disillusion. In practice, furthermore, these workers were supported, morally and to some extent materially and actively, by other poor urban elements during a strike confrontation in 1971 with employers and the state.

Support for Peace's conception of the leading role of the workers is found in Jeffries' study (1978b) of the skilled railway and harbour workers of Sekondi–Takoradi, twin industrial and port cities in western Ghana. These workers, though well-off and secure in relation to the urban poor, still felt deprived in the 1960s because, first, their real income had been lower since 1962 than it had been in 1939, and, second, the gap in living standards (and hence life-styles) between the mass of the wage-earners and the political class was vast and growing. In both 1961 and 1971 these workers vented their grievances in quasi-insurrectional strikes which allegedly went beyond economism to challenge the existing order. Such radical action was possible because populist ideas, easily communicated within a closely-knit working-class community, formed the basis for a shared ideology. Most significantly, these strike actions were supported – either morally or actively – by elements of the urban poor in Takoradi, especially the unemployed and market women. All these strata were unified by a resentment of the widening gap in living standards between the "common people" and the political class.

In this context the conceptual model underlying our study of the

Accra poor can be briefly stated. We use the term "labouring poor" to refer to a heterogeneous collection of working people who are wage-earners, occasionally wage-employed, or self-employed (with no more than a few apprentices or employees) in the urban economy. It includes: workers with varous levels of skill in capitalist production, artisans and craftsmen of all sorts, apprentices, journeymen and workers in petty enterprises, petty traders, market gardeners and petty capitalists, lumpen elements and the unemployed. The peculiar occupational structure in which service occupations proliferate while industrial employment stagnates at a low level is a manifestation of the structural underdevelopment of a "peripheral" capitalist country like Ghana. We hypothesized that the diverse relations of production and distribution in which these strata are involved would influence their political orientations and organizational potential. Most obviously, the concentration of workers in large enterprises not only enhances communication among them, but also aids the development of a sense of solidarity against a common impersonal employer. Workers, in addition, directly confront the power of the state. They cannot but be aware of the effect of governmental regulations upon wage rates and conditions of service, particularly in Ghana where a dynamic trade union movement has sporadically operated. Hence, workers (especially industrial workers) would be more likely to adopt a class-based theory of social inequality and its generation by relations of production and power than other elements of the labouring poor; the individualistic and competitive work situations of these other strata would retard both the communication of ideas and the development of solidarity. The higher educational levels of the skilled and semi-skilled workers would also favour their adoption of such a sophisticated theory.

But, we further supposed, there are other factors working against the separation of a self-conscious "working class" from the urban masses. True, the existence of a large "industrial reserve army", vying for jobs in the urban capitalist sector, might weaken labour's bargaining power and thus depress wages; this is one conflict of interests among the labouring poor. But this potential conflict may be mitigated by other factors. One of these, ironically, is that the life-style of even the skilled and semi-skilled workers is not so different from that of other segments of the labouring poor. . . . In addition, important social ties link the members of the labouring poor; they live side-by-side in the same residential areas; many workers will also be self-employed in an informal occupation in their spare time or when unemployed; and a single household will often contain members employed in different economic sectors. These factors might well tend to augment homogeneity of outlook among the poor. Finally, there are also links created by the economic dependence of much of the rest of the labouring poor upon the permanent workers. The unemployed, for instance, depend upon their employed brothers for assistance in the city; the market women, artisans and petty businessmen rely heavily upon the workers' patronage. In these ways the interests of diverse segments of the poor are interrelated and, in particular, the informal occupations and unemployed just mentioned gain an indirect interest in the economic grievances of the workers.

If these suppositions were correct, we expected to discover that the labouring poor as a whole in Accra manifested a more highly politicized perspective than is usually suspected. For most this perspective would constitute an amorphous populism – an egalitarian, anti-elitist (and *non-tribalist*) "we–they" mentality in which "they" (the elite) are perceived as corrupt, self-interested and supercilious, while "we" (the poor) are regarded as exploited but virtuous. At the same time we expected the workers – especially the better educated skilled and semi-skilled industrial workers – to be more likely to evince a more complex "class" orientation (defined below) toward reality. Of course, we recognized that the existence of a critical, questioning attitude toward the rich and powerful did not imply that any remedial collective political action would necessarily be undertaken by the labouring poor. . . . Moreover, the repressive power of the state, the heterogeneity of the labouring poor, and their lack of political organizational experience, combined with state controls upon trade union activity, made improbable the emergence of non-party organizations dedicated to articulating the collective grievances of the urban poor.

We sought to explore the validity of this model of class formation among the poor through intensive research in two poor neighbourhoods in Greater Accra – Nima and Ashaiman.

Probably the more usual situation in Accra and other West African cities is that represented by Nima. Most workers who live here are employed by the civil service, public agencies or commercial firms, with a minority working in small to medium factories. A minority of the adult population, workers live side-by-side with others of the labouring poor in an environment pervaded by Islamic culture. The educational level of the workers (about half of whom are unskilled) is not significantly higher than that of their neighbours who are primarily engaged in informal occupations. Most inhabitants, regardless of job, have migrated from a rural home with which they maintain contact. Although there is a widespread sense of grievance, the variations in political orientation along occupational lines is not vast. Indeed, the most deprived group – the unemployed – appear to be one of the least dissident elements of the urban poor. Some workers evince a working-class perspective on social reality, but the great majority are either acquiescent or share the popular notions about power and privilege that we typified as populism.

Populism is quite likely not even a uniquely urban phenomenon. The Ghanaian peasants are, after all, just as subject to the exactions of a peripheral mono-cultural economy – including economic insecurity, inflation and bureaucratic dictate (from price-setting agencies) – as the urban poor. Moreover, the constant movement back and forth between villages and city would encourage the wider circulation of popular urban notions. Unfortunately, however, there is not much evidence against which this hypothesis about rural populism can be assessed. One rural attitudinal survey in 1970, covering about 8 per cent of the adults in five villages selected from the Eastern, Volta and Northern Regions, came to rather mixed conclusions. While it apparently showed that most villagers had confidence and faith in their national government, it also revealed . . . that most villagers perceived politicians as untrustworthy, self-interested and dishonest (Hayward, 1972).

Although a populist perspective is common among the Ghanaian poor, a working-class consciousness occurs more rarely. But Peil (1972) goes too far when she concludes on the basis of surveys in Tema, Accra and elsewhere, that ''where they are not working unusual hours, there is little to distinguish factory workers from other men in their urban neighbourhoods. The factory workers are somewhat younger, somewhat more educated than the majority of urban workers, but society appears to have a greater effect on their behaviour than does their industrial employment. . . .'' In the first place, Peil does not provide any comparative evidence about the attitudes and behaviour of non-factory workers to support this thesis. Instead she refers to a variety of factors allegedly tending to eradicate attitudinal distinctions: the maintenance by factory workers of close ties with people in non-industrial employment; their retention of close links with their rural homes; and the (low) frequency of interchange between factory and non-factory employment. Peil also underestimates the extent to which leisure-time experiences can reinforce the effects of work experience – and not only with respect to factory workers working shifts. The factors tending to harmonize the attitudes of the factory workers with other segments of the labouring poor can be neutralized under certain circumstances.

Our study explored these special circumstances. In Ashaiman a significant number of industrial workers not only blame the deprivation they feel upon an unjust politico-economic system, rather than upon fate, chance or personal shortcomings, but also employ explicit, class-based categories to interpret reality and justify illegal strike actions. Their views, furthermore, have apparently exerted a powerful influence upon the political orientations of their neighbours engaged in informal occupations. But these working-class images have arisen only in a situation where relatively well-educated industrial workers from large establishments dominate, numerically and economically, an isolated town in which a nominally Christian, though essentially secular, culture envelops the majority. This is an unusual confluence of circumstances, perhaps only duplicated in Ghana among the skilled railway workers of Takoradi and the Tarkwa gold miners. . . . Consequently one would expect that populism, as in Nima, or widespread acquiescence to the existing political order, are more common in the cities.

But this is not the whole story. It would be misleading not to mention briefly the *ambivalence* which characterizes the outlook of some of the more politicized respondents. At this early stage of semi-industrialism, both populist and class orientations sometimes co-exist with notions concerning the improvement of life-chances through migration to the city and the permeability of the class structure. Many surveys of poor, predominantly migrant neighbourhoods of third-world cities have found that most migrants regard themselves as better off for having moved. . . . Yet, if cities such as Accra are not composed *mainly* of the discontented, this none the less suggests a rather high level of dissatisfaction. Our survey confirmed this impression: only about 60 per cent of the migrant household heads and of the migrant unemployed in Nima and Ashiman felt that life was better there than in their place of origin. Each occupational group in Ashaiman (except petty traders) expressed more dissatisfaction with urban life than its counterpart in Nima. The migrant workers (especially the skilled and semi-skilled ones) were the least satisfied; only a bare majority of these in Ashaiman felt that moving had improved their lives while a large majority would return to their homeplace if they had money or could find a job there. In the absence of the preceding analysis of political orientations, this greater dissatisfaction of the most economically privileged element of the labouring poor would appear paradoxical. Those engaged in the informal sector, and thus dependent upon the urban market, seemed most reconciled to urban life. In short, while discontent was higher than one might have expected, satisfaction with city life co-existed with populist or even class perspectives for a minority of individuals.

Urban surveys have also revealed that many among the poor continue to regard significant upward social mobility as well within the realm of possibility – if not for them, at least for their children. To the extent that this illusion is widely held, it will doubtless tend to moderate popular discontent with the existing social order. Social mobility, after all, represents a personal solution to the generic problems of poverty for the most able and ambitious. In Greater Accra a popular view prevails among the poor that the class structure is indeed open. When asked, ''if the son of a poor man is hard-working, can he become a 'big man', such as a military officer, a top civil servant or a doctor?'', 45 per cent of the household heads answered "yes" and another 36 per cent, "perhaps, it is possible". This view is not, moreover, highly variable among occupations: even among the unemployed one-third responded "yes" and 39 per cent "perhaps". Those who were most realistic about the chances of moving up in the world were the industrial workers living in Ashaiman. For instance, the skilled and semi-skilled elements of the latter were almost twice as likely as their counterparts in Nima to *deny* the likelihood of upward mobility for a hard-working son of a poor man.

The most class-oriented occupational groups evince the most discontent with city life and the most skepticism about the possibility of personal advancement. At the same time there are some with a class orientation and many with a populist one who hold somewhat contradictory notions about the improvement of life-chances through cityward migration and hard work. This ambivalence is far from unique to the Accra poor. It is a common consequence of the incongruence between a person's own experience of life and the values forming his society's dominant bourgeois value system. Among the labouring poor, the industrial workers are not only the most politicized group, but also the most consistent in their views. . . .

While working-class orientations exist, working-class action is limited in the Ghanaian context. The local wildcat strike, an economic action spurred by the animus of broader political discontents, remains the main manifestation of collective behaviour. It could hardly be otherwise. Both the prohibition upon radical movements and the understandable reluctance of trade-union leaders to transcend narrow economic goals militate against radical action. One would also expect neither the parochial neighbourhood development committees nor the religious associations to champion radical aims. . . .

What, finally, is the relevance of these findings to the opening question about the differential possibilities for progressive change in poor countries? In Ghana the conditions for revolutionary change are unlikely to exist in the foreseeable future, though the conditions for sparking occasional urban unrest, such as that in 1961 and 1971, will undoubtedly persist. But implicit in this study is the opinion that a substantial urban political base exists for any leadership, whether military or (eventually) civilian, which espouses a genuine populist-reformist platform. The political consciousness of the labouring poor, though far from monolithic, is neither unduly acquiescent nor deeply divided along ethnic or religious lines. If the political awareness of Accra's poor continues to evolve in a populist and even class direction, their potential power is bound to grow. But whether this will be used to advance their own interests remains to be seen.

Jeff Crisp, *The Labouring Poor, Trade Unions and Political Change in Ghana* (1978)

"Wildcat strikes" express overt and collective discontent by the labouring poor and are frequently a successful means of extracting concessions from recalcitrant representatives of capital and the state. . . . They also frequently represent the working out of contradictions and inequalities within the political economy. The analysis of strikes therefore reveals the workers' perceptions of such contradictions and inequalities and the processes whereby they mobilize collective remedial action. Although, as Sandbrook and Arn suggest, wildcat strikes may appear to be "spontaneous", they are in fact usually dependent on informal networks of organization within a work force and the ability of these networks to mobilize co-ordinated protest. . . .

The tendency, which Sandbrook and Arn share, to regard unofficial strikes as economistic, apolitical actions can be criticized on both empirical and conceptual grounds. The majority of miners' strikes in Ghana have been based on issues other than wages. Like other sectors of the Ghanaian working class, mine workers have experienced a steady decline in real incomes over the last two decades. This has undoubtedly produced a high degree of latent discontent, but the manifestation of such discontent in the form of strikes has usually occurred as a response to managerial policies affecting the nature or rate of work, against disrespectful or disciplinarian members of senior staff, or against measures taken by management to reduce the degree of freedom in the work place. . . .

The non-economistic tradition of mine-worker protest is readily explicable in terms of the nature of mine work, particularly in underground sections, and as a reflection of the high degree of occupational solidarity that has developed among the mining communities. However, such non-economism is not confined to the mining industry. Kraus's invaluable analysis of Ghanaian strike data reveals that since Independence over 54 per cent of all strikes have been concerned with working conditions, dismissals and suspensions, union and worker rights, and management behaviour (Kraus, 1979).

Conventionally, analysts have conceptualized strikes over work-place issues as "industrial", compared with the "economistic" nature of strikes over pay and the "political" motivation of strikes designed to change government policy or to oust the government completely. This traditional division and categorization is rooted in an essentially conservative notion of politics and political activity. In the study of African labour this notion has caused scholars to focus on the activities of organized labour, i.e. trade unions, in the national political process and to pay relatively little attention to the everyday activities and conflicts of the work place. . . . Industrial, economic, and political authority relationships form an indivisible whole, and an attack on any component which assumes the right to assert its authority must be considered "political" and consequently of equal importance in promoting radical change. Of course, authority relationships are hierarchically structured, and attacks on higher levels of the structure may have a more immediate and fundamental impact than attacks on lower levels such as junior management, supervisory personnel in the work place or local government officials. Nevertheless, the importance of worker protest over work-oriented issues should not be underestimated. . . .

Empirical evidence suggests workers do challenge the legitimacy of the institutions of both management and the state. Kraus's statistics reveal that since 1957 management behaviour has been an issue in over 21 per cent of all strikes. . . . The experience of industrialized countries where great thought has been given to the "human relations of the work place" proves that anti-management strikes derive from the fundamental conflict between labour and capital, rather than from individually provocative managers. Similarly, the demands made by mine workers during anti-management strikes – for former workers in managerial posts and for workers' representatives in the mines' administration – demonstrate an explicitly proletarian, rather than populist, consciousness.

Recent Ghanaian labour history also suggests that workers in Ghana do question the institution of the state. The clearest demonstration of this aspect of the workers' political consciousness has been their willingness to engage in conflict with the police and to defy the judicial system. The files of the Labour Department in Accra, Kumasi and Tarkwa are full of such actions by workers, particularly in the mines, on the rubber estates of the Western Region and on some state farms in southern Ghana. As with strikes against management, the threat posed by such incidents to institutional authority does not exist simply in the mind of the scholar, but is a real concern of the Ghanian ruling *elite*. In taking defensive action against workers to restore the authority of the state and management, the Supreme Military Council regime has demonstrated how a large volume of workers, demands over wages, and work-place issues can combine to generate a crisis situation with a potential for progressive political change. The discussion thus far has not acknowledged that the political consciousness of workers can take the form of covert and non-collective work-place protest such as reduced productivity, theft, sabotage, bonus cheating and malingering. The widespread concern in Ghana among managers and government officials about such activities suggests that workers reject the developmentalist ideology propagated by capital, state, and trade union and consistently reaffirm their autonomy in the work place. Again, the continual efforts of management to eliminate such activities by workers reveal the severity of the threat which they pose to managerial and state authority.

The second part of this contribution to the debate on labour and politics in Ghana deals with the role of trade unions as the representatives and mobilizing agents of the labouring poor. . . . The history of the Ghana Mineworkers Union repeatedly demonstrates the influence of rank-and-file political orientations on official ideology and policy. The early leadership of the Mineworkers Union accepted the Labour Department's admonitions to "keep out of politics" and was motivated primarily by concern for social justice in the mines rather than by explicitly political concerns. Nevertheless, the union rapidly attracted Convention People's Party (CPP) activists and by 1950, six years after the union's creation, the General Secretary, S. Bissah, was prepared to call the mine workers out on strike in support of the CPP's Positive Action campaign. The principal reason why Bissah and his successor, D. K. Foevie, ultimately chose to resist overt political affiliations was their awareness that the union had no support among the rank-and-file for such actions. Consequently, the Mineworkers Union leadership made no attempt to mobilize the rank-and-file in the "general strikes" of 1950, 1961 and 1971.

The mine workers' unwillingness to engage in national politics derives from a number of factors. Mine workers form clearly defined occupational communities, and while domestic issues and grievances can be rapidly communicated throughout the workforce, mine workers are relatively isolated from events and ideas in the more heterogeneous urban agglomerations. Many of the mine workers are migrants from northern Ghana which has traditionally remained aloof from the predominantly southern-oriented political system. In this respect the mine workers contrast vividly with the Fante railway workers of Sekondi–Takoradi. Finally, the mine workers' suspicion of political action reflects their historically rooted wariness of leaders and organizations. Since the early days of the mining industry, workers have mobilized autonomous protest action by means of an effective form of direct democracy and have chosen spokesmen rather than leaders.

The political orientation of mine workers has also forced union leaders to adopt a militant stance during periods of strong rank-and-file discontent. The union's two longest official strikes in 1947 and 1955–6 were, according to union leaders, the result of a militant union organization mobilizing its unsophisticated membership into action against exploitive foreign capital. In fact, on both occasions the union hierarchy was forced to take strike action by rank-and-file pressure. This was particularly evident in 1955 when the General Secretary was anxious to negotiate a compromise with the Chamber of Mines, but was ultimately forced to call a strike and prolong it for three months in order to satisfy the workers' demands.

Such ideological responsivity of union leaders to the rank-and-file is, of course, dependent on the maintenance of democratic procedures within the union. The gap which frequently exists between union officials and workers has emerged as a result of the unwillingness of union leaders to maintain internal democracy and their inability to resist external domination. The Mineworkers Union exemplifies the erosion of contact between the rank-and-file and union officials that has occurred in many Ghanian trade unions over the last two decades. In alliance, capital and the state have used every means at their disposal to encourage such a trend. Legislative restrictions, intimidation of union officials, political co-optation, and the bypassing of union officials in branch-level labour/management relations are just a few of the strategies used to alienate union officials from the interests of the rank-and-file. Faced with these restrictions, union officials have often sought to take refuge in the safety of the union hierarchy, to insulate themselves from rank-and-file pressure and, in some cases, to use their impregnable position for personal financial or political advancement. . . . After all, the national officials of the Mineworkers Union have failed to give official support to a single strike since 1955 and have frequently shown their determination to act in conjunction with government and management to suppress unofficial strikes.

Workers who have found their union unresponsive have explored alternate means of defending their interests, including the creation of autonomous workers' associations and the secession of branch unions from national unions. The limitations of such alternatives are only too apparent: ''informal'' modes of protest such as theft, bonus cheating, and reduced productivity may increase the degree of work-place freedom for the worker and provide some psychological redress against management, but these tactics work within the given structure of the organization of production and distribution of benefits. Unofficial strikes have proved extremely effective in securing short-term demands and in forcing government and management to consider the interests of workers in decision-making, but they rarely unite workers on an inter-industry basis or over a prolonged period of time. Autonomous workers' associations reveal the workers' determination to have truly representative and responsive spokesmen, but they enjoy few organizational or financial resources and tend to emerge from those sectors of the working class with the greatest bargaining power. As the general spokesmen of the working class, their potential must be considered small.

Trade unions in Ghana must therefore be accorded a central role in mobilizing formal sector workers, if not the whole of the labouring poor, for progressive political change. Although workers have frequently rejected their union officials, they are clearly not opposed to the concept of a union. Realistically and pragmatically they lend their support to trade unions when those unions are perceived to be democratic, responsive, and uncompromising in their defence and promotion of rank-and-file interests.

Petty Producers and Casual Labour

Chris Gerry, *Urban Poverty, Underdevelopment and "Recuperative" Production in Dakar, Senegal* (1977)

The working poor in underdeveloped capitalist societies, especially in the urban areas, are structurally excluded from access to the means of generating adequate incomes; very small proportions of the total populations of such economies are employed as wage-workers in industry and commerce (at least in the Western senses of the word). Consequently, aside from peasant agriculture, the major means of subsistence available to the urban working poor are those left to them by the dominant capitalist system which controls the commanding heights of the economy; this situation benefits capitalist industry in as much as the industrial labour-force and their dependents have access to selectively cheap mass consumption goods, a factor which exerts a downward pressure on industrial wages and cheapens the cost of production. But this is no "dual economy", with a quaint traditional sector on one side, and the vibrant, dynamic modern sector on the other; though the urban economy is almost invariably analysed along these lines, the linkages between self-employed producers and mainly foreign-owned industrial giants are not insignificant.

Senegal is a relatively small West African republic, with a population of approximately 4 millions. It is a highly urbanised country and while the rural labour-force constitutes 70 per cent of the country's total, its activities contribute only 30–35 per cent of gross domestic product at factor prices. The industrial labour-force numbers 64,000 and yet the number of civil servants and other public sector workers is almost as large. Public sector employment absorbs over half of the total wage-bill, and, indeed, half the budget. The still considerable European presence, and the existence of the relatively wealthy Senegalese and Levantine elites explains the 20,000 domestic servants at work in the urban areas. However, one section of the urban labour-force of interest to many contemporary students of development is the 50,000 self-employed small traders, petty producers and purveyors of services (and their apprentices and family-workers) – the so-called "informal sector". . . .

The typical Senegalese urban petty producer, if he is lucky, becomes dependent upon large-scale producers for his raw materials, his equipment and even his own skills, for many used to work in the large factories during the colonial period. However, for the not-so-lucky, a group which appears to be growing yearly, at least in Dakar, ownership of even the most basic means of production is not a prerequisite for earning an adequate income; merely access will suffice. Apart from the more favoured sections of the non-industrially employed labour-force, there exists considerable production of articles demanded by the mass of the population for their essential consumption, which depends on equipment and materials which have been discarded by capitalist production and consumption. . . . The flotsam and jetsam of capitalist production and consumption can be transformed, or used to transform other materials into marketable articles, from which a meagre income may be earned. . . .

. . . The most basic of mass-consumption products are the stock-in-trade of marginalised "recuperative" production; mattresses, stoves, lighting equipment, housing, clothes and tools fall into this category, and to some extent compete with factory-produced "equivalents" for clients among the urban poor. A large proportion of Dakar's consumer-goods are imported and accompanied by packaging which can be used in petty production. Much of the city's industry also provides by-products and waste which can be re-utilised but petty producers, with "time to spare", access to the cheapest labour, and excluded from other raw materials markets by monopolistic pricing, *must* make use of these inputs. . . .

Though many of the different occupations which can be included within the general framework of recuperative production are striking in their ingenuity, there is another and far more miserable pole to the spectrum of marginal activities. These may nevertheless be characterised by well-developed and complex commercial relations. Many articles are salvaged by impoverished children and the aged from what bourgeois families throw away; old shoes can be sold to shoe-repairers, plastic bags to women peanut-vendors for use as wrapping materials, and plastic bottles can be cut in half to make both a funnel for decanting cooking oil, plus a handy container for condiments. Old newspapers can be sold to the Mauritanian corner-shops as wrapping paper, and, in turn, such shops sell their empty flour and rice-sacks to mattress-makers and repairers. Tin-cans are an important input into artisanal metal-founding, an occupation which provides the urban poor with many of its cooking utensils and market-gardening tools. . . . Everything that has potential value to the working poor is recycled, since they cannot afford to discard such essential raw materials.

A striking example of this enforced "waste-not, want-less" mentality is the utilisation of industrial packaging. Though brick and concrete buildings are rapidly becoming more common, large numbers of the

Dakar poor live in wooden shacks in the peripheral shantytowns; due to the extreme anti-shantytown urbanisation policies undertaken by the Senegalese government, it is not difficult to find African districts in which over half of the constructions are built of wood and other recycled packaging materials. Steel drums are sought after for the manufacture of the local charcoal stove. Used butane canisters can be transformed into serviceable oil lamps for the large proportion of households which either cannot afford, or have no access to electric lighting.

Metal bed-frames are mainly made by Africans and sold through Lebanese wholesalers and retailers, whose mark-ups make the existence of cheaper substitutes very necessary. Consequently, the repairing and renovating of second-hand and/or broken beds is a common occupation. Often such small enterprises work in tandem with a mattress-maker and repairer, who will recuperate old articles, re-use materials which are serviceable and discard what is beyond repair.

The list of such "recuperative" activities is virtually endless, but a mere list would be worthless unless it placed the descriptive elements in a framework which aided the analysis of the complex of urban production. "Recuperation" and recycling, like many aspects of non-capitalist economic activity in underdeveloped economies, are merely manifestations of a deep-rooted structural malaise. Capitalist industry in underdeveloped economies produces mainly either for export or for consumption by the more privileged strata of society. The working poor, like the peasantry, must look after themselves, and, in the face of great adversity and institutionalized discrimination, manage to produce at low cost, many of the basic necessities of life. Petty producers may be looked upon as low productivity workers with little expertise, but such an analysis would ignore a whole range of constraints which deny the labour-force adequate access to the means of production. The level of technology is undoubtedly low, even though European capitalists benefit from small producers' purchases of electric sewing and embroidering machines, woodworking equipment, and the like. Nevertheless, initiative and innovation abound: after Renault, in collaboration with the Senegalese government, ceased exporting spares for the privately operated mini-buses, in order that the state-run and Renault-supplied (and financed) bus company could be secured the monopoly which would ensure its viability, local vehicle-mechanics were forced to improvise spares. Small bus-operators, whose very livelihoods were threatened, were provided with hand-made components and cannibalised engines, enabling them to thwart for many years the monopolizing strategies of the government and its supporters. . . .

Much of this style of subsistence production is so alien to analysts that very superficial explanations ensue. The common tendency is for the *form* of recuperative and recycling activities to be described, whilst its *content* and objective situation are ignored. What are the social and economic relations which give rise to the progressive estrangement of large sections of the urban labour-force from adequate means of subsistence? The answer lies in the fundamental relationship between capitalist development and underdevelopment; the African labour-force is inevitably a victim of the latter, and the more disadvantaged the group, the more profound is its degree of underdevelopment and consequent estrangement from an adequate standard of living. . . .

Hard-won skills are under-utilised and inferior materials used mainly because of the structural constraints located in the national (but nevertheless rooted firmly within the *international*) economy; thus opportunities are restricted in the first instance to the capitalist class in the developed metropolis, and secondly to the privileged strata in the dependent underdeveloped economy. The whole structure of prices, the terms of trade, education and skill-acquisition, market opportunities and credit-availability works against any amelioration of the low standard of living and the marked degree of inequality characterising the mass of the population. The so-called "marginalisation" problem, and the specific phenomenon of recuperative production merely reflect the deep-rooted nature of the complex network of relations and institutions which constitute the base and superstructure of Senegal's capitalist underdevelopment. . . .

Chris Gerry, *Casual Workers and Capitalist Industry in Dakar, Senegal* (1976)

The labour market in the metropolitan districts of an underdeveloped capitalist economy such as Senegal allocates extremely imperfectly, at least from *their* viewpoint, these members of the labour-force who are surplus to the requirements of capitalist industry and commerce, who have little or no skills which they might profit from in the petty-commodity sector, and who have been unsuccessful sellers of the only commodity they possess – their own labour-power. In terms of the capitalist mode of production, however, their intermittent and extremely poorly remunerated employment is entirely consistent with the aims of that dominant mode of production. The existence of a reservoir of unattached labour-power provides considerable benefits to capitalist industry, depressing the wage-rate applicable to more permanent members of the industrial and commercial labour-force by the fact of its very existence. Obviously the knowledge that there are always those "who stand and wait" outside the factory-gate, will ensure an even greater degree of labour compliancy than is guaranteed by the very close links between the trade union movement and the ruling party.

The phrases "surplus members of the labour-force" and "industrial reserve army" may well sound extravagant, yet the type of "development" which has been experienced in most underdeveloped capitalist economies (and particularly manifested in the heavily populated and industrialized urban areas) of necessity produces a relative surplus population of working age, comprising individuals who rely almost exclusively on infrequent and discontinuous employment of various types in the towns and cities. The "superfluity" of these workers is not to be understood as an absolute state; the surplus is a relative phenomenon, due to the fact that capitalist industry is unable and indeed, unwilling, to absorb anything more than a minute proportion of the annual increments in the potentially-active labour-force. This applies to all workers, to a greater or lesser extent, whether they are skilled or unskilled, experienced or otherwise, but is crucially important in the case of new entrants into the labour-market. However, in general it is those who possess few or inappropriate skills who inevitably suffer the worst consequences of a problem which consists of the grossly inefficient utilisation of the available labour-power in an economy in which that resource is in abundance, and the generation of an adequate income is a priority for the mass of the population.

It is clear that the majority of those who are employed in this way by large industrial and commercial concerns are merely transient members of the industrial labour-force; they are barely if at all integrated into the small industrial working class, in terms of their common aims and aspirations, their subjective consciousness of the work-situation, and their attitudes to other members of the labour-force. On the other hand, the cultural, social and economic life of the casual worker has many similarities to that of the self-employed petty producer. Through experience in the industrial sector, and the continual knowledge that work – for him – comes and goes with apparent disregard for his own needs, the casual worker may be regarded as being inextricably linked to what has been called the "informal sector" of petty production, as well as the industrial sector of the city. The casual worker appears as a highly mobile floating labourer, surplus in the long run to the requirements of both the industrial and the petty producing sectors. Unable to find regular employment, he is forced to apply whatever skills and ingenuity he possesses to the task of feeding and supporting both himself and his dependents. In addition, he must search for any kind of employment, unlike the educated unemployed who may well be "parasitical" on friends and family until "something turns up". The response of casual workers to their objective situation is of necessity a defensive one, for it is this group *par excellence* which can be pushed from pillar to post, then left to its own devices when additional labour is no longer required. Casual workers are therefore in no position to act collectively *as such*; their militancy may well be expressed through other organizations, ethnic, community-based, or otherwise, which have internalized appropriate systems of collective responsibility, *"entraid"*, and co-operation. Nor are casual workers in a position to develop a clear consciousness of their role in the overall problem of underdevelopment, of which they are but a part. Their response is defensive and individual, as they circulate between wage-employment, small-scale self-employment, petty services, trading and open unemployment.

The mass of casual workers represents more than just a surplus in the aggregate sense; on an individual level, the degree of integration of the petty producer is small and his active participation in production extremely low. In addition to, and at the margins of, this urban reserve army, there are the unsuccessful petty producers, skilled workers whose small enterprises have failed, pushed aside by the competition that the proliferation of small-scale production promotes, squeezed out by the twin forces of high externally-set input prices and low competitively-set market prices. Such skilled workers circulate near the factories and about the residential areas serching for small jobs or a day's wage-employment. . . .

The following extracts from an interview with a casual worker illustrates some of the points made above:

> . . . Fall considers himself to be unemployed, and has been for five years. He was formerly a farmer . . . after which he became a trader, selling mainly vegetables. Then he moved to Dakar, where he became a tiler's labourer; his trading capital had been completely lost. After . . . [four] years he was laid off. He has since only worked intermittently, occasionally finding day-work, mainly through his friends and former colleagues still active in the trade. Fall says that many craftsmen like himself would be prepared to take even less than [the going rate of 450 francs/day for day-work] . . . in order to secure regular employment. Fall managed [recently] to get six days' work at Les Grands Moulins de Dakar; he was employed as a day-labourer for 3 days, then laid off for a day, then taken on again for a further 3 days. He hoped there would still be work when he returned the following day. Fall learnt of the job through a friend who had already been taken on at Les Grands Moulins . . . and who came to his house. . . .

To leave out of account the mass of temporarily employed workers of this sort, whose social milieu is almost identical to that of the petty producer, itinerant hawker and petty trader, and whose work-situation has extreme locational variability, is to neglect an essential part of the urban labour-force, one about which very little is really known.

Part VI

African Bourgeoisies: Accumulation, Politics and the State

Introduction

African bourgeoisies have been formed by both colonial and post-colonial economies and states (Goulbourne, 1979; Allen, forthcoming). They can be seen as status groups (Weber, 1948), with their own styles of life, values and claims to deference and economic opportunities. Formal education has been the major means of access to such status (Clignet, 1966; Le Brun in R. C. O'Brien, 1979; Court, 1976; Blakemore, 1981); it has legitimated the claims of the educated to political leadership and a disproportionate share of economic resources (*Leys* and *Williams*; Nduka in Gutkind, 1977), while defining the poor, especially the peasants, as ignorant (see Part III). Bourgeois life-styles and values are well illustrated by novelists (Armah, 1969; Achebe, 1966; Ngugi wa Thiongo, 1977; Ousmane, 1976), in various (auto)biographies of military and political figures (Awolowo, 1960; Afrifa, 1966; Post, 1973), and in academic accounts (e.g. Gould, 1980; Schwarz, 1974; Gugler, 1978). Once established, bourgeoisies also form class blocs, expropriating surplus value through political and more directly economic mechanisms. They are composed of competing economic, ethnic and institutional interest groups who all too often have been unable to establish or maintain effective class unity and impose political and social order (*Leys* and *Turner*; Osoba in Gutkind, 1977; Osoba, 1979; Usman, 1979).

The most developed and firmly established bourgeoisie in Africa is that in South Africa. It was originally formed by the displacement of merchant capital by mining and agrarian capital and by the formation of the South African state as outlined by *Marks and Trapido*, above. South African capital has since come to dominate mining and to develop industrial production, with extensive state support and investment (cf. Davies, 1976 with Fransman, 1982). The political alliance of agrarian capital with mining and later manufacturing has proved precarious. The defection of farmers and white workers to the National Party enabled it to take power in 1948 under the leadership of "petty-bourgeois" Afrikaner nationalists, described by *O'Meara*, (see also O'Meara in Webster, 1978; Morris, 1976). The Afrikaner petty-bourgeoisie appropriated the dominant positions in the civil service, armed forces and judiciary, and used state power to protect and expand Afrikaner capital (Giliomee in Adam, 1979). Apartheid legislation was elaborated to protect the labour supply of mining and farming and to provide cheap, controlled labour to industry at the cost of bureaucratic intervention, skilled labour shortages and massive repression (Legassick, 1974a, 1974b; Wolpe, 1972; Davies, 1980; Greenberg, 1980). Bourgeoisies elsewhere in Africa, however, lack the power to impose a comparable system of effective support and controls.

For the bulk of the colonial period, the metropolitan powers concentrated on expanding trade and raising revenues in the colonies. Only after the Depression and in the face of competition from American capitalism did they stress increasing colonial production and industrial development (Gann, 1975; Suret-Canale, 1977; Cowen in Fransman, 1982). European or Asian firms and discriminatory state policies restricted the development of African capital accumulation until the 1950s (Amin, 1967, 1969; Brett, 1973; Kitching, 1980; Kay, 1972) so that post-war nationalist movements drew their leadership and ideology not from established bourgeoisies, but from small elites defined by education and, in some cases, by religious or aristocratic status, though sharing bureaucratic and commercial ambitions (*Hodgkin, Fanon*; Lloyd in Gann, 1975).

Nationalist politicians sought to act as spokesmen for various class-based popular grievances and to appeal for electoral support as representatives of their communities (Hodgkin, 1956a; Allen forthcoming). They co-operated with colonial authorities in bringing about the process of formal decolonization, allowing – as *O'Brien* and *Cohen* indicate – the use of political office and contacts to accumulate money capital from state funds (e.g. Beckman, 1976). Colonial marketing boards were employed to extract the necessary revenues from peasant producers, and privileged relations were established with foreign companies. In Ghana, Guinea, Mali and Tanzania, socialist leaderships extended state economic activity, and control of rural marketing, to limit the development of a commercial bourgeoisie in favour of the party and state bureaucracy (Johnson in Dunn, 1978; Meillassoux, 1970; Shivji, 1975; Samoff, 1979). Ideologically, nationalist and populist appeals gave way to elitism, tribalism, "African socialism", and authoritarian conceptions of representation and the political process (*Williams*; Benot, 1969; Dunn, 1978; Leys, 1975).

Leys's first extract argues that decolonisation in Kenya produced an "auxiliary" bourgeoisie, dependent on the state to fund and protect its activities and allied with and dependent upon foreign capital (cf. for Zambia Baylies in CAS, 1980; for Nigeria Williams, 1976). Such a bourgeoisie, evident in most African countries in recent decades, is marked by its preference for commerce, transporting, real estate and government contracting. Competition for control of these activities, for bureaucratic office and for shares of public spending have prompted conflict among sectional elites, and come to discredit politicians and governments. The military have often captured state power from them and used it to protect their own corporate interests, as *Martin* points out, and as *Dudley* (following Luckham, 1971) and *Turner* show, have engaged in similar forms of accumulation and become vulnerable to the same divisions (First, 1970; Martin, 1976).

Underdevelopment theory, particularly dependency theory, suggests that African bourgeoisies cannot avoid an ''auxiliary'' status nor develop into a class independent of foreign capital. *Leys*'s second extract questions this view, following other recent studies of African entrepreneurs and of the complementary interests of metropolitan and local capitalists (Swainson, 1980; Warren, 1980; Kitching, 1980; Cowen, forthcoming). Leys suggests that in Kenya local capital has successfully moved from agriculture and rural trade, with state support, into sectors previously dominated by Asian or external capital, including manufacturing (see, further, Beckman, 1981, and the debate on Kenya in Fransman, 1982). Nevertheless, throughout Africa the industrial sector continues to depend on the foreign exchange earned by primary exports, even in South Africa (Bienefeld, 1976; Fransman, 1982), and to be dominated by foreign firms, usually in association with and under the political protection of African state or private capital.

Nationalism, Corruption and Accumulation

Thomas Hodgkin, *The African Middle Class* (1956b)

The development of an African middle class, with all its internal gradations, has been a necessary consequence of the growth of towns, the diversification of the economy, the expansion of bureaucracies and the spread of western education. In fact some have argued that the level of educational attainment – primary, post-primary, teacher-training, university – is the sole objective criterion of social status in contemporary Africa. This I doubt. Any working classification must surely take account of the semi-literate or self-educated farmer, middleman, contractor, lorry-owner, trader – an employer of labour, enjoying a relatively comfortable standard of life, with European-style furnishings and equipment. He regards himself, and is regarded, as belonging to a class apart, which can only be described as the middle class. But it remains true that within a society in which illiteracy is still a dominant fact, to be educated constitutes a privilege which opens the door to non-manual jobs, and guarantees immediate prestige. . . .

The external signs of belonging to the African middle class seem fairly universal (except in so far as ''cultural nationalism'' in one or other of its forms has introduced a complicating factor): living in a solid European-style house, equipped with solid European furniture; wearing European clothes (for everyday use, at least); eating European food; listening to the wireless; reading the newspapers; membership of social and sports clubs, old boys' associations, literary societies, progressive unions, etc.; participation in, and direction of, political organisations – where these are permitted to exist. Attitudes – the subjective signs of middle-class membership – are more difficult to assess. A new individualism, an interest in getting on in the world (not merely in the economic sense)? A passionate belief in the value of education as the key to achievement (for oneself, one's children, one's people)? The importance attached to the concept of ''progress'', and to a ''progressive'' outlook in relation to such matters as marriage, the family, religion? A certain consciousness of social superiority and separateness? . . . It has been argued that, correlated with their ambiguous economic status, at the same time privileged (in comparison with the mass of Africans), depressed (in comparison with the European and Asian middle classes), and precarious (given intermittent unemployment, indebtedness, etc.), there develops a kind of political ambivalence – a tendency to oscillate between support for moderate and radical policies. . . . Clearly nationalism, in one of its aspects, expresses the dissatisfaction of an emerging African middle class with a situation in which many of the recognized functions, and rewards, of a middle class – in the commercial, professional, administrative and ecclesiastical fields – are in the hands of ''strangers'', whether European or Asian. The demand for African control of state power is in part a demand for unrestricted access to these functions.

Frantz Fanon, *The National Bourgeoisie* (1965)

The national middle class which takes over power at the end of the colonial regime is an underdeveloped middle class. It has practically no economic power, and in any case it is in no way commensurate with the bourgeoisie of the mother country which it hopes to replace. In its wilful narcissism, the national middle class is easily convinced that it can advantageously replace the middle class of the mother country. But that same independence which literally drives it into a corner will give rise within its ranks to catastrophic reactions, and will oblige it to send out frenzied appeals for help to the former mother country. The university and merchant classes which make up the most enlightened section of the new state are in fact characterized by the smallness of their number and their being concentrated in the capital, and the type of activities in which they are engaged: business, agriculture and the liberal professions. Neither financiers nor industrial magnates are to be found within this national middle class. The national bourgeoisie of underdeveloped countries is not engaged in production, nor in invention, nor building, nor labour; it is completely canalized into activities of the intermediary type. Its innermost vocation seems to be to keep in the running and to be part of the racket. The psychology of the national bourgeoisie is that of the businessman, not that of a captain of industry; and it is only too true that the greed of the settlers and the system of embargoes set up by colonialism has hardly left them any other choice. Under the colonial system, a middle class which accumulates capital is an impossible phenomenon. In an underdeveloped country an authentic national middle class ought to consider as its bounden duty to betray the calling fate has marked out for it, and to put itself to school with the people; in other words to put at the people's disposal the intellectual and technical capital that it has snatched when going through the colonial universities. But unhappily we shall see that very often the national middle class does not follow this heroic, positive, fruitful and just path; rather, it disappears with its soul set at peace into the shocking ways – shocking because antinational – of a traditional bourgeoisie, of a bourgeoisie which is stupidly, contemptibly, cynically bourgeois.

The objective of nationalist parties as from a certain given period is, we have seen, strictly national. They mobilize the people with slogans of independence, and for the rest leave it to future events. When such parties are questioned on the economic programme of the state that they are clamouring for, or on the nature of the regime which they propose to install, they are incapable of replying, because, precisely, they are completely ignorant of the economy of their own country. . . .

The national economy of the period of independence is not set on a new footing. It is still concerned with the groundnut harvest, with the cocoa crop and the olive yield. In the same way there is no change in the marketing of basic products, and not a single industry is set up in the country. We go on sending out raw materials; we go on being Europe's small farmers who specialize in unfinished products.

Yet the national middle class constantly demands the nationalization of the economy and of the trading sectors. This is because, from their point of view, nationalization does not mean placing the whole economy at the service of the nation and deciding to satisfy the needs of the nation. To them, nationalization quite simply means the transfer into native hands of those unfair advantages which are a legacy of the colonial period.

Since the middle class has neither sufficient material nor intellectual resources (by intellectual resources we mean engineers and technicians) it limits its claims to the taking over of business offices and commercial houses formerly occupied by the settlers. The national bourgeoisie steps into the shoes of the former European settlement: doctors, barristers, traders, commercial travellers, general agents and transport agents. It considers that the dignity of the country and its own welfare require that it should occupy all these posts. From now on it will insist that all the big foreign companies should pass through its hands, whether these companies wish to keep on their connexions with the country, or to open it up. The national middle class discovers its historic mission: that of intermediary. . . . In the colonial countries, the spirit of indulgence is dominant at the core of the bourgeoisie; and this is because the national bourgeoisie identifies itself with the Western bourgeoisie, from whom it has learnt its lessons. It will be greatly helped on its way towards decadence by the Western bourgeoisies, who come to it as tourists avid for the exotic, for big-game hunting and for casinos. The national bourgeoisie organizes centres of rest and relaxation and pleasure resorts to meet the wishes of the Western bourgeoisie. Such activity is given the name of tourism, and for the occasion will be built up as a national industry.

Donal O'Brien, *The Politics of Corruption in Senegal* (1975)

For an outside evaluation of the Senegalese political style one may begin by remembering the victims, those who fall outside the moral boundaries surrounding political or economic transactions. The Senegalese writer Sembène Ousmane, in his short story and film *The Money Order* (1972) offers a bitter and relevant parable. An elderly, simple citizen receives a money order for some fifty pounds from his nephew, a Paris street-cleaner. His ultimately futile efforts to cash the order lead him helpless into the maze of Dakar bureaucracy, while he is hoodwinked and swindled by cynical functionaries, by usurer-traders, then last, most bitterly and most comprehensively, by his own family. Cynical and parasitic elite as against trusting shantytown victim, it is not difficult to read the moral and the political lesson.

One must I think recognize the force of this "imaginative" vision, but one must also understand that "the elite" and "the mass" are no more than convenient labels to cover a diverse social reality. From among the mass, one may find a higher proportion of true innocents in fiction than in real social life. The victims are not unaware of the political games which go on around them, often at their expense: they take the trouble to try to learn the rules, and to use them (so far as possible) to their own advantage. The elite predators may be distinguished into given categories, each with a distinct style of operation. Four principal categories, four styles of more or less corrupt activity, will be briefly reviewed here: the bureaucrat, the party politician, the private trader, and the saint.[1]

Senegalese state officials not merely account for over half the national budget in official salaries, they use their control of administrative and marketing institutions to make further illicit profits on a scale roughly proportional to each invididual's standing within the official hierarchy. The local bureaucrat, whose style of life is still modelled on that of his French predecessors, finds that he cannot hope to attain such relative luxury without systematically breaking the rules of his organisation. The differential exercise of administrative power can be a means to draw cash subsidies from the bureaucrat's wealthier clients, and protection money from the politically weak (e.g. the local Lebanese). Private commerce can be conducted under the formal auspices and protection of state

---

[1] I.e. the leadership of the Islamic Mouride brotherhood; see Jeffries, above, and D. O'Brien (1971).

authority, and (at its simplest) cash can just be stolen from the till. In these procedures certain limited bases of commercial and political solidarity do emerge; with party politicians who can (at a price) provide security from the harassment of official investigation, with traders who can provide remunerative outlets for administrative funds, and of course with family members (not many) who help to consume the funds. These are solidarities of the privileged, of an elite which shows little concern for patronage expenditures to the subject masses.

The bureaucrat's crucial advantages are his education and specialized training, which make his activities mysterious and unintelligible to many of the subjects, as well as his institutional position as an officer of the state. Though systematically breaking his own supposed rules, he can in fact manipulate the rules to hoodwink quite a proportion of the people some of the time. The people may not have the means to understand just *how* they are being swindled, but it must be said that they do (at least among the Wolof) realize that they *are* swindled. The apparatus of Senegalese officialdom is locally seen at least in broad outline as a parasitic body, and it certainly does seem to provide small proportional return for the legal and illegal salaries of its sixty thousand employees.

The party politician, even when Senegal was a single-party state, must regard his position as dependent to some degree on popular support (or at the very least, a plausible appearance of popular support). Officials of the ruling *Union Progressiste Sénégalaise* are at least in principle chosen by election from below, and must always in fact bear their supporters in mind. To neglect the constituency, at any level in the party hierarchy, is to risk losing one's job. Thus the party officer, though involved in many elite intrigues for private financial gain (corruption), is also concerned to redistribute some of the proceeds especially to the more influential of his supporters. The bureaucrat, who has no constituency but only a temporary area of jurisdiction, need only be concerned with the good opinion of his superiors (and that too can be bought): the proceeds of his malversation ultimately find their way to Dakar. The party official is valued by his superiors largely for the support which he is deemed to command in his constituency (a term which may be understood in broad sociological terms rather than a legal and restrictive sense). To command that support, it is well understood that he must be shown to have secured favourable government consideration for his constituents. This is the corruption of machine politics, in which the party man may be seen as counterpose to the bureaucrat: you can't swindle all the people all the time, not even country people.

The private trader may seem a dubious candidate for analysis in this perspective of corruption. He is after all by profession dedicated to the pursuit of private gain, and thus apparently cannot violate his own commercial norms in the maximization of profits. From the rural Wolof he buys peanuts, to them he lends money and sells a range of (largely imported) commodities. But money-lending and peanut-buying are each conducted outside the boundaries of Senegalese law, which means that the goal of profit-maximization can only be achieved with the help of political protection. Bureaucrats and party officials receive their cut, and the successful trader is in fact one who is as skilful in political intrigue as in strictly commercial transactions. He may not break his own rules, but his success depends on breaking the rules of others. His "clientele" is not to be understood as a constituency of candidates for patronage redistribution, rather as those with whom he does business (buys and sells) and who are dependent usually because they owe him money. He is from the peasant's standpoint naturally enough often a detested figure, however indispensable his services on occasion may be. From the outside he appears above all as the ally of the state bureaucracy in a whole range of corrupt manipulations – corruption of and for the elite. The peasants indeed are necessarily and permanently the losers in their encounters with bureaucratic/commercial graft of this type.

The saint does of course take his part in the politics of the elite, he does further his political and commercial ends by alliances with given bureaucrats, traders and party representatives. But he is to be distinguished from these allies by the nature of his relations with his own disciples. Alone among the privileged in this respect, he has his roots in peasant society: the saint's relation to his disciples, including the differential exchange of goods and services, has a real, locally recognized moral sanction – the promise of paradise. The saint, like the trader, may participate in violating the supposed norms of others at an elite level. In dealing with his own peasant disciples, however, he must take his own divinely-sanctioned principles more seriously. These principles are shared by the disciples, who indeed have done much to develop their implications in the material world. The client is far from helpless before his holy patron, indeed he expects his saint to act as his protector in dealing with the other superordinate agents of the Senegalese state. It is the very effectiveness of the saintly intermediary in this respect which makes the agencies of state authority acceptable to the Muslim peasant. The charismatic community also depends for its survival on the material services which accompany the divine gift, in other words on the ways in which the saintly variant of elite corruption can be shown to have brought some real benefits to the peasant masses.

The Wolof peasants, though they are in many respects and to varying degrees the victims of the ruling elite, cannot thus be seen as inert objects of exploitation from above. Through the saints, and to a lesser extent through local party representatives, peasants can assert their own particular claims. These claims (for the preferential allocation of government services) can often only be satisfied by procedures in violation of formal institutional arrangements. So corruption does not work solely to the advantage of the already privileged: indeed the total eradication of corruption from the Senegalese state (admittedly a remote eventuality) might well leave the peasants altogether defenceless before a technically qualified bureaucracy.

Dan O'Meara, *Afrikaner Nationalism and the State* (1977)

[The character of twentieth-century Afrikaner nationalism in South Africa was largely the outcome of the nature of] economic and political incorporation of the Afrikaans-speaking petty-bourgeoisie in the broad South African social formation. Within the imperialist colonial states a clear cultural oppression operated against Afrikaans-speakers. Long before the Anglo-Boer war ended the independence of the northern Republics, so generating a fierce cultural response, the language movement of the Cape had inspired a strong cultural nationalism. More importantly, in an essentially peripheral economy dominated by the ideology of imperialist interest, for those Afrikaners unprepared to accept cultural assimilation and who possessed a modicum of training rendering them unsuitable for manual labour, employment opportunities were limited. English was the language of the economy. Law, the Church, education and the lower levels of the state bureaucracy were the only real, if limited, avenues available for Afrikaans-speakers. Thus for the Afrikaner petty-bourgeoisie, economic opportunities were limited both by class position and language. Yet these occupations placed the petty-bourgeois individual in a unique position from which to experience and at the same time to mediate the effects of ''imperialism'' – seen as the economic and political domination of South Africa by Britain through the Empire – for virtually all Afrikaans-speakers. He interpreted its law for farmers and workers, taught its curriculum to their children, implemented its policies and, as a cleric, was particularly responsible for the interpretation of the entire experience – its explanation in cosmic and symbolic terms – to a confused *volk*. Thus, in a sense, the experience of ''imperialism'' was synthesized in the Afrikaner petty-bourgeoisie. Nor did the structure of South African capitalism in its imperialist phase provide the culturally aware Afrikaner fraction of the petty-bourgeoisie with any real potential allies within the dominant capitalist class, except perhaps in the Cape. Such alliances would involve total cultural assimilation and, more important, an acceptance of the long-term dominance of the interests of imperialist mining and finance capital. Many Afrikaners did make such alliances. Specific fractions of agricultural capital, particularly in the eastern and western Transvaal, increasingly identified their interests with "imperialism" after the 1913 Land Act. Botha and Smuts personified this alliance. But the petty-bourgeoisie did not have this independent basis on which to act. By nature a dependent class, alliances had to be sought elsewhere.

In the Cape, conditions were less traumatic than in the north and the potential alliance clear. The long-established and prosperous commercial agriculture of the western Cape and Boland provided a viable basis for political and economic alliance as well as the possibilities of independent accumulation. . . . In the north, and the Transvaal particularly, no such potentially viable economic alliances were available. The petty-bourgeoisie were politically more isolated and required to interpret an economically much more hostile world for the great bulk of Afrikaans-speakers, who had never known the prosperity of the Cape. The political struggle of the northern petty-bourgeoisie was thus built on an alliance not with a strong fraction of capital as in the Cape, but with poorer farmers and (potentially, for it took a long time to develop) a class fraction which grew out of this group, Afrikaner workers. This could only be anti-imperialist in tone.

The differential class alliances which comprised Afrikaner Nationalism in the Cape, the Orange Free State and Transvaal before 1934 not only represented different forms of rural interest, but each incorporated the petty-bourgeoisie in a secondary, though varying, position. The Nationalist Party, particularly after it came to power in the 1924 Labour–Nationalist "Pact" government, operated to guarantee the interests of the Afrikaner petty-bourgeoisie. With the entrenchment of language rights in the state bureaucracy, the assertion of South African sovereignty against the Empire, the "civilized labour" policies of the Pact government, and its promotion of a form of industrialization heavily dependent on state intervention, the position of the petty-bourgeoisie appeared to be secured *independent* of "imperialism". During this period, too, their position as political and ideological functionaries, now of the state rather than mere party, was further advanced and entrenched. However, these gains and this new security all rested on the maintenance of anti-imperialist alliances with the various rural interests. The petty-bourgeoisie could not sustain state power on their own. If these alliances were threatened the petty-bourgeoisie would be isolated, as happened in 1934. [The Nationalist MPs under General Hertzog had formed a coalition with General Smuts's South African Party (SAP), splitting the party. A year later the northern Nationalist MPs followed Hertzog into "fusion" with the SAP to form the United Party (UP), leaving a rump of Cape Nationalist MPs. . . .]

At the economic level Fusion was partially a response to the changing structure of production of South African capitalism. The development of industry during the period of the Pact government, the changes in the labour-process within industry and the extension and development of capitalist relations of production in this period (particularly the proletarianization of rural whites), all placed extreme pressure on both the traditional and new petty-bourgeoisie. The disruption of the communities of the platteland (countryside) and the general pressure of proletarianization placed the new petty-bourgeoisie in an extremely insecure position during this period. Teachers in rural areas saw their classes shrink; those in the cities were faced with all the problems of recently uprooted pupils and limited educational resources. The disruption of rural congregations, the apparently growing attraction of white workers to various forms of labour movements, and the rise of apostolic denominations in this period similarly changed and threatened the role of the clerics of the established Calvinist churches. And given the impoverishment of the Depression years, many of these petty-bourgeois agents were themselves faced with pressures of proletarianization.

Further, the split in the Nationalist Party threatened the role which the Afrikaner petty-bourgeoisie had managed to carve out for themselves. The South African Party represented the monopoly mining industry and its numerous "imperialist" interests. It was immediately clear that in fusion with the SAP, the ideological role and niche of the Afrikaner petty-bourgeoisie would be altered. The relative independence from "imperialist" domination established under the Nationalist Party would be lost as not only would the new party be dominated by monopoly interests of the mining industry, but the ideological functionaries of this party were much more likely to be drawn from the "sophisticated" ranks of the SAP, than from those of the NP. Fusion thus left the petty-bourgeois elements of the old Nationalist Party in an extremely isolated position.

Fusion thus marked two related developments in Afrikaner Nationalism. First, it changed its class basis, more particularly, the relationship between rural and petty-bourgeois elements in the North. Under Hertzog, rural interests dominated the concerns of Afrikaner Nationalism. The petty-bourgeoisie were relegated to a supportive position. Given the nature of its economic concerns, heavily dependent on the state and discriminated against by "imperialism", the Afrikaner petty-bourgeoisie were left isolated in the North. Almost without exception Northern commercial agriculture supported the UP. Rural support for the rump Nationalists, such as it was, came from poorer farmers or professional groups in the platteland towns. In its isolation the petty-bourgeoisie was reduced to articulating the interests of "the small man". . . . A second related result of Fusion was the emergence of a new generation of ideological and political leaders, again predominantly in the North. These younger men had not fought in the Anglo-Boer war and had lived most of their lives in a unified South Africa. Given a chance at leadership and an influence they would otherwise have had to wait long for, they brought to Afrikaner Nationalism new vigour, ideas and perspectives. . . . [In this they were strongly influenced by ideologues and journals associated with the Afrikaner Broederbond, founded in Transvaal in 1919, but spreading throughout the Afrikaner petty-bourgeoisie from 1931.]

In an environment of perceived (Imperialist) economic domination the Bond strove to interpret the world and formulate a counter-policy for their petty-bourgeois membership. It recognized that political power was the key to an inversion of this process. Yet the petty-bourgeoisie were isolated. Allies had to be found. These consisted potentially of two major groups, the poorer farmers, and Afrikaans-speaking workers. But their support could not simply be appropriated. As the enthusiastic rural support for Fusion indicated, poorer farmers tended to follow the lead of wealthier land-owners, and Afrikaner workers displayed an unhealthy attraction for class organizations. Given the existence of a large group of poor whites, a real danger existed that they could be mobilized in class terms, thereby undermining any potential mass base for Afrikaner Nationalism. An obsession with the dangers of class division and class mobilization is a major theme of Nationalist ideologues of this period. These groups had to be saved for the *volk* and mobilized in cultural terms. Yet underlying all these problems was the almost complete exclusion of Afrikaans-speakers from control in any sector of the economy bar farming. If the basis of imperialist domination was economic the mere capture of state power would not end it. Rather, Afrikaners would have to move into positions of economic control. The petty-bourgeoisie would have to transform themselves into a bourgeoisie on the savings of Afrikaner workers and farmers – the proven Cape formula. Thus, throughout the thirties, the Bond directed their attention to these interrelated problems, operating in three broad areas: the ideological redefinition of Afrikanerdom and its Nationalism – *kultuurpolitiek*; the organization of Afrikaner workers into separate trade unions; and the establishment and promotion of Afrikaner business interests.

. . . Sufficient common ground existed among Bond ideologists to enable debate to take place within agreed parameters. Four broad areas of agreement emerged: the relationship between culture and nationalism; the dangers of class divisions; the need for the economic mobilization of Afrikaners; and Republicanism. All groups agreed that nations are products of Divine Will, each with an allotted task, distinguished from each other by culture in its broadest sense. Culture is thus to be developed for itself. During the thirties this divinely created Afrikaner nation was politically divided, culturally disunited and wracked by severe class divisions. Afrikaner workers had little contact with the *volk*, displayed scant interest in its culture, and behaved economically and politically in class terms. The huge ''poor white problem'' was the most glaring manifestation of this division. Rapid ''denationalization'' of urban Afrikaners, particularly poor whites, disturbed all the ideologues. They agreed on the major theme of the period, the overriding need for unity and more particularly the need to win workers to Afrikaner Nationalism. Hankering after the ''unity'' of the Great Trek and the Republics, in terms of whose mythology all were farmers and united against external enemies, class divisions were seen as the product of ''imperialism'' and its alter ego, ''foreign'' capitalism. While Afrikaners had suffered under capitalism, the solution lay in improving their position in the *industrial* economy, to take control of South African capitalism itself and develop a *volkskapitalisme*. And, finally, this transformation of *kultuur*, classes and the economy was to be encapsulated in a Republic, freed from British political domination.

This common ideological ground incorporated a consensus on the role of the individual in national endeavour, and the relationship between political power and the economic struggle. Entrepreneurship was seen as the highest form of creative activity, provided the entrepreneur gave ''service'' in return for the just reward of profit. . . . Workers must work in return for a fair wage. The common good lies in common effort allowing those with ability to rise to their natural level. The state should provide the infrastructure for national development in South Africa, ensure the services needed by local entrepreneurs. Further, the state is the prime agent of economic struggle against ''imperialist'' domination of the economy guaranteeing not only the profits and labour needs of the entrepreneur, but employment for all members of the polity, which was of course defined to exclude blacks. In this vision the state is very clearly the instrument of the petty-bourgeois attack on monopoly control of the economy by ''imperialist'' interests, and the means for the transformation of its class position. Political power then becomes the *sine qua non* of the success of the economic struggle. The two are indivisible as the transformation of economic consciousness aimed at by the Bond is, in effect, a transformation of political consciousness, indeed a redefinition of nationalism itself.

The Bureaucracy and Accumulation

Colin Leys, *The Kenyan Bureaucracy* (1975)

The significance of the higher bureaucracy has been somewhat obscured in the literature on African underdevelopment, perhaps under the influence of Fanon (1965), who appeared to run together the idea of the higher bureaucracy and that of the bourgeoisie or would-be bourgeoisie when he wrote of a "bourgeoisie of the civil service". But the important point about higher echelons of the state apparatus is less their class origins or ambitions than their specific function in relation to the ruling alliance of classes and class-strata. Concentrating on the tendency of state officials to try to acquire property is apt to divert attention from this more important point.

This is not to say that the higher bureaucracy in Kenya, as in other African states, did not do what it could in the 1960s to acquire wealth. As the Ndegwa Commission put it in 1971, "it is understandable that civil servants should have taken their opportunities like other citizens". But it is questionable whether the thrust of this activity was to enable the higher bureaucracy to constitute themselves as a "fraction" of the bourgeoisie. For what the bureaucrat needs is income which can be obtained without leaving his bureau; and although there are always borderline cases the main aim of the bureaucrat must be to draw rent rather than look for profits.

This is why house-ownership was so important for the higher bureaucracy. It suited the salaried official because it did not involve any enterprise. From 1964 onwards there was an intense demand for real estate of all kinds in Nairobi, mainly as a result of the private foreign-investment boom. Property was reckoned at this time to yield 18 per cent per annum after tax, so that the capital outlay could be recovered in just over five years. Foreign missions and companies preferred not to own property, partly for political reasons, and were willing to pay extremely high rents, sometimes in the form of several years' advance payment on a lease. The civil servant, and to only a very slightly lesser extent, the executive of a large foreign company, was regarded as a good risk by the lending institutions, which in any case had the security of the property itself. Credit for house purchase therefore expanded dramatically. It was significant that the loans tended to be repaid at a faster rate than expected; this was because borrowers typically let the house, paid off the loan as quickly as possible out of the difference between their repayment commitment and the rent charged, and then took a new loan on a second house.

Obviously not all the new rentiers were bureaucrats, and certainly not all bureaucrats, even in the most senior cadres, were rentiers. Farming was also a favoured line of activity for them; there was a precedent established by the colonial administration, which had allowed British administrators to buy farms of up to 50 acres while still serving in Kenya, and it was a sphere in which management could be devolved on to a paid manager, and where loan funds were also available to senior officials. In the nature of the case there are no statistics on the question; but it does seem likely that there was a fairly clear distinction between the private interests of the salariat and those of other "middle-class" Kenyans in the 1960s, with the salariat predominantly involved in urban real estate and to a much lesser extent in activities calling for enterprise and management.

But in any case, although the evidence is mainly impressionistic, I think that the higher bureaucracy had by this time formed a definite conception of themselves, based on their professional function, and distinct from that of the entrepreneurial bourgeoisie. They did not on the whole see themselves as "businessmen" or future businessmen. It was clear to them that "modern" means of production were corporately owned, and that the important question was who controlled and staffed the corporations, and what relationship existed between them and the state. Working with expatriate experts and managers, senior officials and senior African company executives found themselves in effect collaborating in the framing of policies and in taking decisions which day by day defined more and more clearly the relations between the different modes of production in Kenya, and their own increasingly pivotal function in these relations. This is not to say that all the higher bureaucracy shared a single, comprehensive view of their situation, let alone one free from illusions. But there was a lot of recognized common ground, and as time passed their particular experiences gradually fused into a more general collective consciousness.

The decision at the end of the decade to appoint a commission of inquiry into the structure and remuneration of the public service (the Ndegwa Commission) threw some light on all this.

For one thing, it brought out the great importance of the private sector as a "reference group" for higher civil servants, both as a model of "efficiency" and as an index of the "market" rates of pay for administrative talent. The widespread feeling that the public service and the private-sector bureaucracy had fundamentally common tasks and interests was well expressed in the composition of the commission itself, which was drawn predominantly from the private sector, mainly from senior executives of multinational companies, under the chairmanship of the Governor of the Central Bank. And the submissions made to the commission by civil servants at its hearing were notable for their constant repetition of a single theme, namely that unless civil servants were paid as much as private-sector personnel, they would join the private sector. . . .

One submission, however, was concerned with wider issues, and deserves to be quoted for the glimpse it affords of the sort of ideas which animated a minority, but an energetic and powerful one, among the highest ranks of the civil service:

> We are too concerned with Trade Licensing and all that. . . . The Treasury must be staffed by personnel of sufficiently high calibre who can think on broader economic horizons. Commerce and Industry must also have capable officers who are bereft of narrow commercial or industrial interests. . . . The City of Nairobi has now achieved the status of an international centre and its future planned development must be approached in that light. . . . We must not spare our efforts in keeping Nairobi facilities etc. well above those of Johannesburg, our only competitor in this part of the world. . . .

In this scenario Kenya was destined for continued and dramatic growth as a regional centre for international capital, and the task of the higher bureaucracy was to plan and facilitate this process, acting partly through general policy, partly through statutory boards, and partly through direct partnership with foreign companies. For this it should be paid something near the "international market rate".

Whatever else may be said about this it is not the ideology of Fanon's "greedy little caste, avid and voracious, with the mind of a huckster, only too glad to accept the dividends that the former colonial power hands out to it . . . incapable of great ideas of inventiveness". This might or might not be fair to the petty-bourgeoisie, but what we have here is a glimpse of something much more self-confident and ambitious, with a clear consciousness of mission: the image of a bureaucratic *corps d'élite* controlling and dramatically expanding the "modern sector" in partnership with Western capital. The vision is chauvinist ("obtain the maximum possible amount of scarce world resources") and elitist; the peasants and workers, the great mass of the ordinary people, barely figure in the scenario, let alone as its central participants. They are at most the presumed ultimate beneficiaries of the dramatic changes to be wrought at the "centre" by their educated sons.

This was, to repeat, only one view among many. In the outlook of other senior bureaucrats, as well as of politicians, the peasantry featured more centrally, though nearly always, as objects of policy, not subjects, as in the rhetoric of "rural development", "African socialism", etc. The higher bureaucracy mediated between the capitalist and peasant modes of production in the political and economic tradition in which it had been trained. Few senior officials saw any discrepancy between the aims of official economic policy, their own social and economic position, and the interests of the majority in the countryside and in the towns. They believed that the government they served was, within limits, popularly chosen; at any rate no more popular alternative was available. They also considered that it was genuinely benevolent in intention, if not always in practice; it was not unconcerned about poverty, lack of opportunity, and similar problems, and it permitted civil servants a good deal of freedom in formulating programmes for productive investment and for providing social services.

This apparent harmony of aims, interests and functions was reinforced by the closeness of senior public servants – and Kenyan executives in foreign-owned companies – to their extended families in the countryside, a bond not yet too seriously weakened by social distance. All this did not mean that the Kenyan bureaucracy fulfilled less of a "comprador" function than in other parts of the third world; it meant only that this was perhaps less apparent, both to them and to the peasants and workers.

Michael Cohen, *Public Policy and Class Formation* (1974)

The decline of the party within the one-party state in Africa has emphasized the dominant position of the government as the source of public resources and opportunities. This dominance, illustrated by the many public policies implemented by the government, has been the determining factor in emerging patterns of social stratification. Although there has been much debate about the degree of social mobility in post-independence Africa, little attention has been paid to the role of national administrations in resource distribution. . . .

Discussion about social stratification in post-independence Africa often starts with erroneous assumptions about traditional society. In spite of important social differences such as castes or traditional authority structures, much of the "popular anthropology" used in analysis of Africa emphasizes communal egalitarianism and democratic patterns of authority. This "indigenous" pattern is supposed to continue after independence, with unlimited social mobility arising from free education, urban employment, and the rapid expansion of opportunities. Fluid paths of social mobility, added on to traditional egalitarianism, are supposed to obliterate social distinctions arising from political position or economic wealth. Therefore, lacking classes or obstacles to mobility, all the interests of the people are similar, if not identical. This analysis serves as a justification for the single party, which represents those common interests. Public policy reflects the united will of the people and is not understood as a source of conflict in itself.

These kinds of arguments are presented forcefully by political leaders in the Ivory Coast, where . . . the ideology of classlessness became official doctrine, asserting that no divergent interests existed in the society. A more recent statement on the subject, by Philippe Yace[1] at the 1970 PDCI Congress, shows how the party *now* seeks to affiliate itself with the common interests of recognized, divergent groups in the population. This statement is notable for its admission that distinct groups do exist and its use of that fact in justifying the existence of the single party:

> Social phenomena have created an African society of classes. In effect, the traditional families of chiefs had under their direct authority the villager populations; the large planters of the years 1925 to 1945 who were the base of the creation of the *Syndicat Agricole Africain* constituted a class; the businessmen and transporters who enjoy a certain ease were also a social category; the intellectuals of today of high competence. Directors of services or managers of enterprises also formed a distinct group. Thus, social classes have existed here. But for a long time they have been confused and mixed in a mode of life identical with the lower moral effects of the colonization. Their misery from the master and his requirements provoked a crisis of conscience which, concerning the Ivory Coast, led to the creation of the great movement of the *Rassemblement Démocratique Africain.*
>
> Together, the African nations are poor nations and their alienation is not from one social class to another, it is between a dominated country and a dominating country. The conclusion is that there are no divergent interests in our society. Consequently, everyone must unite to struggle together against poverty of individuals and the underdevelopment of countries. Guided by this desire for economic independence which becomes the primary objective, we wish to reject the theory of class struggle here and adopt rather a theory of the single party in the name of higher interests, including a scarcely differentiated society.

This argument, while urging the need for economic independence, cleverly ignores the fundamental differences between rulers and ruled. The interests of the two groups, reflecting their differential access to national resources and opportunities, are not identical, but sharply

---

[1] President of the National Assembly; former Secretary of the single party, the PDCI.

opposed. Contrary to the above statements, the ruling class and the government it controls operate as separate entities with specific interests, goals, and methods to achieve them. Diverting attention away from these differences "in the name of higher interests" – that is, the common African struggle for economic independence – is merely an attempt to confuse understanding of real sources of discontent and political opposition.

The data from the Ivory Coast suggest that the most important cleavage is between the rulers and ruled, all other intermediate distinctions being of lesser importance. This position contradicts the Marxist analysis of Samir Amin (1967) who describes three "classes" in the urban Ivory Coast: the masses, the middle class, and the ruling group of some 2000 heads of families. This classification, and particularly the breakdown which Amin presents: 150,000 workers, 10,000 in the middle class, and 10,000 at the top, is allegedly the same stratification system as existed in 1950. This assertion, and particularly his conclusion that the stratification system, like the economy, has experienced growth without development, ignores the importance of a two-stage process of rural–urban transfer of political and economic power, accompanied by the formation of a politico-administrative class. On the basis of the evidence contained in this study, a different definition of the class structure seems better suited to African conditions: *classes are categories of people sharing common political and economic interests arising from their access to public authorities and the public resources and opportunities which they control.* Other classifications ignore the fundamental *political origins of social mobility.* Distinctions between small shopkeepers, considered by Amin as "middle class" and "artisans", included among the "masses", are simply less important than the political and economic differences resulting from access to public authority. Although urban growth involves increasing differentiation and therefore Amin's distinctions may become relevant at later stages of development, there are presently only two important analytic classes which deserve recognition as politically and economically significant – the rulers and the ruled. . . .

The distribution of public resources and opportunities permits social mobility for only a small portion of the urban population. The Minister of Construction and Town-Planning has been emphasized as all-powerful in the distribution of urban land. Table 1 illustrates the pattern of distribution of all *concessions définitives* and *concessions provisoires* from 1960 to 1970, showing gradual percentage increases in the number of recipients serving in the administration or having administrative connections. In 1970 the percentage of all urban land allocated by the government to administrative-connected people had reached 49.9 per

Table 1   *Land concessions granted (percentage)*

	1960	1961	1962	1963	1964	1965	1966	1967	1968	1969	1970
French	12	20	22	6	8.5	7	5	3	3	2	0.2
Merchants	14	19	11	7	8.5	6	2	3	4	5	8.6
Planters	15	15	9	2	17	10	4	3	2	1	1
Administration	4	9	14	30	0	13	20	27	26	33	43.8
Personalities	8	5	13	12	8.5	9	5	6	9	6	6.1
Administration and personalities	12	14	27	42	8.5	22	25	33	35	39	49.9
Others	48	32	32	42	58	55	65	58	56	49	40.3
Concessions:	102	78	79	282	12	120	462	398	346	690	397

cent. This remarkable share of urban land has grown through the past decade with only one slump – in 1964, after the plots against the government and the ouster of the Minister of Construction and Town-Planning, Jerome Kacou Aoulou. Within the administrative share of land grants, the percentage of land allocated to ''personalities'' in the government, was highest in the first years after independence and then gradually decreased, permitting lower-level officials to have their opportunity to secure urban land. The category of ''administration'', not including ''personalities'', has grown steadily since 1964, suggesting a widening of the administrative class after the first years of consolidation after independence. Table 1 shows a decrease in the percentages of land allocated to Frenchmen, merchants, and planters during the same period. This pattern suggests the following conclusions: (1) the French are no longer in control of the process and are not to be granted public land; (2) the merchants are important, but have invested their money in other areas; and (3) the planters have lost both their early political power and their ability to successfully request urban resources. In comparison to these three categories, the ''others'' column has grown substantially, but due to the increases in the administrative share of land grants, it nevertheless is not experiencing continuous growth.

. . . In 1963 land was granted to the ten leading members of the government, including seven ministers. Most of these grants were in the elite residential quarter of Cocody. Between 1965 and 1968 Minister of Construction and Town-Planning Goly Kouassi granted plots to five other leading figures. One official, an important préfet and a member of the Bureau Politique, received land in Attiécoubé in 1960 and, in 1969, in Danga-Sud, a part of Cocody, indicating a rise in his status during the intervening years. Other people who received plots included the pastry chef and chauffeurs at the Presidential Palace, and some political leaders of African states with close ties to the Ivory Coast.

The above data suggest administrative and political control of urban land concessions, and this process turns out to be an extraordinarily sensitive measure of political status within the ruling class. Administrative appointments or promotions are often accompanied by approval of an individual's application for land in Abidjan. For example, the Chief of Protocol at the Ivory Coast Embassy in Paris was appointed to his position on 23 December 1969. On 8 December 1969 he had been granted a lot of 1800 sq. metres in the fashionable area of Cocody near the Centre Hospitalier Univérsitaire. These coincidences are frequent. More interesting, however, are the 1970 announcements of land grants to a series of former officials, all imprisoned after the 1963–4 plots, including three former ministers and a former député. What are the effects of this pattern on the mass of population? Although land allocation is officially justified by the government in terms of improvement criteria for urban land, the extraordinary share of land given to officials seems to defy any explanation other than that the members of the government take care of their own. The rest of the population, consequently, complains that there is a shortage of allotted land for housing construction, thereby keeping rents high and lowering the housing standards of most families. The government tends to give large plots to members of the administration, usually the only people who can afford to improve them. Many families are forced to live in bidonvilles and other crowded conditions on land not yet claimed by the government for lotissement and subsequent distribution. Some residents of bidonvilles remarked that their landlords are in fact members of the administration, so their housing is relatively secure even though the land is not officially owned by anyone.

A large portion of urban land, therefore, is effectively controlled by members of the administrative class, and what they do not control they influence through the creation of market conditions which make life increasingly difficult for the mass of population.

The Military and Accumulation

Billy Dudley, *The Social Characteristics of the Nigerian Military* (1973)[1]

As the ultimate instrument of coercion, the army was not only the institution over which the colonial administration was last to relinquish formal control, it was also the last to be "indigenized". At the time of independence in 1960, only 17 per cent of the officer corps of the army was Nigerian. The top command was almost exclusively British. This slow rate of indigenization is in sharp contrast to what obtained either in the police force or in the public services, both of which at that period had been more or less completely indigenized with Nigerians holding the top offices. One result of the slow rate of "localization" of the personnel of the army was to place it at the lower end of prestige rankings of occupations by Nigerians. As an occupation, the army offered fewer and less attractive prospects to Nigerians than the other services or professions. It was therefore the last choice for most Nigerians and those with any ability or academic qualifications avoided it. Those who sought recruitment into the army therefore came to be those who were unable to obtain or were incapable of obtaining alternative forms of employment. Given the educational differential between the North and the South, it was therefore to be expected that most of those who sought a career in the army would be from the North, and even here, the majority came from the riverain areas – the so-called Middle Belt – of the North since in the "far" or "dry" North, the Hausa/Fulani/Kanuri areas, the barely literate found a ready employment in the Native Authorities (NA). In the East, particularly the Ibo areas, where there was population pressure on resources and hence enforced migration in search of employment, a number of Ibo men also entered the army, but since they were, in the main, better educated than their Northern counterparts, most joined the service sections of the army. The outcome of this set of factors was that Nigeria inherited an army whose rank-and-file was dominated largely by men from the North. When the January 1966 military coup took place Northerners formed some 80 per cent of the "other ranks" and of these, about two-thirds were drawn from the riverain North; while Easterners predominated among the "tradesmen".

---

[1] Much of the empirical data presented here are drawn from Luckham (1971).

When, however, one turns to the commissioned ranks, one finds a reverse distribution. By 1960 when Nigeria became a sovereign state, 83 per cent of the serving officers in the Nigerian Army were British. Two years later, this had fallen to 11 per cent, and by 1966 the percentage of British officers serving in the army had fallen to zero. This change in the composition of the officer corps was a product of two main factors. The first was the prospect of independence which in the mid-fifties encouraged the political leaders to demand that Nigerians should increasingly replace British officers. The second was the independence of Ghana in 1957 which made the breakup of the old Royal West African Frontier Force and the setting up of separate national armies in the various territories imperative.

As the prospect of independence loomed and it became both desirable and necessary to have Nigerians among the commissioned ranks, the first of them had to be found among those who had been promoted from the ranks to positions of non-commissioned officers. Of the seven men to be commissioned between 1949 and 1954 who had risen to the rank of colonel and above by 1965, 71 per cent (5) had been NCOs while 29 per cent (2) held direct commissions, both of whom came from the North. By 1955/6 and 1959/60, the percentage of those commissioned in those years who had been NCOs had fallen to 38 per cent and 27 per cent respectively, falling to zero for those recruited between 1963/4. Thus, as localization of the officer corps opened new career opportunities for Nigerians in the military, better educated men took to the military as a profession. Most of them had had a secondary education and a majority came from the East. By 1962 when a regional quota system was introduced, of the 157 Nigerians who had got their commissions, roughly two-thirds were from the Eastern Region of the Federation. The rationale and effect of the quota system are perhaps best shown by contrasting the distribution by rank and region of those recruited into the commissioned ranks between 1955 and 1960 on the one hand, and 1963/4 on the other. Of those recruited in the former period, who by 1965 had risen to the ranks of Lieutenant-Colonel and Major, 36 per cent of the former category (Lt-Col.) were from the East, 14 per cent from the West, 21 per cent from the North and 29 per cent from the Mid-West. Among the rank of Major, 66 per cent came from the East, 22 per cent from the West and 6 per cent from the North and Mid-West respectively. In contrast, of the 163 commissioned in 1963/4 and who were Second-Lieutenants by 1965, 25 per cent were from the East, 19 per cent came from the West, 42 per cent from the North and 14 per cent from the Mid-West.

From the circumstances of its origin, the rate of its career liberalization and the effects of the quota system emerged a pyramidally structured army with four principal layers. At the top of the pyramid, the level of Colonel and above, Westerners, mainly Yoruba, predominated. They were followed in the second layer of the hierarchy of command by Easterners, who were mainly Ibo, occupying the ranks of Lieutenant-Colonel and Major. At the bottom of the command hierarchy, in the ranks between Second-Lieutenant and Captain, came the Northerners, in the main of ''Middle Belt'' origin, the same group who also filled the base of the hierarchy, the rank-and-file. From this relative ''fit'' between strata and region – and hence of party orientation – we might expect two possible outcomes should the military be unable to maintain its organizational boundaries: first, that the military was unlikely to be capable of acting collectively as an institutional whole; second, and conversely, that the different strata would react differently to the stimuli making for boundary fragmentation. Whether, however, the military would be able to maintain its boundaries or not would depend on the cleavage – stratificational pattern of the military and the impulses from the surrounding environment – principally the nature and structure of political and economic conflict found in the society.

Sources of cleavage and environmental inputs as factors of boundary fragmentation have to be counterbalanced against possible cohesive forces such as institutionalized norms of authority and command and the extent or degree of professionalism. The degree of professionalism can be indicated by contrasting the experience levels (measured in terms of years of service in a given institution for instance) of members of the officer corps of the armed forces with equivalent ranks from the civil bureaucracy (federal) and the police. By the end of 1965 some 80 per cent of the officer corps of the military had not had more than 4 years' experience, in contrast to the public service where some 41 per cent had had between 5 and 7 years. With the police, roughly 36 per cent had had a service experience of not less than 9 years. The contrasts become more pronounced, particularly between the military and the public service, when other variables such as age and education are considered. In terms of age, where 62 per cent of the military fall within the age range 20–24 years, the comparable figure for the civil bureaucracy and the police is 1 per cent. Educationally, while 58 per cent of the administrative class of the federal public service had a university degree, 66 per cent of the military (combat and non-combat officers) had no more than a secondary school education before being commissioned. In contrast to both, most of the police officers with the rank of Assistant Superintendent of Police and above (71 per cent) rose from the ranks. In the army (all officers) and the police (ASP and above) only 13 per cent and 3 per cent respectively had a university education.

These comparisons point to one possible source of cleavage within the military, arising from the educational differential between the top command and the medium and lowest parts of the command hierarchy. While the top command (Colonel and above) have been recruited from the ranks with no more than a primary school education, their subordinates have been, in the main, men with a secondary education who have been directly commissioned. The cleavage potential of the educational differentiation between the various levels of the commissioned ranks of the military becomes more salient when related to promotional opportunities. The modal length of period of promotion from the rank of Captain to Major for those commissioned between 1949 and 1954, for example, was 64 months. In the later half of the 'fifties, however, as opportunities became more open for Nigerians in the army, the promotional period became shorter. For those commissioned between 1958 and 1961, the average promotional period from Lieutenant to Captain was 22 months and that for Captain to Major was roughly 28 months. Given the size of the military, it was obvious there was a limit to such rapid promotions. By 1965 there was in operation what was more or less a moratorium on promotions. This meant little opportunity for upward mobility for those commissioned during these periods, the outcome of which was a sense of relative deprivation among these later groups, a relative deprivation which was heightened by the fact that they tended to be better educated than their superiors. The problem was made no less poignant by the fact that some of those feeling so deprived had been not only school-mates but even classmates of their superiors, but also had overlapped with them at the military academies to which they were sent. Thus, while some in the upper command ranks may have been liked for their personal qualities, not many commanded the respect of their subordinates. . . .

The stresses deriving from differentials in age and education, relative occupational mobility and career opportunities and regional differences are not necessarily additive. Their respective salience may in fact be near negative if mediated by institutionalized norms and values. Much of this is a function of the socialization processes to which military personnel have been subjected. And for the Nigerian Army, this meant British training. Thus, all those who had attained the rank of Captain and above in 1965 had at some stage or the other been through either Sandhurst or the cadet officers school at Mons or Eaton Hall. Of the whole commissioned complement of 514 officers, only some 19 per cent had had their military training outside Britain. The proportion of those trained outside the Commonwealth is even smaller – in fact negligible. The effect of this form of socialization has been to inculcate in the military the organizational norms and values associated with the British Army with its emphasis on respect for duly constituted authority, initiative, an *esprit de corps* and behaviour becoming an "officer and a gentleman".

Michel Martin, *Corporate Interests and Military Rule* (1973)

"Corporate expectations" are a key variable in explaining military interventions in Africa. Coups can be seen both as a means of defending corporate military interests – or of satisfying corporate expectation – and as a means of enhancing the corporate standing of the army. The latter normally occurs through the army acquiring a greater share of national resources, in the form of increases in pay and in the share of the budget. Acquiring political power provides the most effective means of doing so as the rapid post-coup increase in the size and spending of the armed forces in Zaïre, Nigeria and other states indicates. Censure is pointless in this context; it is more important to consider the effects on development, from two perspectives: the direct developmental consequences of a given distribution of public spending; and its political implications.

Developmentally, the satisfaction of the army's corporate interests is expensive and no gains in production arise; rather resources must be withdrawn from other sectors. Levels of military spending in Africa are only a little less than those on education, and many times more than those on health. As a proportion of the budget, they range from Niger's 11 per cent to Mali's 21 per cent. The cost of each member of the army is higher than in other underdeveloped regions – such as South-East Asia – which have larger and more active armies: the small francophone states were spending $3000 a year by 1970, and the Central African Republic $6000, on each soldier. Yet it is unlikely that these costly armies could ever be used in combat: they are hardly logistically capable of such use.

These high levels of spending reflect not developmental needs but the tendency of the African military to satisfy their corporate expectations. Data on salary levels, for example, shows considerable variations but one common feature: the privileged position of the army (e.g. Lee, 1969: 89–97). Even a private can sometimes earn ten times the minimum unskilled wage, in addition to what he receives in kind. To this must be added hidden spending, often referred to by the term "corruption", though the moral overtones of this are misleading. Corruption often serves as a means of enhancing the corporate status of the army in the eyes of the community, which tends to judge individuals by the services they can perform, or their visible standard of living, however achieved.

The satisfaction of corporate tendencies not only consolidates the standing of the army but also allows individual self-enrichment. Many officers have bought land or properties which they offer at high rents or with which they speculate; Kamitatu (1971) cites the cases of the Zaïrian chief of staff, Col. Njufula, who owned four blocks of flats, and the commander of President Mobutu's bodyguard, owner of several properties.

Such accumulation can undermine development policy by helping to crystallize rival factions whose conflicts over access to and distribution of public wealth can resemble class conflict (cf. *Turner*, below). In such conflicts the army has a double advantage in its combination of military and political strength. To the extent that development implies the equalization of opportunity to share in national resources, economic or social, the army must sooner or later oppose those social forces which support, or at least benefit from, such development, and reject reforms which might redistribute authority or resources to those who seek to restrain their corporatist tendencies.

Thus once in power the military appear to confine themselves to policies designed at the most to increase the gains arising within existing structures. This produces a sort of collusion or merging between the interests of the officer corps and those of the national bourgeoisie. Other classes then identify the military with the national bourgeoisie, which does not oppose social and economic reforms in so far as their interests are not threatened. Similarly, although the African military do not have a well-defined social origin (unlike Latin American or Middle Eastern armies), it identifies through its social and political gains with the privileged social strata. It constitutes a sort of ''shadow elite'' in relation to the national bourgeoisie (which does not imply there are no internal divisions based on rank, types of leadership, or material interests). But this identification is readily destroyed, may indeed be only apparent, for it confuses class and corporate interests; such interests are sometimes symmetrical, sometimes divergent. Accumulation by the national middle class is at least productive, since it often involves developmental investment; the basis for the existence and reproduction of this bourgeoisie lies essentially in such entrepreneurial capacity. Military accumulation by contrast is not developmental: they do not invest, nor does their reproduction depend on investment, the character of the army being largely bureaucratic.

Terisa Turner, *State Power and the Nigerian Military* (Williams and Turner, in Dunn, 1978)

In 1966 the Nigerian Army officer corps overthrew the civilian government, and after a brief period of rule by largely Igbo officers, installed Lt.-Col. Gowon as head of state. The assumption of state power by military commanders and top civil servants did not eliminate the politics of resource allocation. It simply changed its form. Access to opportunities was now controlled, not by elected politicians with constituents to reward, but by military governors, permanent secretaries, army officers and civilian and military commissioners. At both federal and state levels, resources were allocated by a clique of insiders. Far more resources passed through fewer hands, and were allocated to a narrower clientele.

The state controls access to oil supplies and lucrative contracts. The state itself, and its civil servants, thus become the focus of a mass of distributive conflicts. Bureaucrats act as "gatekeepers", monitoring the outflow of oil and agricultural exports and the inflow of imported goods and services. As they open and close the gate, they can exact a toll on the exchange. Foreign buyers and sellers secure supplies and contracts by gaining the favour of state officials. "Commercial triangles" are formed of private Nigerian middlemen, state "gatekeepers" or compradores, and representatives of foreign firms. Foreign businessmen come to Nigeria to sell their firms' products. They hire Nigerians to act as go-betweens with state officials. If the official who has jurisdiction over the particular matter awards a contract, the Nigerian middleman may reward him appropriately. The "triangle" manifests itself in many forms, since the state issues a variety of dispensations, oil sales, import and foreign exchange permits, and contracts. Alternatively the private Nigerian middleman is simply cut out and the "triangle" is replaced by a bilateral relationship between the state comprador and foreign firm.

Commercial triangles are exemplified by the billion naira cement racket, which clogged Lagos roadsteads with ships, without solving the cement shortage. Increased government and private spending created a massive shortage of cement. Under the authority of the permanent secretary in the Ministry of Defence, and the Defence Commissioner, General Gowon himself, contracts were freely awarded to overseas suppliers operating through the small ring of local middlemen. Sixteen million tons of cement, far in excess of Nigeria's import capacity was contracted and paid for by the Ministry of Defence alone. Much of the world's surplus shipping was then loaded with cement and anchored off Lagos at the expense of the Nigerian government. Military arms purchasers established bilateral relations with suppliers: ''To be an army officer means to be the granter of licences for deliveries to the armed forces.'' Bilateral relations were formed between the Ministry of Mines and Power and the largest oil producer in Nigeria, Shell–BP, which was assured access to supplies of oil on favourable terms. Rival US and European oil companies sought allies within the state opposed to the special relationship between the oil ministry and Shell–BP.

The expansion of the direct economic activities of the state increased the scope for senior officials to deal directly with foreign firms, at the expense of private middlemen, and their bureaucratic collaborators. Businessmen resented state officials who had privileged access to information about, and to the patronage of, foreign companies selling shares to comply with the Indigenization Decree. They similarly opposed the purchase of firms or shares by state governments at the expense of out-of-state businessmen. State involvement in commerce and manufacturing threatens to pre-empt the intermediary position which Nigerian businessmen occupy between foreign capital and the local state or consumer market. The full rhetoric of unfettered private enterprise was marshalled by the Chamber of Commerce against state capitalist usurpation of their middlemen's activities.

The dynamics of resource allocation generated divisive conflicts. Military and bureaucratic officials competed to control the allocation of revenue, jobs and contracts. Middlemen competed for access to state officials. Foreign corporations competed by proxy through their local agents. The operations of commercial ''triangles'' perpetuated nepotism, tribalism and statism. The clique of ''insiders'' swelled. The form of commercial relations led towards closed government. The more triangles formed around a particular contract, the more competition; the fewer triangles involved, the easier the settlement. The shift towards bilateral deals further increased the premium on secrecy and the concentration of decision-making.

The public resented the increasing corruption and incompetence of government. Politicians, businessmen and academics resented the appropriation of opportunities by small cliques of military rulers and ''super'' permanent secretaries. They saw themselves as qualified and competent to share in the government of Nigeria. Army officers, including those who had brought the regime to power, resented their exclusion from decision-making and opportunities. In 1974 civilian rule was postponed indefinitely. The rejection of civilian rule would perpetuate the domination of, and appropriation of, resources by a small clique of military and bureaucratic rulers and their local and foreign associates. Army officers decided to remove their seniors.

The Bourgeoisie and the State

Gavin Williams, *Class Relations in the Nigerian Political Economy* (1976)

Decolonization altered the patterns of participation and influence in public affairs. Power was effectively devolved to the bourgeoisie who commanded the skills and resources necessary to determine public policy at the regional and national levels. The scale of the resources required to take advantage of the new opportunities for political participation was well beyond the reach of the petty traders and contractors who had previously been able to exercise some influence with the customary authorities at the local level. Allocation of resources at the local level was now determined by the interests of the ruling party at the regional, and ultimately the Federal, level. Thus local influence depended on patronage relations with regional politicians, and the imposition of military rule deprived people of even these limited opportunities for patronage.

Decolonization thus paved the way for capitalist development in Nigeria. But the development of capitalism consolidated rather than undermined foreign economic domination. It depended on the increasing exploitation of export-crop farmers, and restricted the development of peasant and petty commodity production. The transition from the colonial to the neocolonial political economy both required and led to changes in class relations, and generated contradictions that could not be resolved within the framework of representative political institutions.

Expatriate domination of investment opportunities, thanks to their superior access to credit, supplies, and the technology and managerial skills necessary to industrial production, inhibits the accumulation and reinvestment of capital by indigenous entrepreneurs who lack the resources necessary to compete with vertically integrated multinational corporations. Consequently, indigenous entrepreneurs became "compradores", i.e. intermediaries between foreign interests and the indigenous polity and economy, and/or turned to the state as a source of both capital and contracts. Lucrative profits have accrued to those able to establish control of monopolistic niches in the distribution of commodities, rather than to those who have organized their production most efficiently. Consequently, politics and the favour of foreign companies, itself a product of political influence, became the primary sources of capital accumulation by Nigerians. Initially, this capital was accumulated from the surplus value appropriated from the peasants by the Marketing Boards. Tariff protection and monopolistic distributive arrangements for imported and factory-produced goods increased profits at the expense of consumers. Professionals, bureaucrats, and merchants used state power to establish themselves as a bourgeoisie.

Nigerian governments perpetuated the highly inegalitarian colonial administrative, salary, and tax structure, with its complex of fringe benefits (car and child allowances, health facilities and housing, subsidies available to the earners of high salaries). The state regulated expatriate quotas to encourage foreign companies to employ Nigerian managerial and professional staff. The lucrative salaries offered in the private sector and, by necessity, offered for professional and technical staff in the public sector led administrators, followed by academics, to demand equivalent salaries for themselves. . . .

The bourgeoisie sought to establish areas of economic activity in which they would be protected from foreign competition, or in which foreign companies would have to operate through them. Initially this was provided by the withdrawal of foreign companies from retail trading, by the exclusion of foreigners from land ownership, and by the established position of Nigerian entrepreneurs in such fields as produce and passenger transport. This did not resolve the conflict between indigenous businessmen and multinational corporations over the terms of their relationship. The initial focus of African aspirations has been to exclude Lebanese merchants from their position in the distributive trades and certain assembly industries. The 1972 Indigenization Decree reserved large areas of economic activity for indigenous businessmen, including advertising and public relations, pools, assembly of radios, record-players, etc., blending and bottling of alcoholic drinks, block and brick making, bread making, clearing and forwarding, and retail trading. Multinational companies had only peripheral interests in these fields, in which Lebanese merchants were well-represented. Local participation in equity shares and a minimum size are required for foreign firms operating in a wider range of activities. Finance for indigenous participation in foreign industries or takeover of them has been provided by banks, now 40 per cent government-owned, and required to allocate at least 40 per cent of their loans to Nigerian businessmen, by the legally and illegally gained wealth of the state-sponsored bourgeoisie, and by employees of foreign companies who have been lent money by firms to buy their shares at favourable prices. Civil servants are reported to be among the main recipients of bank loans for share purchases. Thus managers and bureaucrats have assimilated themselves to Nigeria's capitalist class. Nigeria has expanded and consolidated its capitalist class. Geographically, its operations and the operations of the businesses which have been taken over are concentrated in Lagos and Kano, the major areas of industrial expansion. Increasing access to money and opportunities for the few will strengthen their ability to deny opportunities to the many. Multinational corporations have taken a leading role in sponsoring the acquisition of shares by Nigerians, and establishing on a firmer footing their alliance with Nigerian capitalism. This does not preclude future conflict over the relative share of foreign and indigenous capitalists in the profits of the neocolonial economy.

The ambiguous position of the bourgeoisie within the neocolonial political economy is expressed in its ideological ambiguity. Its nationalism is the outcome of its wish to appropriate resources back from the foreigner; its commitment to foreign investment is the outcome of its concrete dependence on the neocolonial political economy. National unity and reconciliation express its ambition to act as an hegemonic class, providing moral and political leadership at the national level and within the international political arena; its tribalism is the outcome of its lack of control of the productive resources of the economy and hence of the competition among the bourgeoisie for favoured access to scarce resources, and the need to manipulate particularistic interests and sentiments among the poor to maintain the bourgeoisie's political domination. The bourgeoisie lacks the commitments of a religious, socialist, or nationalist character of the rationalizing, capital-accumulating, surplus-expropriating classes which directed the industrialization of Britain, Russia, Germany, and Japan. Perhaps it is this which lies behind the repeated call for a "national ideology" which seeks to subordinate the energies of the people behind a single national goal. In fact, the Nigerian bourgeoisie do have an ideology, in the sense of a theoretical legitimation of the status quo. It is expressed in the concept of "development", which is "that which we are all in favour of", and given statistical respectability in figures measuring the growth of commodity production, particularly production by capitalist mining and manufacturing industries. The demand for Nigerianization gives it a nationalist colouring. But this demand falls short of the demand for expropriation of foreign capitalists on whom the Nigerian bourgeoisie remains dependent. In this way, the ideology of "national development" presents the bourgeoisie's image of itself as providing national leadership in the public interest, with its contradictions abolished and its immediate material interests preserved. What the bourgeoisie lacks, to use Mannheim's terminology, is a Utopia, a set of ideas to inspire the transformation of the existing order and the liberation of human capacities.

Colin Leys, *Indigenous Accumulation in Kenya* (1978)

While several aspects of Kenya's development may at first sight seem to be illuminated by means of the concepts of underdevelopment and dependency, the process of domestic capital accumulation since the early 1940s does not lend itself so easily to analysis from this perspective. This is particularly apparent in the period since independence. Once the uncertainties of the transition had been resolved, the high overall growth rate of the 1940s and '50s was resumed. . . . The relatively high and sustained level of capital accumulation was accompanied by an extension of capitalist relations of production. A growing proportion of households came to depend on wage labour, and the reproduction of labour power was increasingly commercialised. . . . In manufacturing, labour productivity rose, though in agriculture productivity appeared to stagnate in the 1970s, after rising in the 1960s. These developments attracted and were in turn reinforced by a net inflow of capital from abroad, . . . while the level of foreign indebtedness remained low, and was still further reduced in real terms by inflation.

What is the explanation of the Kenyan growth process, and what significance does the explanation have for the prospects of capitalist development in Kenya in the future?

Kenya has not been in receipt of exceptionally large flows of official capital or technical assistance, nor has it had any exceptional growth of primary commodity exports or, in general, any major advantage in terms of endowment or location over neighbouring countries. Nor, on the other hand, has its overall rate of growth been due to exceptional growth rates in one or two "enclaves" sectors unrelated to the rest of the economy. While some marked geographic and sectoral imbalances exist, growth has been more or less equally pronounced both in agriculture and outside it, in small- and large-scale farming, in manufacturing and in commerce, in the private and the public sectors, etc.

A more plausible explanation of Kenyan economic growth since the 1940s lies, rather, in the specific social relations of production developed before, during and since the colonial period, and particularly – but in no sense exclusively, as will be seen – in the key role of the class formed out of the process of indigenous capital accumulation.

In a series of important but largely unpublished papers, Michael Cowen (see e.g. Cowen, 1979) has established that before the colonisation of East Africa the relations of production existing in what is now Central Province – the most populous, productive and economically strategic area of Kenya – determined the formation of a class of accumulators of the principal means of production – land and livestock – through migration on to new land, raiding, and long-distance trade. The tendency of this accumulation, which was in large measure "primitive", was to concentrate the means of production more and more in a few hands, excluding others from access to them, a tendency which those threatened with exclusion could overcome, by and large, only through migrating themselves (usually as labourers clearing land for others in return for stock and a share of the new land). Colonial settlement closed off further migration, by alienating land to white settlers. On the other hand the colonial state launched some, at least, of the precolonial accumulators on a fresh path of accumulation by appointing them "chiefs" who were enabled to loot their new "subjects" by means of unregulated taxes and fines, and to further accumulate land within the now restricted African land areas by engaging in costly litigation.

The transformation of this class into a class of agrarian capitalists (appropriating surplus value through wage labour proper) was, however, thwarted by (a) the settler farmers' monopoly, enforced by the colonial state, over most of the available African surplus labour; (b) parallel settler monopolies over the production of most of the agricultural commodities (notably coffee) or over markets (e.g. for maize), on which capitalist agriculture could be based; (c) the intervention of international capital – as opposed to small and medium settler capital – in commodity production, either through plantation production (in the case of wattle), or through permitting the still existing mass of smallholders to produce commodities under the supervision of large-scale foreign capital. This permitted the smallholdings to survive as units of production (a situation confirmed by the universal issue of freehold land titles from 1955 onwards) and deprived the indigenous class of capital of the opportunity to further enlarge their landholdings and exploit the labour of those who became proletarianised.

Meanwhile, the route of entry to the "accumulator" class, and the basis of further accumulation for the individual agents within it, had necessarily shifted from the old forms of primitive accumulation to wage income, increasingly based on education; and to the sphere of commerce, the avenues for which were gradually widened by political pressure brought to bear on the colonial state by new organizations such as the Kikuyu Central Association and the Kavirondo Taxpayers Welfare Association – whose ascendancy also signified the displacement of the older, "primitive" accumulating element within the indigenous class of capital, by the "modern", educated element. Although these efforts preserved and even permitted some enlargement of the accumulated capital of this class, it was wholly confined to the sphere of circulation and hence to the limited share of surplus value to be obtained there, in face of unremitting pressure both from Asian merchant capital and from the growing weight of international productive capital.

By the end of the Second World War a direct challenge to this limitation was finally articulated by the militant wing of the Kenya African Union, leading in 1952 to the declaration of emergency. Meanwhile international capital had moved into Kenya on a much larger scale, and in the context of Britain's interest in expanding colonial commodity production as a contribution to the solution of the dollar shortage, the colonial state also began to dismantle the barriers to indigenous capital accumulation. African exclusion from the "white highlands", the ban on African-grown coffee, restriction on credit for Africans and opposition to the issue of individual land titles all disappeared. Finally, white settler capital was largely removed from the configuration of class forces by the independence settlement agreed in outline in 1961. . . .

Contemporary Accumulation

When negotiations for independence were begun in 1960, the economic and political weight of the indigenous owners of capital was already decisive.

The often-cited expansion of smallholder farm output that occurred in the decade 1955 to 1964, for example – from K£5.2m to K£14.0m per annum – is remarkable not least for the capital investment it implies, especially when we consider that down to 1964 the cumulative total of government and bank lending to smallholders was only K£1.7m. The size distribution of the output tells the same story. In Murang'a in 1970–1 14 per cent of the members of one coffee co-operative studied by Lamb (1974) (i.e. all the growers of a given area in Kikuyu country) supplied 64 per cent of the crop, and in the same season in two tea-growing locations of the neighbouring Nyeri District, studied by Cowen, 20 per cent of the growers supplied 55 per cent of the crop (in 1965 20 per cent had supplied 64 per cent of the total; in other words, the initial impetus came even more markedly from those with the capital to make the necessary investment and pay the necessary wages). Similar reflections are prompted by the fact that from 1959, when Africans became eligible to buy land in the former "white highlands", down to 1970, at least K£7m and perhaps as much as K£10m of privately-owned capital, mostly from Central Province, was invested in large-farm purchase. Bearing in mind the degree of concentration involved in both the expansion of smallholder production, and the purchase of large farms from white settlers, these figures serve as useful if very rough indicators of the scale of accumulation which had been achieved during the colonial

period by the indigenous class of capital, in spite of massive competition
from foreign capital of all kinds, and with very little support from the
colonial state.

Besides the scale of their capital, the indigenous class of capital had a
further highly significant asset. It was heavily concentrated in not only
the largest ethnic group – composing with closely related neighbouring
people about 25 per cent of the total population, but also in the economic
and political centre of the country. Combined with its strong
representation in the state apparatus (due to its heavy investment in
education) the indigenous bourgeoisie was exceptionally well placed to
convert its natural dominance in the nationalist movement into a
position of strategic control over the postcolonial political realignments
needed for the next phase of accumulation. By mid-1966 – 2½ years
after independence – these realignments had been completed and the
framework of an effective ''power bloc'' under the hegemony of the
Kikuyu bourgeoisie was clearly established.

From this time onward the state apparatus superintended a series of
measures which rapidly enlarged the sphere and the rate of indigenous
capital accumulation. The principal measures used were trade licensing,
state monopolies, state finance capital, state direction of private credit,
and state capitalist enterprise. Their effects may be seen in a broadly
sequential pattern whereby in one sector after another, according to the
relative difficulties posed for indigenous capital by varying technical and
capital requirements, African capital became first significant, and then
preponderant. The movement into the former ''white highlands'' began
in 1959. By 1977 it was estimated that only 5 per cent of the mixed farm
area within the former white highlands remained in expatriate hands.
The transfer to African owners of expatriate-owned ranches and coffee
plantations was well advanced and the transfer of the much more
concentrated tea estates was no longer impossible to envisage. By 1974
the Development Plan claimed that most ''small commercial firms have
already been transferred to citizen ownership'' and that ''larger and
more intricate'' firms still in foreign hands would be Kenyanized by
1978: by 1977 the evidence suggested that this target would be
substantially met. The transfer to African capital of urban real estate,
already well advanced by 1976, received a fresh impetus from the
sudden rise in liquidity due to the exceptional coffee sales of that year,
and led to a rush to purchase the remaining foreign-owned large office
blocks in central Nairobi, suggesting that the complete African
occupation of this sector was no longer a distant prospect. Passenger
road transportation was largely in African hands by 1977 as were tour
companies, laundries and dry cleaning, and a rapidly growing share of
the hotel and restaurant sectors. Sectors still substantially in foreign or at

least non-African hands were those still protected against African entry by a combination of technical and capital barriers, often reinforced by a degree of monopoly: e.g. construction, financial services, insurance, mining, and manufacturing. But in each of these fields a significant degree of penetration had already begun, and in manufacturing, the most important of all, a new phase of African entry seemed to be beginning by 1977. . . .

In commerce, returns are quick and the capital outlay is relatively small, but in the long run profits are liable to be forced down by competition from other commercial capitals and by industrial capital, in relation to a share of surplus value the total of which is determined at the point of production. In Kenya, this was experienced by the leading African capitalists as a rapidly narrowing scope for further displacement of foreign capital from the sphere of circulation, coupled with a growing awareness of the limitations of that sphere. . . . It was interesting to note how the shift from the sphere of circulation to that of production was reflected in a shift of class imagery, as evidenced in several interviews: ''People think they must be a manufacturer to be someone. If you have a beer distributorship, that's nothing to be.''

It would be misleading to say that by 1977 African capital was moving primarily into manufacturing production. There was still considerable scope for movement in the sphere of distribution and services. But the movement into manufacturing was under way, with the following specific features:

(a) Capital as being *concentrated* in sufficient volume and in *appropriate forms* for industrial investment. Five specific forms were in evidence. Most common (especially in new investments), and perhaps in the long run most significant, there were *syndicates*, usually of 4 or 5 individual capitalists, formed to make one or sometimes several investments in manufacture, usually taking 25–30 per cent of the equity together with a state investment corporation and a foreign manufacturer, but sometimes with a controlling interest. Second, *co-operatives* of various types had begun investing in manufacturing; usually these were agricultural (producer) co-operatives, moving into a project connected with farming (e.g. to produce fertilizer) but other types of co-operative were also increasingly moving along the now familiar path from agricultural through commercial to manufacturing investment. Third, there were *mass investment companies*, of which the prototype was Gema Holdings Corporation, an offshoot of the Gikuyu, Embu and Meru Association, and controlled by a group of leading Kikuyu capitalists. Other ''ethnic'' investment companies were planning to follow this example. An earlier example, with different origins, was the ICDC Investment Company, an offshoot of the state-owned Industrial and Commercial Development

Corporation. Set up in 1967 with initial funding and continuing management provided by the parent ICDC, its shares were sold to Africans. Fourth, a variety of *state economic institutions* had begun to act as industrial investment companies, in addition to the longer-established investment corporations. This was particularly true of some of the large number of agricultural parastatals, which were beginning to invest in the processing of agricultural commodities. Finally, there had been a notable growth of *merchant and industrial banks*, some of them tapping new sources of foreign capital. This was true of the state-owned Industrial Development Bank, established in 1973, which by 1976 had increased its original capital by about 200 per cent by drawing on World Bank funds.

(b) Skills and knowhow had been accumulated. One of the most striking changes in Kenya since 1971 was the coming "on stream" of a new generation of technically trained state economic functionaries. The Industrial Development Bank staff were a leading example of this, combining advanced technical (economic and accounting) qualifications with considerable specialised experience, but the pattern was being repeated in other organizations. Some of these new economic functionaries were themselves spearheading the entry of private African capital into manufacturing, under the freedom given to officials in 1971 to engage in private enterprise. The financial controller of one large parastatal had, thus, also established three manufacturing companies in which he had a controlling interest, the largest of which had assets worth K£1.7m. . . .

Formation of an Indigenous Bourgeoisie

To examine properly the process of class formation associated with indigenous capital accumulation would be far beyond the scope of this paper. Here we can simply note certain rather obvious indicators of this process.

(a) An increasingly evident differentiation during the decade in which the accumulators had spread out of their original base in circulation. Distinct fractions of African capital – primarily merchant, agricultural and industrial, but also financial (e.g. stockbroking) and rentier (e.g. real estate), and within the first two of these, large-scale/modern and small or medium scale/archaic – had begun to crystallize around various recurrent issues: for instance, the scope and level of protection afforded to manufacturing (merchant capital favouring more limited protection), wage controls (more important for smaller, more archaic forms of capital, with lower levels of productivity). Besides the formation of these class fractions the formation of certain significant strata (determined by political and ideological practices) could also be discerned: in particular, a small, older political stratum, heavily involved in the various forms of modern primitive accumulation, increasingly giving way to a younger generation more equipped to dispense with primitive forms of accumulation and oriented strongly towards fully capitalist valorization of the inherited family capital: the higher-level "straddlers", i.e. holders of salaried positions, state, parastatal and corporate, using their salaries and their privileged access to credit to create independent basis of accumulation: and a stratum of low-profile entrepreneurs, in the classical mould, with sometimes surprisingly large capitals invested in relatively advanced fields of production, a stratum destined to assume greater importance through the long-run growth and deepening of its investments.

(b) A notable development of adjutant, auxiliary ranks immediately subordinate to and serving the African bourgeoisie: lawyers, accountants, stockbrokers, insurers, heart specialists and psychiatrists, as well as a layer of ideologists, including academics and journalists.

(c) A parallel development of bourgeois culture: increasing resort to private schooling, followed by university education at the family's expense in Britain or the USA, a distinctive bourgeois life-style in terms of housing, entertainment, etc.; a bourgeois marriage circuit with a manifestly dynastic aspect; the growth of a weekly and monthly magazine culture which reflected these tastes and interests, but also some of the more political concerns of its younger, more sophisticated elements for institutional reform and for the establishment of civil rights seen as essential in creating stable and reliable conditions for economic life.

(d) A progressive development of bourgeois class consciousness through a series of struggles with other classes and fractions. The decisive years here were 1965–9, during which the political challenge of the petty-bourgeois/urban trade union/rural landless alliance led by Odinga and Kaggia was outmanœuvred and finally destroyed in the banning of the Kenya Peoples Union in 1969. In the course of these struggles, the unionized working class was brought effectively under control of the state, first through a state-controlled union central organization, and subsequently by a ban on strike action and an effective system of wage controls. The petty-bourgeoisie was also decisively neutralized as an independent political force. The populist tendency maintained, after the breakup of the KPU, by a group of parliamentary backbenchers, was ultimately curbed through the murder of J. M. Kariuki and the subsequent detention (or exemplary jailing on conviction for offences) of his most effective successors; while the middle and poor peasants were as far as possible organized as clients under the patronage of the bourgeoisie through a comprehensive system of ethnic organizations with their associated "self-help" movements, rival ethnic colleges of technology, ethnic investment holding companies, etc. These organizations and their offshoots, ostensibly trans-class, must be understood as class organizations of the bourgeoisie in its relations with the peasantry, just as much as the Federation of Kenyan Employers was the principal class organization of the bourgeoisie in relation to the organized working class; and as KANU – through its very lack of organization and effectiveness – was the class organization of the bourgeoisie in relation to all other classes, perpetuating their disorganization, their under-determined condition, *vis-à-vis* the bourgeoisie which "led" it (superintending its endless factional struggles, and the repeated campaigns for party revitalization and reorganization, apparently preparing for an exercise in mass democracy which never came).

Bibliography

Abbreviations

AA	*African Affairs*
CEA	*Cahiers d'Etudes africaines*
CJAS	*Canadian Journal of African Studies*
CUP	Cambridge University Press
JMAS	*Journal of Modern African Studies*
JPS	*Journal of Peasant Studies*
JSAS	*Journal of Southern African Studies*
OUP	Oxford University Press
RAPE	*Review of African Political Economy*
SALB	*South African Labour Bulletin*

Achebe, C. 1966. *A Man of the People.* London: Heinemann.
Adam, H., and Giliomee, H. 1979. *Ethnic Power Mobilised: Can South Africa Change?* New Haven: Yale UP.
Adams, A. 1978. "The Senegal River Valley: What Kind of Change." *RAPE* 10: 33–59.
Adeleye, R. A. 1971. *Power and Diplomacy in Northern Nigeria 1804–1906.* London: Longman.
Afrifa, A. A. 1966. *The Ghana Coup.* London: Cass.
Aghassian, M., *et al.*, 1976. *Les Migrations africaines.* Paris: Maspero.
Al Hajj, M. 1967. "The Thirteenth Century in Muslim Eschatology: Mahdist Expectations on the Sokoto Caliphate", *Research Bulletin* (Centre of Arabic Documentation, Ibadan), 3, 2: 100–13.
Allen, C. H. (forthcoming). *Colonial Government and African Nationalism.* Brighton: Harvester.
Amin, S. 1967. *Le Développement du Capitalisme en Côte d'Ivoire.* Paris: Minuit.
——. 1969. *Le Monde des Affaires Sénégalais.* Paris: Minuit.
Amselle, J. L. 1978. "La Conscience paysanne: La Révolte de Ouolossebougou" (juin 1968, Mali), *CJAS* 12, 3: 339–55.
Ardener, S. 1973. "Sexual Insults and Female Militancy", *Man* 8, 3: 422–40.
Armah, A. K. 1969. *The Beautyful Ones Are Not Yet Born.* London: Heinemann.
Aronson, D. R. 1980. *The City is Our Farm: Seven Migrant Ijebu Yoruba Families.* Cambridge, Mass.: Shenkman; Boston: G. K. Hall.
Arrighi, G., and Saul, J. S. 1973. *Essays on the Political Economy of Africa.* New York: Monthly Review Press.

Awolowo, O. 1960. *Awo*. London: CUP.

Barnett, A. S. 1977. *The Gezira*. London: Cass.

Bates, R. H. 1971. *Unions, Parties and Political Development: A Study of Mineworkers in Zambia*. New Haven: Yale UP.

Beckman, B. 1976. *Organising the Farmers: Cocoa Politics and National Development in Ghana*. Uppsala: SIAS.

——. 1981. "Imperialism and Capitalist Transformation", *RAPE* 19: 48–62.

Beer, C. E. F. 1975. *The Politics of Peasant Groups in Western Nigeria*. Ibadan: Ibadan UP.

Benot, Y. 1969. *Idéologies des Indépendances africaines*. Paris: Maspero.

Bernstein, H. 1979. "African Peasantries: A Theoretical Framework", *JPS* 6, 4: 412–43.

Berry, S. S. 1975. *Cocoa, Custom and Socioeconomic Change in Rural Western Nigeria*. Oxford: OUP.

Beti, M. 1971. *The Poor Christ of Momba*. London: Heinemann.

Bienfeld, M., and Innes, D. 1976. "Capital Accumulation and South Africa", *RAPE* 7: 31–55.

Blakemore, K., and Cooksey, B. 1981. *A Sociology of Education for Africa*. London: Allen & Unwin.

Bondestam, L. 1974. "People and Capitalism in the North-Eastern Lowlands of Ethiopia", *JMAS* 12, 3: 423–39.

Boserup, E. 1970. *Women's Role in Economic Development*. London: Allen & Unwin.

Bozzoli, B., ed., 1979. *Labour, Townships and Protest*. Johannesburg: Ravan.

Brett, E. A. 1973. *Colonialism and Underdevelopment in East Africa*. London: Heinemann.

Bryceson, D. 1980. "The Proletarianization of Women in Tanzania", *RAPE* 17: 4–27.

Bundy, C. 1979. *The Rise and Fall of the South African Peasantry*. London: Heinemann.

Burawoy, M. 1972. *The Colour of Class on the Coppermines*. Lusaka: University of Zambia Institute for African Studies.

CAS. 1980. *The Evolving Social Structure in Zambia*. Edinburgh: Centre of African Studies.

Clarke, D. 1977. "Social Security and Aged Subsistence: Roots of the Predicament in Zimbabwe", *SALB* 3, 6: 38–53.

Clayton, A., and Savage, D. S. 1974. *Government and Labour in Kenya, 1895–1963*. London: Cass.

Cliffe, L., and Saul, J. S., eds, 1973. *Socialism in Tanzania*, 2 vols. Nairobi: East African Publishing House.

——. 1976. "Rural Class Formation in East Africa", *JPS* 4, 2: 195–224.

Clignet, R., and Foster, P. 1966. *The Fortunate Few*. Northwestern UP.

Cock, J. 1980. *Maids and Madams*. Johannesburg: Ravan.

Cohen, A. 1969. *Custom and Politics in Urban Africa*. London: Routledge & Kegan Paul.

Cohen, M. A. 1974. *Urban Policy and Political Conflict in Africa: A Study of the Ivory Coast*. Chicago: Univ. of Chicago Press.

Cohen, Ronald. 1960. "The Structure of Kannyi Society." Ph.D., University of Wisconsin.

——. 1981. "Resistance and Hidden Forms of Consciousness among African Workers", *RAPE* 19: 8–22.

——., and Michael, D. 1973. "The Revolutionary Potential of the African Lumpenproletariat: A Sceptical View", *IDS Bulletin* 5, 2/3: 31–42.

——. Gutkind, P., and Brazier, P., eds, 1979. *Peasants and Proletarians.* London: Hutchinson and New York: Monthly Review Press.

Cooper, F. 1981. "Peasants, Capitalists and Historians", *JSAS* 7, 2: 284–314.

Copans, J., ed., 1975. *Sécheresse et Famine dans le Sahel.* Paris: Maspero.

——. 1980. *Les Marabouts de l'Arachide.* Paris: Sycamore.

Court, D. 1976. "The Education System as a Response to Inequality", *JMAS* 14, 4: 661–90.

Cowen, M. P. 1979. "Capital and Household Production : Kenya's Central Province 1903–64". Thesis, Cambridge University.

——., and McWilliam, S., eds, (forthcoming). *Essays on Capital and Class in Kenya.* London: Longman.

Crisp, J. 1978. "The Labouring Poor, Trade Unions and Political Change in Ghana", *Manpower and Unemployment Research* 11, 2: 93–100.

Cross, S. 1973. "The Watch Tower Movement in South-Central Africa 1908–45." Thesis, Oxford University.

Davidson, B. 1969. *The Africans: An Entry into Cultural History.* London: Longman.

——. 1978. *Africa in Modern History.* London: Allen Lane.

Davies, R., *et al.*, 1976. "Class Struggle and the Periodisation of the State in South Africa", *RAPE* 7: 14–30.

Davies, R. 1979. *Capital, State and White Labour in South Africa, 1900–60.* Hassocks: Harvester.

Davies, R., and Kaplan, D. 1980. "Capitalist Development and the Evolution of Racial Policy in South Africa", *Tarikh* 6, 2: 46–62.

Derman, W. 1972. *Serfs, Peasants and Socialists.* Berkeley: Univ. California Press.

Diop, A. A. B. 1960. "Enquête sur la Migration Toucouleur à Dakar", *Bulletin de l'IFAN*, ser. B., 22, 3: 393–418.

Du Toit, D. 1981. *Capital and Labour in South Africa.* London: Routledge & Kegan Paul.

Dudley, B. 1973. *Instability and Political Order.* Ibadan: University Press.

Dunn, J., ed., 1978. *West African States.* Cambridge: CUP.

Echenberg, M. 1975. "Military Conscription in French West Africa 1914–29", *CJAS* 9, 2: 171–92.

Epstein, A. L. 1958. *Politics in an Urban African Community.* Manchester: University Press.

Fanon, F. 1965. *The Wretched of the Earth.* London: McGibbon & Kee.

Farrah, N. 1970. *From a Crooked Rib.* London: Heinemann.

First, R. 1970. *Barrel of a Gun.* Harmondsworth: Penguin.

——. 1982. *Black Gold: Proletarians and Peasants.* Brighton: Harvester.

Forde, D., and Scott, R. 1946. *The Native Economies of Nigeria.* London: Faber & Faber.

Fox, R. C., *et al.*, 1965. "The Second Independence: A Case Study of the Kwilu Rebellion in the Congo", *Comparative Studies in Society and History* 8, 1: 78–109.

Frank, A. G. 1967. *Capitalism and Underdevelopment in Latin America.* New York: Monthly Review Press.

——. 1969. *Latin America: Underdevelopment or Revolution.* New York: Monthly Review Press.

Fransman, M., ed., 1982. *Industry and Accumulation in Africa.* London: Heinemann.

Gann, L. H., and Duignan, P., eds, 1975. *Colonialism in Africa 1870–1960:* vol. 4: *The Economics of Colonialism.* Cambridge: CUP.

Gerold-Scheepers, T. 1978. "The Political Consciousness of African Urban Workers", *African Perspectives* no. 2: 83–98.

Gerry, C. 1976. "Casual Workers and Capitalist Industry in Dakar". *Manpower and Unemployment Research* 9, 2: 17–27.

——. 1977. *Urban Poverty, Underdevelopment and Recuperative Production in Dakar.* Swansea University: Centre for Development Studies.

Gibbal, J. 1974. *Citadins et Paysans dans la Ville africaine: l'Example d'Abidjan.* Paris: Maspero.

Gluckman, M. 1971. "Tribalism, Ruralism and Urbanism in South and Central Africa", *Colonialism in Africa 1870–1960* III: 127–66, ed. V. Turner. Cambridge: CUP.

Gordon, R. 1975. "A Note on the History of Labour Action in Namibia", *SALB* 1, 10: 7–17.

——. 1977. *Mines, Masters and Migrants.* Johannesburg: Ravan.

——. 1978. "Some Organisational Aspects of Labour Protest among Contract Workers in Namibia", *SALB* 4, 2: 116–23.

Goulbourne, H. 1980. *Politics and State in the Third World.* London: Macmillan.

Gould, D. T. 1980. *Bureaucratic Corruption and Underdevelopment in the Third World: The Case of Zaïre.* New York: Pergamon.

Gran, G., ed., 1979. *Zaïre: The Political Economy of Underdevelopment.* New York: Praeger.

Greenberg, S. B. 1980. *Race and State in Capitalist Societies.* New Haven: Yale UP.

Grillo, R. 1973. *African Railwaymen.* Cambridge: CUP.

Gugler, J., and Flanagan, W. 1978. *Urbanisation and Social Change in West Africa.* Cambridge: CUP.

Gutkind, P. 1967. "The Energy of Despair: Social Organisation of the Unemployed in Two African Cities", *Civilisations* 17: 186–214, 380–405.

——. 1968. "The Poor in Urban Africa", *Power, Poverty and Ban Policy,* ed. W. Bloomberg and H. Schmandt (Beverley Hills: Sage), 355–96.

——. 1973. "From the Energy of Despair to the Anger of Despair", *CJAS* 7, 2: 179–98.

——. 1974. *The Emergent African Proletariat.* Montreal. McGill University, Centre for Developing Area Studies.

——., *et al.*, 1975. "The View from Below: Political Consciousness of the Urban Poor in Ibadan", *CEA* 57: 5–55.

Gutkind, P., and Wallerstein, I., eds, 1976. *The Political Economy of Contemporary Africa*. Beverley Hills: Sage.

——., and Waterman, P., eds, 1977. *African Social Studies*. London: Heinemann and New York: Monthly Review Press.

——., *et al.*, eds, 1978. *African Labour History*. Beverley Hills: Sage.

Hafkin, N., and Bay, E., eds, 1975. *Women in Africa*. Stanford: University Press.

Harries-Jones, P. 1975. *Freedom and Labour*. Oxford: Blackwell.

Harriss, B. 1979. "Going Against the Grain", *Development & Change* 10, 3: 363–84.

Hart, K. 1973. "Informal Income Opportunities and Urban Employment in Ghana", *JMAS* 11, 1: 61–89.

Haswell, M. 1953. *Economics of Agriculture in a Savanna Village*. London: HMSO.

Hayward, G. 1972. "Rural Attitudes and Expectations about National Government", *Rural Africana* 18: 40–58.

Heyer, J., *et al.*, eds, 1981. *Rural Development in Tropical Africa*. London: Macmillan.

Hill, P. 1963. *Migrant Cocoa Farmers of Southern Ghana*. Cambridge: CUP.

——. 1969. "Hidden Trade in Hausaland", *Man* 4, 3: 392–409.

——. 1972. *Rural Hausa*. Cambridge: CUP.

——. 1977. *Population, Prosperity and Poverty: Rural Kano in 1900 and 1970*. Cambridge: CUP.

Hirson, B. 1979. *Year of Fire, Year of Ash*. London: Zed.

Hobsbawm, E. J. 1959. *Primitive Rebels*. Manchester: Univ. Press.

Hobson, J. A. 1900. *The South African War*. London: Nisbet.

Hodgkin, T. L. 1956a. *Nationalism in Colonial Africa*. London: Muller.

——. 1956b. "The African Middle Class", *Corona* 8, 3: 85–8.

——. 1980. "The Revolutionary Tradition in Islam", *Race and Class* 21, 3: 221–38.

Holt, P. M. 1958. *The Mahdist State in the Sudan*. Oxford: Clarendon Press.

Hopkins, A. G. 1973. *An Economic History of West Africa*. London: Longman.

Horton, R. 1971. "African Conversion", *Africa* 41, 2: 85–108.

——. 1975. "On the Rationality of Conversion to Islam", *Africa* 45, 3: 219–35 and 45, 4: 373–98.

Howard, R. 1980. "Formation and Stratification of the Peasantry in Colonial Ghana", *JPS* 8, 1: 61–80.

Hugon, P., *et al.*, 1977. *La Petite Production marchande et l'Emploi dans le Secteur informel*. Paris: Université de Paris 1.

Hyden, G. 1980. *Beyond Ujamaa in Tanzania: Underdevelopment and an Uncaptured Peasantry*. London: Heinemann.

Ifeka-Moller, C. 1975. "Female Militancy and Colonial Revolt", *Perceiving Women*, ed. S. Ardener (London: Malaby), 127–57.

Iliffe, J. 1979. *A Modern History of Tanganyika*. Cambridge: CUP.

Isaacman, A. 1978. *A Luta Continua: Creating a New Society in Mozambique*. Binghampton, NY: Braudel Center.

Isichei, E. 1976. *A History of the Igbo People*. London: Macmillan.

Jeffries, R. 1978a. "Political Radicalism in Africa", *AA* 77: 308: 335–46.

Jeffries, R. 1978b. *Class, Power and Ideology in Ghana.* Cambridge: CUP.

Jessop, B. 1982. *The Capitalist State.* London: Martin Robertson.

Johnstone, F. R. 1970. "White Prosperity and White Supremacy in South Africa Today", *AA* 69, 275: 124–40.

——. 1976. *Class, Race and Gold.* London: Routledge & Kegan Paul.

Joseph, R. 1977. *Radical Natinonalism in Cameroun.* Oxford: OUP.

Kamitatu, C. 1971. *La Grande Mystification de Congo-Kinshasa.* Paris: Maspero.

Kapferer, B. 1972. *Strategy and Transaction in an African Factory.* Manchester: University Press.

Kasfir, N. 1976. *The Vanishing Political Arena.* Berkeley: University of California Press.

Kay, G. 1972. *The Political Economy of Colonialism in Ghana.* Cambridge: CUP.

Kitching, G. 1980. *Class and Economic Change in Kenya.* New Haven: Yale UP.

Kjekshus, H. 1977. *Ecology Control and Economic Development in East African History: The Case of Tanganyika 1850–1950.* London: Heinemann.

Klein, M., ed., 1980. *Peasants in Africa.* Beverley Hills: Sage.

Kraus, J. 1979. "Strikes and Labour Power in Ghana", *Development and Change* 10, 2: 159–86.

Kuper, L., and Smith, M. G., eds, 1969. *Pluralism in Africa.* Berkeley: University of California Press.

Lacey, M. 1981. *Working for Boroko: Origins of a Coercive Labour System in South Africa.* Jonannesburg: Ravan.

Lamb, G. 1974. *Peasant Politics.* Lewes: Julian Friedmann.

Le Brun, O., and Gerry, C. 1975. "Petty Producers and Capitalism", *RAPE* 3: 20–32.

Lee, J. M. 1967. *Colonial Development and Good Government.* Oxford: OUP.

——. 1969. *African Armies and Civil Order.* London: Chatto & Windus.

Leftwich, A., ed., 1974. *South Africa: Economic Growth and Political Change.* London: Allison & Busby.

Legassick, M. 1974a. "Legislation, Ideology and Economy in post-1948 South Africa", *JSAS* 1, 1: 5–35.

——. 1974b. "South Africa: Capital Accumulation and Violence", *Economy & Society* 3, 3: 253–91.

Leonard, D. K. 1977. *Reaching the Peasant Farmer.* Chicago: University Press.

Leys, C. 1975. *Underdevelopment in Kenya.* London: Heinemann.

——. 1976. "The 'Over-developed' Post-colonial State: A Re-evaluation", *RAPE* 5: 39–48.

——. 1978. "Capital Accumulation, Class Formation and Dependency: The Significance of the Kenyan Case", *Socialist Register:* 241–66.

Linden, I., and J. 1971. "John Chilembwe and the New Jerusalem", *Journal of African History* 12, 4: 629–51.

Lipton, M. 1979. "The Debate about South Africa: Neomarxists and Neoliberals", *AA* 78, 310: 57–88.

Little, K. 1973. *African Women in Towns.* Cambridge: CUP.

Lloyd, P. 1975. *Power and Independence.* London: Routledge & Kegan Paul.

Long, N. 1968. *Social Change and the Individual.* Manchester: University Press.

Luckham, R. 1971. *The Nigerian Military 1960–67.* Cambridge: CUP.

Machel, S. 1975. "Women's Liberation is Essential for the Revolution", *African Communist* 61: 37–51.

Mackintosh, M. 1977. "Reproduction and Patriarchy", *Capital and Class* 2: 119–27.

——. 1979. "Domestic Labour and the Household", *Fit Work for Women*, ed. S. Burman (London: Croom Helm), 173–91.

Mafeje, A. 1971. "The Ideology of 'Tribalism' ", *JMAS* 9, 2: 253–61.

Mamdani, M. 1976. *Politics and Class Formation in Uganda.* London: Heinemann and New York: Monthly Review Press.

Marcum, J. 1969, 1978. *The Angolan Revolution*, vols 1 and 2. Cambridge, Mass.: MIT Press.

Marks, S., and Trapido, S. 1979. "Lord Milner and the South African State", *History Workshop Journal* 8: 50–80.

Martin, M. 1973. "Un Aspect de l'Insertion des Militaires dans le Processus de Développement national en Afrique", *CJAS* 7, 2: 267–85.

——. 1976. *La Militarisation des Systèmes Politiques africains 1960–72.* Quebec: Éditions Naaman.

Matshoba, M. 1979. *Call Me Not a Man.* Johannesburg: Ravan.

Mayer, P., and I. 1961. *Townsmen or Tribesmen.* Cape Town: OUP.

Mbeki, G. 1964. *The Peasants' Revolt.* Harmondsworth: Penguin.

Mbilinyi, M. 1973. "Education, Stratification and Sexism in Tanzania", *African Review* 3, 2: 327–40.

Meillassoux, C., ed., 1967. *The Development of Indigenous Trade and Markets in West Africa.* London: OUP.

——. 1970. "A Class Analysis of the Bureaucratic Process in Mali", *Journal of Development Studies* 6, 2: 97–110.

——. 1975. *Femmes, Greniers et Capitaux.* Paris: Maspero; English version: *Maidens, Meal and Money.* Cambridge: CUP, 1980.

Melson, R., and Wolpe, H., eds, 1971. *Nigeria: Modernisation and the Politics of Communalism.* East Lansing: Michigan State UP.

Mihyo, P. 1975. "The Struggle for Workers' Control in Tanzania", *RAPE* 4, 62–84.

Mitchell, J. C. 1956. *The Kalela Dance.* Manchester: Rhodes–Livingstone Institute.

Moore, B. 1966. *The Social Origins of Dictatorship and Democracy.* London: Allen Lane.

Moorsom, R., ed., 1978. "Focus on Namibia", *SALB* 4, 1/2.

Morris, M. 1976. "The Development of Capitalism in South African Agriculture", *Economy & Society* 5, 3: 292–343.

Murray, C. 1977. "High Bridewealth, Migrant Labour and the Position of Women in Lesotho", *Journal of African Law* 21, 1: 79–96.

——. 1980. "Migrant Labour and the Changing Family Structure in the Rural Periphery of Southern Africa", *JSAS* 6, 2: 139–56.

——. 1981. *Families Divided: The Impact of Migrant Labour in Lesotho.* Cambridge: CUP.

Mwase, G. 1975. *Strike a Blow and Die.* London: Heinemann.

Myint, H. 1971. *Economic Theory and the Underdeveloped Countries*. New York: OUP.

Ndadi, V. 1974. *Breaking Contract*. Richmond, BC: LSM Press.

Nelson, N., ed., 1981. *African Women in the Development Process*. London: Cass.

Netting, R. 1968. *Hill Farmers of Nigeria*. Seattle: University of Washington Press.

Newsinger, J. 1981. "Revolt and Repression in Kenya: The 'Mau Mau' Rebellion 1952–60", *Science & Society* 45, 2: 159–85.

Ngugi wa Thiongo. 1977. *Petals of Blood*. London: Heinemann.

Nichols, T., ed., 1980. *Capital and Labour*. Glasgow: Collins.

Obbo, C. 1980. *"Town Migration is not for Women": African Women's Struggle for Economic Independence*. London: Zed.

O'Brien, D. C. 1971. *The Mourides of Senegal*. Oxford: OUP.

——. 1975. *Saints and Politicians*. Cambridge: CUP.

——. 1977. "A Versatile Charisma: the Mouride Brotherhood 1967–75", *Archives Européenes de Sociologie* 18, 1: 84–106.

O'Brien, R. C., ed., 1979. *The Political Economy of Underdevelopment: Dependence in Senegal*. Beverley Hills: Sage.

Ochieng', W. R., and Janmohamed, K. K., eds, 1977. "Perspectives on the Mau Mau Movement", *Kenya Historical Review* 5, 2: 169–403.

O'Meara, D. 1975. "The 1946 African Mineworkers' strike and the Political Economy of South Africa", *Journal of Commonwealth and Comparative Politics* 13, 2: 146–73.

——. 1977. "The Afrikaner Broederbond 1927–48, Class Vanguard of Afrikaner Nationalism", *JSAS* 3, 2: 156–86.

Oppong, C. 1973. *Marriage Among a Matrilineal Elite*. Cambridge: CUP.

Osoba, S. 1979. "The Deepening Crisis of the Nigerian National Bourgeoisie", *RAPE* 13: 63–77.

Ousmane, S. 1970. *God's Bit of Wood*. London: Heinemann.

——. 1972. *The Money Order*. London: Heinemann.

——. 1976. *Xala*. London: Heinemann.

Oxaal, I., *et al.*, eds, 1975. *Beyond the Sociology of Development*. London: Routledge & Kegan Paul.

Paden, J. 1973. *Religion and Political Culture in Kano*. Berkeley: University of California Press.

Palma, G. 1978. "Dependency: A Formal Theory of Underdevelopment or a Methodology for the Analysis of Concrete Situations of Underdevelopment", *World Development* 6, 7/8: 881–924.

Palmer, R., and Parsons, N., eds, 1977. *The Roots of Rural Poverty in Central and Southern Africa*. London: Heinemann.

Peace, A. 1979a. *Choice, Class and Conflict*. Brighton: Harvester.

——. 1979b. "Prestige , Power and Legitimacy in a Modern Nigerian Town", *CJAS* 13, 1/2: 25–51.

Peel, J. D. Y. 1968. *Aladura*. London: OUP.

Peil, M. 1972. *The Ghanaian Factory Worker*. Cambridge: CUP.

Perrings, C. 1979. *Black Mineworkers in Central Africa*. London: Heinemann.

Phillips, A. 1977. "The Concept of Development", *RAPE* 6: 7–20.

Post, K. W. J. 1972. " 'Peasantisation' and Rural Political Movements in Western Africa", *Archives européennes de Sociologie* 13, 2: 223–54.
——., and Jenkins, G. 1973. *The Price of Liberty*. Cambridge: CUP.
Raikes, P. 1978. "Rural Differentiation and Class Formation in Tanzania", *JPS* 5, 3: 285–325.
Ranger, T. O. 1967. *Revolt in Southern Rhodesia 1896–7*. London: Heinemann.
——., and Kimambo, T., eds, 1972. *The Historical Study of African Religion*. London: Heinemann.
——. 1975. *Dance and Society in Eastern Africa 1890–1970*. London: Heinemann.
——. 1978. "Growing from the Roots: Reflections on Peasant Research in Central and South Africa", *JSAS* 5, 1: 99–133.
Rex, J. 1970. *Race Relations in Sociological Theory*. London: Weidenfeld & Nicolson.
——. 1974. "The Compound, Reserves and the Urban Location", *SALB* 1, 2: 4–17.
Richardson, P. 1982. *Chinese Mine Labour in Transvaal*. London: Macmillan.
Rivière, C. 1977. *Guinea: Mobilisation of a People*. Ithaca, NY: Cornell UP.
Roberts, A. 1970. "The Lumpa Church of Alice Lenshina", *Protest and Power in Black Africa*, ed. R. I. Rotberg and A. A. Mazrui (New York: OUP), 513–68.
Roux, E. 1942. *Time Longer than Rope*, 2nd edn, 1966. Madison: University of Wisconsin Press.
Samoff, J. 1979. "The Bureaucracy and the Bourgeoisie: Decentralisation and Class Structure in Tanzania", *Comparative Studies in Society and History* 25, 1: 30–62.
Samuel, R., ed., 1981. *People's History and Socialist Theory*. London: Routledge & Kegan Paul.
Sandbrook, R. 1975a. *Proletarians and African Capitalism*. Cambridge: CUP.
——. 1982. *The Politics of Basic Needs*. London: Heinemann.
——., and Cohen, R., eds, 1975b. *The Development of an African Working Class*. London: Longman.
——., and Arn, J. 1977a. *The Labouring Poor and Urban Class Formation: the Case of Greater Accra*. Montreal: McGill University Centre for Developing Area Studies.
——. 1977b. "The Political Potential of Urban African Workers", *CJAS* 11, 3: 411–33.
——, 1982. *The Politics of Basic Needs*. London: Heinemann.
Saul, J. S. 1979. *State and Revolution in Eastern Africa*. London: Heinemann and New York: Monthly Review Press.
Schapera, I. 1947. *Migrant Labour and Tribal Life*. Oxford: OUP.
——., and Roberts, S. 1975. "Rampedi Revisited: Another Look at a Kgatla Ward", *Africa* 45, 3: 258–79.
Schwarz, A. 1972. "Illusion d'une Émancipation et Alienation réelle de l'Ouvrière zaïroise", *CJAS* 6, 2: 183–212.
——. 1974. "Mythe et Réalite des Bureaucraties africaines", *CJAS* 8, 2: 255–84.
Shanin, T., ed., 1972. *Peasants and Peasant Societies*, Harmondsworth: Penguin.
Shivji, I. 1975. *Class Struggles in Tanzania*. London: Heinemann and New York: Monthly Review Press.

Skinner, E. P. 1960. "Labour Migration and its Relationship to Socioeconomic Change in Mossi Society", *Africa* 30, 4: 375-99.

Smith, M. 1954. *Baba of Karo*. London: Faber & Faber.

Sundkler, B. G. M. 1961. *Bantu Prophets in South Africa*. London: OUP.

Suret-Canale, J. 1971. *French Colonialism in Tropical Africa*. London: Hurst.

——. 1977. *Afrique noire Occidentale et Centrale: de la Colonisation aux Indépendances (1945-60): I*. Paris: Editions Sociales.

Swainson, N. 1980. *The Development of Corporate Capitalism in Kenya 1918-78*. London: Heinemann.

Taylor, J. G. 1979. *From Modernisation to Modes of Production*. London: Macmillan.

Themba, C. 1972. *The Will to Die*. London: Heinemann.

Tlali, M. 1979. *Muriel et Metropolitan*. Johannesburg: Ravan.

Trapido, S. 1971. "South Africa in the Comparative Study of Industrialisation", *Journal of Development Studies* 7, 3: 309-20.

Urdang, S. 1979. *Fighting Two Colonialisms: Women in Guiné-Bissau*. New York: Monthly Review Press.

Usman, Y. B. 1979. *For the Liberation of Nigeria*. London: New Beacon.

Vail, L., and White, L. 1980. *Capitalism and Colonialism in Mozambique*. London: Heinemann.

Van Binsbergen, W. M. J., and Meilink, H. A., eds, 1978. "Migration and Transformation of Modern African Society", *African Perspectives* 1.

——. 1980. *Religious Change in Zambia*. London: Routledge & Kegan Paul.

van Hekken, P., and van Velzen, Bonno Thoden. 1972. *Land Scarcity and Rural Inequality*. The Hague: Mouton.

van Onselen, C. 1976. *Chibaro*. London: Pluto.

——. (forthcoming). *New Babylon*; and *New Nineveh*, 2 vols. London: Longman.

van Velsen, J. 1960. "Labour Migration as a Positive Factor in the Continuity of Tonga Society Tribal Society", *Economic Development and Cultural Change* 8, 3: 265-78.

van Velzen, Bonno Thoden. 1972. "Controllers in Rural Tanzania", *Sociologische Gids* 19, 2: 126-35.

Verhaegen, B. 1967/9. *Rébellions au Congo*. Brussels: CRISP.

Vidal, C., ed., 1977. "Des Femmes sur l'Afrique des Femmes", *CEA* 65.

Warren, W. 1980. *Imperialism: Pioneer of Capitalism*. London: New Left Books.

Waterman, P., ed., 1979. *Third World Strikes*. Zug: Interdocumentation.

Watson, W. 1958. *Tribal Cohesion in a Money Economy*. Manchester: University Press.

Watts, M., and Shenton, R. 1980. "Capitalism and Hunger in Northern Nigeria", *RAPE* 15: 53-62.

Weber, M. 1948. *From Max Weber*. London: Routledge & Kegan Paul.

Webster, E., ed., 1978. *Essays in Southern African Labour History*. Johannesburg: Ravan.

Weiss, H. 1967. *Political Protest in the Congo*. Princeton: University Press.

Wickens, P. 1978. *The Industrial and Commercial Workers Union of Africa*. Cape Town: OUP.

Williams, G. P. 1974. "Political Consciousness among the Ibadan Poor",

Sociology and Development, ed. E. de Kadt and G. P. Williams. London: Tavistock, 109–39.

Williams, G. P., ed., 1976. *Nigeria, Economy and Society*. London: Collins.

——. 1978. "Imperialism and Development", *World Development* 6, 7/8: 925–36.

Wilson, F. 1971. "Farming", *The Oxford History of South Africa*, ed. M. Wilson and L. Thompson, vol. 2, 104–71 (Oxford: OUP).

——. 1972. *Migrant Labour in South Africa*. Johannesburg: SPRO–CAS.

Wilson, G. 1942. *An Essay on the Economics of Detribalisation in Northern Rhodesia*. Livingstone: Rhodes–Livingstone Institute.

Wipper, A. 1971. "The Politics of Sex: Some Strategies Employed by the Kenyan Power Elite", *African Studies Review* 14, 3: 463–82.

——. 1975. "The Maendeleo ya Wanawake Movement", *African Studies Review* 18, 3: 99–120.

——. ed., 1975/6. "Rural Women: Development or Underdevelopment?", *Rural Africana* 29.

——. 1978. *Rural Rebels*. Nairobi: OUP.

Wolf, E. R. 1972. *Peasant Wars of the Twentieth Century*. New York: Harper & Row and London: Faber & Faber.

Wolpe, H. 1972. "Capitalism and Cheap Labour Power in South Africa", *Economy & Society* 1, 4: 425: 56.

Young, C. 1976. *The Politics of Cultural Pluralism*. Madison: University of Wisconsin Press.

Index

214